Microsoft®

Excel

Functions
in Practice

by Patrick Blattner

201 West 103rd Street
Indianapolis, IN 46290

Microsoft® Excel Functions in Practice

Copyright © 1999 by Que

International Standard Book Number: 0-7897-2045-0

Library of Congress Catalog Card Number: 99-65638

Printed in the United States of America

First Printing: *September 1999*

01 00 99   4   3   2   1

Trademarks

Warning and Disclaimer

EXECUTIVE EDITOR
John Pierce

ACQUISITIONS EDITOR
Jamie Milazzo

DEVELOPMENT EDITOR
Laura Bulcher

MANAGING EDITOR
Thomas F. Hayes

PROJECT EDITOR
Leah Kirkpatrick

COPY EDITOR
Kay Hoskin

INDEXER
Heather Goens

PROOFREADER
Tricia Sterling

TECHNICAL EDITORS
Robert Rosenberg
Alex Holtz

SOFTWARE DEVELOPMENT SPECIALIST
Andrea Duvall

INTERIOR DESIGNER
Dan Armstrong

COVER DESIGNER
Anne Jones

LAYOUT TECHNICIANS
Liz Johnston
Cheryl Lynch

Table of Contents

1 Functions Overview   5

Function Fundamentals   5
Functions Versus Formulas   5
Arguments   5
Operators   6
Operator Order   7
Custom Functions   7

Database- and List-Management
Functions   8

Date and Time Functions   8

DDE and External Functions   9

Engineering Functions   9

Financial Functions   11

Information Functions   14

Logical Functions   15

Lookup and Reference Functions   15

Math and Trigonometry Functions   16

Statistical Functions   18

Text Functions   21

2 Managing Your Business with Functions   23

An Overview   23

Using Functions for Lookup and
Reference, Math, and Trigonometry   24
VLOOKUP   24
MATCH   24
OFFSET   24
SUMIF   24
SUMIF with a Conditional Month   24
SUMIF with a Cell Reference Year
Conditional and Month   25
SUBTOTAL   25
INDEX (Reference Form)   25
INDEX with a MATCH Condition   25

Working with Date and Time   26
TODAY   26
NOW   26
EDATE   26
NETWORKDAYS   27

Computing Statistics   27
AVERAGE   27
COUNTA   27
COUNTIF   27
MAX   28
MIN   28
STDEVA   28
FORECAST   28

Generating Financial Results   28
CUMIPMT   28
CUMPRINC   29
IPMT   29
FV   29

Producing Logical and Informational
Data   30
IF   30
ISNUMBER   30
ISBLANK   30

Working with Text   31
CONCATENATE   31
PROPER   31
UPPER   31
RIGHT   31
MID   31

Important Tools for Any Business   32
Sell In Versus Sell Through   32
Channel Velocity   32
Cascading Schedules   33
Reverse Schedules   35
Summing the Total Velocity   36
Automating Projected Cash Flows   36
Transposing Tables with Formulas
(without Absolute Referencing)   37
Averaging Positive Numbers Only in a
Range   38
International Rate Converters   39
Rate Exchange Tables   40
Using the EUROCONVERT
Formula   40
Applying a Named Range to
Formulas   41

P&L—Direct Contribution 42
Financial Ratios 43
Resource Pools 46
Building Custom Functions 48
Producing a Line Item Milestone
Management Chart 49
Ramping Up Production on a
Single-Line Item 50
Counting Unique Items in a List 51

3 Database- and List-Management Functions 53

Database Functions Overview 53

General DFUNCTION Syntax 54

DAVERAGE 54

DCOUNT 55

DCOUNTA 56

DGET 56

DMAX 57

DMIN 58

DPRODUCT 58

DSTDEV 59

DSTDEVP 59

DSUM 60

DVAR 61

DVARP 62

GETPIVOTDATA 63

4 Date and Time Functions 65

Date and Time Functions Overview 65

DATE 66

DATEVALUE 66

DAY 67

DAYS360 68

EDATE 68

EOMONTH 69

HOUR 70

MINUTE 70

MONTH 71

NETWORKDAYS 72

NOW 73

SECOND 73

TIME 74

TIMEVALUE 74

TODAY 74

WEEKDAY 75

WEEKNUM 76

WORKDAY 77

YEAR 77

YEARFRAC 78

5 Engineering Functions 79

Engineering Functions Overview 79

BESSELI 80

BESSELJ 80

BESSELK 81

BESSELY 82

BIN2DEC 83

BIN2HEX 84

BIN2OCT 84

COMPLEX 85

CONVERT 86

DEC2BIN 89

DEC2HEX 90

DELTA 90

ERF 91

ERFC 92

GESTEP 92

Microsoft®

Excel

Functions
in Practice

HEX2BIN 93

HEX2DEC 94

HEX2OCT 94

IMABS 95

IMAGINARY 96

IMARGUMENT 97

IMCONJUGATE 97

IMCOS 98

IMDIV 99

IMEXP 100

IMLN 101

IMLOG10 101

IMLOG2 102

IMPOWER 103

IMPRODUCT 104

IMREAL 105

IMSIN 106

IMSQRT 106

IMSUB 107

IMSUM 108

OCT2BIN 109

OCT2DEC 110

OCT2HEX 110

6 Financial Functions 113

Financial Functions Overview 113

ACCRINT 114

ACCRINTM 115

AMORDEGRC 115

AMORLINC 116

COUPDAYBS 117

COUPDAYS 118

COUPDAYSNC 119

COUPNCD 119

COUPNUM 120

COUPPCD 121

CUMIPMT 122

CUMPRINC 122

DB 123

DDB 124

DISC 125

DOLLARDE 126

DOLLARFR 126

DURATION 127

EFFECT 127

FV 128

FVSCHEDULE 129

INTRATE 129

IPMT 130

IRR 131

ISPMT 132

MDURATION 132

MIRR 133

NOMINAL 134

NPER 134

NPV 135

ODDFPRICE 136

ODDFYIELD 138

ODDLPRICE 138

ODDLYIELD 139

PMT 140

PPMT 140

PRICE 141

PRICEDISC 142

PRICEMAT 143

PV 144

RATE 145

RECEIVED 146

SLN 147

SYD 148

TBILLEQ 148

TBILLPRICE 149

TBILLYIELD 150

VDB 151

XIRR 152

XNPV 152

YIELD 153

YIELDDISC 154

YIELDMAT 155

7 Information Functions 157

Information Functions Overview 157

CELL 158

COUNTBLANK 160

ERROR.TYPE 161

INFO 162

IS Functions 163

Using the ISBLANK Function 164

ISNUMBER 164

N 165

NA 166

TYPE 166

8 Logical Functions 167

Logical Functions Overview 167

AND 168

FALSE 169

IF 170

NOT 171

OR 172

TRUE 172

9 Lookup and Reference Functions 173

Lookup and Reference Functions Overview 173

ADDRESS 174

AREAS 174

CHOOSE 175

COLUMN 176

COLUMNS 177

HLOOKUP 177

HYPERLINK 178

INDEX (Array Form) 179

INDEX (Reference Form) 180

INDIRECT 182

LOOKUP (Array Form) 183

LOOKUP (Vector Form) 184

MATCH 184

OFFSET 185

ROW 188

ROWS 188

TRANSPOSE 188

VLOOKUP 189

10 Math and Trigonometry Functions 191

Math and Trigonometry Functions Overview 191

ABS 192

ACOS 192

ACOSH   193

ASIN   193

ASINH   194

ATAN   195

ATAN2   195

ATANH   196

CEILING   197

COMBIN   197

COS   198

COSH   199

COUNTIF   199

DEGREES   200

EVEN   201

EXP   201

FACT   202

FACTDOUBLE   203

FLOOR   203

GCD   204

INT   204

LCM   205

LN   205

LOG   206

LOG10   206

MDETERM   206

MINVERSE   207

MMULT   207

MOD   208

MROUND   208

MULTINOMIAL   208

ODD   209

PERMUT   209

PI   210

POWER   210

PRODUCT   210

QUOTIENT   211

RADIANS   211

RAND   212

RANDBETWEEN   212

ROMAN   213

ROUND   213

ROUNDDOWN   214

ROUNDUP   214

SERIESSUM   214

SIGN   215

SIN   215

SINH   216

SQRT   216

SQRTPI   216

SUBTOTAL   217

SUM   218

SUMIF   219

SUMPRODUCT   220

SUMSQ   221

SUMX2MY2   222

SUMX2PY2   222

SUMXMY2   222

TAN   223

TANH   223

TRUNC   223

11 **Statistical Functions   225**

Statistical Functions Overview   225

AVEDEV   226

AVERAGE   226

AVERAGEA   227

BETADIST 227

BETAINV 228

BINOMDIST 228

CHIDIST 230

CHIINV 230

CHITEST 231

CONFIDENCE 231

CORREL 232

COUNT 233

COUNTA 234

COUNTBLANK 234

COUNTIF 235

COVAR 236

CRITBINOM 236

DEVSQ 237

EXPONDIST 238

FDIST 239

FINV 240

FISHER 240

FISHERINV 240

FORECAST 241

FREQUENCY 241

FTEST 242

GAMMADIST 243

GAMMAINV 244

GAMMALN 244

GEOMEAN 244

GROWTH 245

HARMEAN 246

HYPGEOMDIST 246

INTERCEPT 247

KURT 248

LARGE 248

LINEST 249

LOGEST 250

LOGINV 251

LOGNORMDIST 252

MAX 252

MAXA 253

MEDIAN 253

MIN 254

MINA 254

MODE 254

NEGBINOMDIST 255

NORMDIST 256

NORMINV 257

NORMSDIST 258

NORMSINV 258

PEARSON 258

PERCENTILE 259

PERCENTRANK 260

PERMUT 261

POISSON 261

PROB 262

QUARTILE 263

RANK 264

RSQ 264

SKEW 265

SLOPE 266

SMALL 267

STANDARDIZE 267

STDEV 268

STDEVA 269

STDEVP 269

STDEVPA 270

STEYX 270

TDIST 271

TINV 272

TREND 272

TRIMMEAN 273

TTEST 274

VAR 274

VARA 275

VARP 275

VARPA 276

WEIBULL 276

ZTEST 277

PHONETIC 289

PROPER 290

REPLACE 290

REPT 291

RIGHT 291

SEARCH 292

SUBSTITUTE 292

T 293

TEXT 293

TRIM 294

UPPER 295

VALUE 296

YEN 296

Index   297

12 Text Functions   279

Text Functions Overview 279

ASC 280

CHAR 280

CLEAN 281

CODE 281

CONCATENATE 282

DOLLAR 282

EXACT 283

FIND 284

FIXED 285

JIS 286

LEFT 286

LEN 287

LOWER 288

MID 288

About the Author

Patrick Blattner has authored and co-authored *Special Edition Using Microsoft Excel 2000* and *Special Edition Using Microsoft Word and Excel in Office 2000*. Patrick has been using Excel for more than 12 years in corporate and private business. After graduating from Northeast Louisiana University, he started out in the contracting and gold-mining industry. He then branched off into product development where he received a United States Utility Patent (5,031,865). A member of the Academy of Interactive Arts and Sciences, he spent several years in interactive media development with Disney Interactive. Most recently, he moved to Silicon Valley for new media initiatives and vertical application software development. He can be contacted at Patrick@Blattnerbooks.com or you can visit his Web site at www.Blattnerbooks.com.

Dedication

To my wonderful mother, Jean Blattner, who graced this earth for only a short time before Multiple Sclerosis took her life.

Although here a short time, you instilled a lifetime of memories for everyone you came in contact with. You are a true inspiration in every day that passes in my life and you are severely missed.

Acknowledgments

Although there is one name on the cover of this book it takes a dedicated team of talented individuals to put a book of this nature together. First, I would like to begin by giving special thanks to Jamie Milazzo my acquisitions editor, and Laura Bulcher my developer, who had to sift and wade through the countless layout revisions and spend countless hours talking with me on the phone. I would also like to give special thanks to the added contributions by Laura Stewart, the author of *Using Microsoft Excel 97* and *Platinum Edition Using Microsoft Office 2000*. In addition I would like to thank Leah Kirkpatrick, Kay Hoskin, Tricia Sterling, and Robert Rosenberg for their detailed and countless corrections and revisions.

Tell Us What You Think!

As the reader of this book, *you* are our most important critic and commentator. We value your opinion and want to know what we're doing right, what we could do better, what areas you'd like to see us publish in, and any other words of wisdom you're willing to pass our way.

As the Executive Editor for the Que team at Macmillan Computer Publishing, I welcome your comments. You can fax, email, or write me directly to let me know what you did or didn't like about this book—as well as what we can do to make our books stronger.

Please note that I cannot help you with technical problems related to the topic of this book, and that due to the high volume of mail I receive, I might not be able to reply to every message.

When you write, please be sure to include this book's title and author as well as your name and phone or fax number. I will carefully review your comments and share them with the author and editors who worked on the book.

Fax: 317.581.4663

Email: que@mcp.com

Mail: Executive Editor
        Macmillan Computer Publishing
        201 West 103rd Street
        Indianapolis, IN 46290 USA

Introduction

Because Microsoft Excel is such a daunting program with regards to flexibility and the number of tools involved, *Microsoft Excel 2000 Functions in Practice* was designed to break out the automated functions in Excel. You might be asking "What is a function, anyway?" A function is a predetermined calculation built into Excel. The function with its arguments activates the software to perform the calculation. You'll notice that this book contains nearly as many screen captures as there are functions in Excel. We've also included a CD with the functions shown in this book—this way you can refer to the CD and practice using the functions while reading the text.

Who Should Read This Book?

If you're just beginning to use Excel or have used Excel for years, chances are, functions have been a bit confusing at times. This book was designed for all users as a true reference guide—which is why all of the chapters are broken into their respective functions. It allows you to gain quick access, and in most cases, the function is accompanied with a screen capture in addition to being accessible on the CD. The spirit of this book was not to create gadget functions, but functions that are used and are useful. Hopefully you'll find this reference an invaluable resource for using Microsoft Excel Functions.

How This Book Is Organized

This book is organized in a straightforward fashion that allows you to go directly to the category in which you're working. For example, if you want help looking up information from a list in Excel, go to the Lookup and Reference chapter of this book. Organizing a book that contains so many functions by their respective categories helps you save countless hours searching for the right function to compute the task.

Chapter 1 "Functions Overview"

In this chapter, you'll learn some fundamentals that describe the basics of function construction. Chapter 1 covers all the basic conventions of syntax and syntax priorities in constructing functions.

Chapter 2 "Managing Your Business with Functions"

This chapter is dedicated to showing business situations and solutions using proper spreadsheet design and functions.

Chapter 3 "Database- and List-Management Functions"

Learn all the current database functions with examples in Microsoft Excel 2000 in this chapter.

Chapter 4 "Date and Time Functions"

This chapter covers all the current date and time functions with specific examples.

Chapter 5 "Engineering Functions"

This chapter covers all the current Engineering functions.

Chapter 6 "Financial Functions"

Explore examples of the current Financial functions.

Chapter 7 "Information Functions"

This chapter covers all the current Information functions.

Chapter 8 "Logical Functions"

This chapter covers all the current Logical functions with specific examples.

Chapter 9 "Lookup and Reference Functions"

This chapter covers all the current Lookup and Reference functions.

Chapter 10 "Math and Trigonometry Functions"

Examine all the Excel 2000 Math and Trigonometry functions.

Chapter 11 "Statistical Functions"

Learn about all the current Statistical functions with specific examples.

Chapter 12 "Text Functions"

This chapter covers all the current Text functions and examples of what are available in Excel 2000.

Conventions Used in This Book

Certain text formats will help you read and understand the text in *Microsoft Excel 2000 Functions in Practice*. Each function is broken into the following format structure.

1. Function—The function to be described.

2. Syntax—The elements included in the proper order to make the function work.

3. Brief Description—A brief overview of what the function calculates.

4. Elongated Description—A longer version of the description with examples of how to use the function.

5. Argument Description—The description of each element of the function's syntax.

6. Example—In most cases, an example is included to show the function being used in practice.

7. Example Description—A brief description of the example shown in the figure, where appropriate.

In Excel, you can use either the mouse or the keyboard to activate commands and choose options. You can press a command or menu hotkey, use the function keys, or click items with the mouse to make your selections.

I'll also use a mixture of the following to draw out important things you need to pay attention to.

N O T E Notes provide additional information that might help you avoid problems or offer advice or general information related to the current topic.

 T I P Tips provide extra information that supplements the current topic. Often, tips offer shortcuts or alternative methods for accomplishing a task.

Functions Overview

Function Fundamentals

What is a function? A function in Excel is a built-in calculation that performs a mathematical operation. For example, if I had a list of a thousand numbers and wanted to manually look for the highest value, it could take a while. That's where Excel can help you out. It has a Max formula that searches a specified range and places the highest value in the cell with the formula. Using another example, if you wanted to calculate the average from a list of numbers, you could use the Average function to calculate the average. In all, Excel has more than 450 mathematical calculations already created, so if you know which ones do what, you can save countless hours. In addition to the numerous calculations already created, you'll also learn how to create your own functions. If you have specific calculations that are customized to you or your business, it may warrant creating your own set of custom functions.

Functions Versus Formulas

The function is the built-in mathematical calculation provided by Excel. The formula is the function with its arguments. Each function is activated by the = sign. For example, if you place the formula Average(B3:B20), where Average is the function and (B3:B20) is the argument, nothing happens; however, place an = sign in front of Average and it activates the formula. Think of it in terms of using a key to start your car.

Arguments

An argument is the reference behind the function. The reference being the number, cell reference, or worksheet names. For example, if I were to calculate the average of cells B3:B20 in a list, the argument is the cell-range reference shown as (B3:B20) behind the function. Table 1.1 shows examples of arguments used in Excel.

Table 1.1   Argument Types

Argument	Example
Numbers	1,2,3
Text	"January"
Logical Values	(True or False)
Cell References	B7 or B7:B20

Operators

Operators are really broken into four categories: arithmetic operators, comparison operators, text operators, and reference operators. An operator simply tells Excel what kind of calculation you want to perform. For example, if I wanted to divide 7 by 3, the operator is the front slash key and tells Excel to divide. In essence, it's a language used to talk to Excel and to tell it what you want to do. You could use voice recognition to tell Excel to divide or you could learn the keystroke language as shown in Table 1.2.

Table 1.2   Keystroke Operators

Arithmetic	Explanation	Example
+	Addition	2+3
-	Subtraction	5-1
	Negation	-7
*	Multiplication	7*3
/	Division	7/2
%	Percent	90%
^	Exponentiation	7^2
Comparison	**Explanation**	**Example**
=	Equal to	B1=D1
>	Greater than	B1>D1
<	Less than	B1<D1
>=	Greater than or equal to	B1>=D1
<=	Less than or equal to	B1<=D1
<>	Not equal to	B1<>D1

Table 1.2	Keystroke Operators	
Text	**Explanation**	**Example**
&	Adjoins text	"Scott" & "Blattner" produce "ScottBlattner"
Reference	**Explanation**	**Example**
:	One reference between all cells	B3:B20
,	Separates arguments in a function	(B3,B20)

Operator Order

When creating complicated formulas or formulas that include more than one operator, there is a specific order to use. The order is listed in Table 1.3. Meaning, if I were to create a formula that contained % and the operator +, the % would come first.

Table 1.3	Excel's Operator Order
Operator Order	**Example**
1	% Percent
2	^ Exponentiation
3	* / Multiplication before Division
4	+ – Addition and then Subtraction
5	& Ampersand (adjoins text)
6	>, >=, <, <=, =, <> Comparisons

Custom Functions

You can create custom functions in Excel, however, be sure Excel has not already addressed a function that will work for your specific needs. Note the following custom function example.

> If I was in the construction industry, and had a specific calculation that included a formula with rates that were specific to my company and equipment, and a profit rate that was also specific to my company, I would want to create the custom function =TRUCKRATE(xxx). Now, every time that I estimate an amount of material to be moved and it includes the use of a Cat 777 truck, it would calculate the amount of material based on the 777 truck base rate plus overhead. See Chapter 2, "Managing Your Business with Functions," to learn more about creating custom functions.

The following quick reference will help you find a function that will work for your specific needs. To learn more about the function, see its detailed description in the corresponding chapter. As you will see, the lists below are grouped to reflect the structure and layout of this book.

For example, to learn more about the DCOUNT function, you'd go to the Chapter 3, covering "Database- and List-Management Functions."

Database- and List-Management Functions

DAVERAGE	Indicates the average of the values that meet the specified criteria.
DCOUNT	Counts the number of cells that contain numbers that meet the specified criteria.
DCOUNTA	Counts nonblank cells containing numbers or text that meet the specified criteria.
DGET	Returns a single value that meets the specified criteria.
DMAX	Extracts the highest value that meets the specified criteria.
DMIN	Extracts the lowest value that meets the specified criteria.
DPRODUCT	Returns the product of multiplying the values that meet the specified criteria.
DSTDEV	Returns the calculation of the standard deviation of a population, based on the sum of the whole population.
DSUM	Returns the total of the values that meet the specified criteria.
DVAR	Estimates the variance of a sample population, based on the values that meet the specified criteria.
DVARP	Returns the calculation of the variance of an entire population, based on the values that meet the specified criteria.
GETPIVOTDATA	Returns a value of data stored in a pivot table.

Date and Time Functions

DATE	Returns the DATEVALUE as a serial number.
DATEVALUE	Converts a text date to a DATEVALUE as a serial number.
DAY	Returns the corresponding day of the month as a serial number, from 1 to 31.
DAYS360	Returns the number of days between two set dates that you specify.
EDATE	Returns the value or serial number of the date specified by you and the number of months before or after the specified date. Use EDATE to calculate the maturity date or date due that falls on the same day of the month as the date of issue.
EOMONTH	Returns the calculated maturity dates or dates due that fall in the last day of the month.

HOUR	Returns the hour as a serial number integer between 0 and 23.
MINUTE	Returns the serial number that corresponds to the minute.
MONTH	Returns the corresponding serial number of the month between 1 and 12.
NETWORKDAYS	Returns the number of working days between two dates. Excludes weekends and specified holidays.
NOW	Returns the current date and time in the form of a serial number. There are no arguments for this function. This function updates the date and time each time the worksheet it appears on re-calculates.
SECOND	Returns the corresponding serial number of seconds as an integer between 0 and 59.
TIME	Returns the corresponding serial number of time as a fraction or decimal between 0 and 0.99999999.
TIMEVALUE	Returns the serial number represented by text as time.
TODAY	Returns the current date as a serial number. There are no arguments for this function. This function updates the date each time the worksheet it appears on re-calculates.
WEEKDAY	Returns the corresponding day of the week as a serial number.
YEAR	Returns the corresponding year as a serial number in the form of an integer.
YEARFRAC	Returns the calculated fraction of the year represented by whole numbers between two dates.

DDE and External Functions

For information on the following DDE and External functions, see Chapter 2, "Managing Your Business with Functions."

CALL	Calls up the procedure in a dynamic link library or code resource. Syntax 1 is used in conjunction with the REGISTER function, Syntax 2 uses the CALL function by itself.
REGISTER.ID	Supplies the registered ID of the dynamic link library or code resource.
SQL.REQUEST	Runs a query from a worksheet and connects an external data source.

Engineering Functions

BESSELI	Returns the Bessel function in modified form for imaginary arguments.

BESSELJ	Returns the actual Bessel function. X is the value at which to evaluate the function. Y is the order of the Bessel function.
BESSELK	Returns the Bessel function in modified form for imaginary arguments.
BESSELY	Returns the Bessel function, also known as the Weber or Neumann function. X is the value at which to evaluate the function. N is the order of the function.
BIN2DEC	Converts a binary number to decimal form.
BIN2HEX	Converts a binary number to hexadecimal.
BIN2OCT	Converts a binary number to octal.
COMPLEX	Converts real and imaginary coefficients into a complex number of the form x + yi or x + yj.
CONVERT	Converts from one measurement system to another.
DEC2BIN	Converts decimal numbers to binary.
DEC2HEX	Converts decimal numbers to hexadecimal.
DEC2OCT	Converts decimal numbers to octal.
DELTA	Tests whether numbers or values are equal.
ERF	Returns the integrated error function between lower limit and upper limit.
ERFC	Returns a complementary ERF function integrated between x and infinity. X is the lower bound for integrating ERF.
GESTEP	Returns the value of 1 if the number is greater than or equal to the step, otherwise 0.
HEX2BIN	Converts hexadecimal numbers to binary.
HEX2DEC	Converts hexadecimal numbers to decimal.
HEX2OCT	Converts hexadecimal numbers to octal.
IMABS	Returns the absolute value (Modulus) of a complex number in x + yi or x + yj text format.
IMAGINARY	Returns the coefficient of a complex number x + yi or x + yj in text format.
IMARGUMENT	Returns the Theta argument as an angle expressed in radians.
IMCONJUGATE	Returns the complex conjugate of a complex number x + yi or x + yj in text format.
IMCOS	Returns the cosine of a complex number x + yi or x + yj in text format.
IMDIV	Returns the quotient of complex numbers x + yi or x + yj in text format.

IMEXP	Returns the exponential of complex numbers x + yi or x + yj in text format.
IMLN	Returns the natural logarithm of complex numbers x + yi or x + yj in text format.
IMLOG10	Returns the common logarithm (base 10) of complex numbers x + yi or x + yj in text format.
IMLOG2	Returns the base 2 logarithm of complex numbers x + yi or x + yj in text format.
IMPOWER	Returns a complex number raised to a power x + yi or x + yj in text format.
IMPRODUCT	Returns the product from 2 to 29 complex numbers x + yi or x + yj in text format.
IMREAL	Returns real coefficients of complex numbers x + yi or x + yj in text format.
IMSIN	Returns the sine of complex numbers x + yi or x + yj in text format.
IMSQRT	Returns the square root of complex numbers x + yi or x + yj in text format.
IMSUB	Returns the difference of two complex numbers x + yi or x + yj in text format.
IMSUM	Returns the sum of two complex numbers x + yi or x + yj in text format.
OCT2BIN	Converts an octal number to binary.
OCT2DEC	Converts an octal number to decimal.
OCT2HEX	Converts an octal number to hexadecimal.
SQRTPI	Returns the square root of a positive number multiplied by pi. This value cannot be less than zero. Also found under Trigonometric functions.

Financial Functions

ACCRINT	Returns the accrued interest for security that pays periodic interest.
ACCRINTM	Returns the accrued interest for security that pays interest at maturity.
AMORDEGRC	Returns appreciation for each accounting period.
AMORLINC	Returns depreciation for each accounting period.
COUPDAYBS	Returns the number of days from the start date of the coupon period to the settlement.

COUPDAYS	Returns the number of days in the coupon period that includes the settlement date.
COUPDAYSNC	Returns the number of days from the settlement date to the next coupon date.
COUPNCD	Returns the number of days from the next coupon date after the settlement date.
COUPNUM	Returns the total number of coupons payable between the settlement and maturity date, rounded up to the nearest whole coupon.
COUPPCD	Returns the number of the previous coupon date before the settlement date.
CUMIPMT	Returns the cumulative interest on a loan between start and stop dates.
CUMPRINC	Returns the cumulative principal amount between start and stop dates.
DB	Returns the asset depreciation for a period using the fixed-declining balance method.
DDB	Returns the asset depreciation for a period using the double-declining balance method, or another method you specify.
DISC	Returns the security discount rate.
DOLLARDE	Converts a fraction dollar price into a decimal dollar price.
DOLLARFR	Converts a decimal dollar price into a fraction dollar price.
DURATION	Returns the duration for an assumed par value of $100 using the Macauley method.
EFFECT	Returns the effective interest rate annually, giving the nominal annual interest rate and the number of compounding periods per year.
FV	Returns the future value of periodic payments and a constant interest rate.
FVSCHEDULE	Returns the future value of the initial principal after applying several compound interest rates.
INTRATE	Returns the interest rate of a fully invested security.
IPMT	Returns the interest payment for a period of time based on an investment with periodic constant payments and a constant interest rate.
IRR	Returns the internal rate of return for a series of cash flows represented by numbers in the form of values.
MDURATION	Returns a modified duration of a security with an assumed par value of $100.

MIRR	Returns a modified internal rate of return for several periodic cash flows.
NOMINAL	Returns the nominal annual interest rate given an effective rate and a number of compounding periods per year.
NPER	Returns the number of periods for an investment based on periodic constant payments and a constant interest rate.
NPV	Calculates the net present value of an investment with the discount rate and several future payments and income.
ODDFPRICE	Returns the value of a security based on a per $100 face value and an odd first period.
ODDFYIELD	Returns the security yield with an odd first period.
ODDLPRICE	Returns the per $100 face value of a security having an odd last coupon period.
ODDLYIELD	Returns the security yield that has an odd last coupon period.
PMT	Calculates the loan payment for a loan based on constant payments and constant interest rates.
PPMT	Returns the principal payment for a period of an investment based on periodic constant payments and a constant interest rate.
PRICE	Returns the value of a security based on price per $100 face value and periodic payments.
PRICEDISC	Returns the value of a discounted security based on a price per $100 face value.
PRICEMAT	Returns the value of a security that pays interest at maturity and price per $100 face value.
PV	Returns the present value based on an investment.
RATE	Returns per period the interest of an annuity.
RECEIVED	Returns the amount received at maturity based on a fully invested security.
SLN	Returns the straight-line depreciation on an asset based on one period.
SYD	Returns the sum-of-years-digits depreciation of an asset based on a specified period.
TBILLEQ	Returns the bond equivalent yield for a treasury bill.
TBILLPRICE	Returns the price per $100 face value for a treasury bill.
TBILLYIELD	Returns the yield for a treasury bill.
VDB	Returns the depreciation of an asset for a period you specify.
XIRR	Returns the internal rate of return for a schedule of cash flows that are not necessarily periodic.

XNPV	Returns the present value for a schedule of cash flows that are not necessarily periodic.
YIELD	Returns the yield of the security based on a yield that pays periodic interest.
YIELDDISC	Returns the annual yield for a discounted security.
YIELDMAT	Returns the annual yield based on a security that pays interest at maturity.

Information Functions

CELL	Returns information about a cell's location, formatting, or contents in the upper-left cell in a reference.
COUNTBLANK	Counts the number of empty cells in a specified range.
ERROR.TYPE	Returns the corresponding number value associated with an error type in Microsoft Excel.
INFO	Returns operating environment information.
ISBLANK	Returns the value associated with the number of empty cells.
ISERR	Returns the error value associated with an error in Microsoft Excel, except #NA.
ISERROR	Returns the error value associated with an error in Microsoft Excel.
ISEVEN	Returns TRUE or FALSE if the number is even or odd, TRUE being even and FALSE being odd.
ISLOGICAL	Returns TRUE if the value is logical.
ISNA	Returns the value associated with the error type #NA.
ISNONTEXT	Returns the value of any item that is nontext and returns TRUE if the value refers to a blank cell.
ISNUMBER	Returns a value if the cell has a number.
ISODD	Returns FALSE if the number is even and TRUE if the number is odd.
ISREF	Returns the value associated with a reference.
N	Returns the value converted to a number.
NA	Returns the error value associated with #NA.
TYPE	Returns the type of value, for example, Number = 1, Text = 2, Logical Value = 4, Error Value = 16, and Array = 64. Use type when the behavior of another function depends on the type of value in a particular cell.
U	Returns the logical value TRUE or FALSE associated with text.

Logical Functions

AND	Returns TRUE if the arguments are true in the formula, and FALSE if they're false.
FALSE	Returns the value FALSE. There are no arguments associated with this function.
IF	Returns a value if one condition is TRUE, and returns another value if the condition is FALSE.
NOT	Returns the reverse value of its arguments.
OR	Returns FALSE if all arguments are false, and TRUE if all arguments are true.
TRUE	Returns the value TRUE. There are no arguments associated with this function.

Lookup and Reference Functions

ADDRESS	Creates a cell address as text given specified row and column numbers.
AREAS	Returns the number of areas based on a reference.
CHOOSE	Returns the index number from the list based on a list of arguments.
COLUMN	Returns the column number based on a given reference.
COLUMNS	Returns the number of columns based on an array or reference.
HLOOKUP	Searches for a specified value in an array or a table's top row.
HYPERLINK	Creates a shortcut to jump to a document stored within a workbook or on a network server. You can also use the hyperlink function to link to a URL, such as a stock page on the Web.
INDEX (Array Form)	Returns the value of an element selected by the row number and column letter indexes based on a table or array.
INDEX (Reference Form)	Returns the reference of the cell based on the intersection of a particular row and column.
INDIRECT	Returns the reference based on a text string.
LOOKUP (Array Form)	Looks in the first row or column of an array, and returns the specified value from the same position in the last row or column of the array.
LOOKUP (Vector Form)	Returns the value from the same position in a second row or column based on a range of one row or one column.

MATCH	Returns the position of an item in an array that matches a specified value and order.
OFFSET	Returns a reference to a range that is a specific number of rows and columns from a cell or range of cells.
ROW	Returns the row number based on a reference.
ROWS	Returns the number of rows based on a reference or array.
TRANSPOSE	Returns a horizontal range of cells as vertical or vice versa.
VLOOKUP	Looks for a value in the leftmost column of a table and returns a value from the column number you specify.

Math and Trigonometry Functions

ABS	Returns the absolute value of number.
ACOS	Returns the arccosine of number. The arccosine is the angle whose cosine is number.
ACOSH	Returns the inverse hyperbolic cosine of number.
ASIN	Returns the arccosine of number.
ASINH	Returns the inverse hyperbolic sine of number.
ATAN	Returns the arctangent of number.
ATAN2	Returns the arctangent of the specified x and y coordinates.
ATANH	Returns the inverse hyperbolic tangent of number.
CEILING	Returns number rounded up, away from zero, to the nearest multiple of significance.
COMBIN	Returns the number of combinations for a given number of items.
COS	Returns the cosine of a given angle.
COSH	Returns the hyperbolic cosine of number.
COUNTIF	Counts the number of cells in a specified range that meet the criteria you specify.
DEGREES	Converts radians into degrees.
EVEN	Returns number rounded up to the nearest integer.
EXP	Returns E raised to the power of number.
FACT	Returns the factorial of number.
FACTDOUBLE	Returns the double factorial of number.
FLOOR	Rounds number down, toward zero, to the nearest multiple of significance.
GCD	Returns the greatest common divisor of two or more integers.
INT	Rounds number down to the nearest integer.

LCMN	Returns the least common multiple of integers.
LN	Returns the natural logarithm of a number.
LOG	Returns the logarithm of a number to the base you specify.
LOG10	Returns the base 10 logarithm of a number.
MDETERM	Returns the matrix determinant of an array.
MINVERSE	Returns the inverse matrix for the matrix stored in an array.
MMULT	Returns the matrix product of two arrays.
MOD	Returns the remainder after number is divided by divisor.
MROUND	Returns number rounded to the desired multiple.
MULTINOMIAL	Returns the ratio of the factorial of a sum of values to the product of factorials.
ODD	Returns number rounded to the nearest odd integer.
PI	Returns the number 3.14159265358979, the mathematical constant pi, accurate to 15 digits. There are no arguments associated with this function.
POWER	Returns the result of a number raised to a power.
PRODUCT	Multiplies all the numbers given as arguments and returns the product.
QUOTIENT	Returns the integer portion of a division.
RADIANS	Converts degrees to radians.
RAND	Returns an evenly distributed number greater than or equal to 0 and less than 1. There are no arguments associated with this function.
RANDBETWEEN	Returns a random number between the numbers you specify.
ROMAN	Converts an Arabic numeral to Roman, as text.
ROUND	Rounds a number to a specified number of digits.
ROUNDDOWN	Rounds a number down toward 0.
ROUNDUP	Rounds a number up away from 0.
SERIESSUM	Returns the sum of a power series based on the formula.
SIGN	Determines the sign (positive or negative) of number.
SIN	Returns the sine of the given angle.
SINH	Returns the hyperbolic sine of number.
SQRT	Returns the positive square root of number.
SQRTPI	Returns the square root of (number*pi).

SUBTOTAL	Returns a subtotal from a list or database. It has 11 commands. Subtotal can tally AVERAGE, COUNT, COUNTA, MAX, MIN, PRODUCT, STDEV, STDEVP, SUM, VAR, and VARP.
SUM	Adds the numbers in a range of cells.
SUMIF	Adds the cells specified by criteria.
SUMPRODUCT	Multiplies corresponding components in the given array, and returns the sum of those products.
SUMSQ	Returns the sum of the squares of the arguments.
SUMX2MY2	Returns the sum of the difference of squares of corresponding values in two arrays.
SUMX2PY2	Returns the sum of the sum of squares in corresponding values in two arrays.
SUMXMY2	Returns the sum of squares of differences of corresponding values in two arrays.
TAN	Returns the tangent of the given angle.
TANH	Returns the hyperbolic tangent of number.
TRUNC	Truncates number to an integer, removing the fractional part of the number.

Statistical Functions

AVEDEV	Returns the average of the absolute deviations of data points from their mean.
AVERAGE	Returns the average of the arguments.
AVERAGE A	Calculates the average of the values in the list of arguments.
BETADIST	Returns the cumulative beta probability density function.
BETAINV	Returns the inverse of the cumulative beta probability density function.
BINOMDIST	Returns the individual term binomial distribution probability.
CHIDIST	Returns the one-tailed probability of the chi-squared distribution.
CHINV	Returns the inverse of the one-tailed probability of the chi-squared distribution.
CHITEST	Returns the test for independence.
CONFIDENCE	Returns the confidence interval for a population mean.
CORREL	Returns the correlation coefficient of the array1 and array2 cell ranges.
COUNT	Counts the number of cells that contain numbers within the list of arguments.

COUNTA	Counts the number of cells that are not empty and the values within the list of arguments.
COVAR	Returns covariance, the average of the products of deviations for each data-point pair.
CRITBINOM	Returns the smallest value for which the cumulative binomial distribution is greater than or equal to a criterion value.
DEVSQ	Returns the sum of squares of deviations of data points from their sample mean.
EXPONDIST	Returns the exponential distribution.
FDIST	Returns the F probability distribution.
FINV	Returns the inverse of the F probability distribution.
FISHER	Returns the Fisher transformation at X.
FISHERINV	Returns the inverse of the Fisher transformation.
FORECAST	Calculates or predicts a future value by using existing values.
FREQUENCY	Calculates how often values occur within a range of values, and then returns a vertical array of numbers.
FTEST	Returns the result of an Ftest.
GAMMADIST	Returns the gamma distribution.
GAMMAINV	Returns the inverse of the gamma cumulative distribution.
GAMMALN	Returns the natural logarithm of the gamma function.
GEOMEAN	Returns the geometric mean of an array or range of positive data.
GROWTH	Calculates predicted exponential growth by using existing data.
HARMEAN	Returns the harmonic mean of a data set.
HYPGEOMDIST	Returns the hypergeometric distribution.
INTERCEPT	Calculates the point at which a line will intersect the y-axis by using existing x-values and y-values.
KURT	Returns the Kurtosis of a data set.
LARGE	Returns the k-th largest value in a data set.
LINEST	Calculates the statistics for a line by using the "least squares" method to calculate a straight line that best fits your data, and returns an array that describes the line.
LOGEST	Calculates an exponential curve that fits your data and returns an array of values that describes the curve in regression analysis.
LOGINV	Returns the inverse of the lognormal cumulative distribution function of X, wherein (x) is normally distributed with parameters MEAN and STANDARD_DEV.
LOGNORMDIST	Returns the cumulative LOGNORMAL distribution of X, wherein (x) is normally distributed with parameters MEAN and STANDARD_DEV.

MAX	Returns the largest value in a set of values.
MAXA	Returns the largest value in a list of arguments.
MEDIAN	Returns the median of the given numbers.
MIN	Returns the smallest number in a set of values.
MINA	Returns the smallest value in a list of arguments.
MODE	Returns the most frequently occurring, or repetitive, value in an array or range of data.
NEGBINOMDIST	Returns the negative binomial distribution.
NORMDIST	Returns the normal cumulative distribution for the specified mean and standard deviation.
NORMINV	Returns the inverse of the normal cumulative distribution for the specified mean and standard deviation.
NORMSDIST	Returns the standard normal cumulative distribution function.
NORMSINV	Returns the inverse of the standard normal cumulative distribution.
PEARSON	Returns the Pearson product moment correlation coefficient, r, a dimensionless index that ranges from –1.0 to 1.0 inclusive and reflects the extent of a linear relationship between two data sets.
PERCENTILE	Returns the k-th percentile of values in a range.
PERCENTRANK	Returns the rank of a value in a data set as a percentage of the data set.
PERMUT	Returns the number of permutations for a given number of objects that can be selected from number objects.
POISSON	Returns the Poisson distribution and predicts events over time.
PROB	Returns the probability that values in a range are between two specified limits.
QUARTILE	Returns the quartile of a data set.
RANK	Returns the rank of a number in a list of numbers.
RSQ	Returns the square of the Pearson product moment correlation coefficient through data points in known_y's and known_x's.
SKEW	Returns the skewness of a distribution.
SLOPE	Returns the slope of the regression line through data points in known_y's and known_x's.
SMALL	Returns the k-th smallest value in a data set.
STANDARDIZE	Returns a normalized value from a distribution characterized by MEAN and STANDARD_DEV.
STDEVA	Estimates standard deviation based on a sample. STDEVA acts upon values.
STDEVE	Estimates standard deviation based on a sample. STDEVE acts upon numbers.

STDEVP	Calculates standard deviation based on the entire population given as arguments.
STDEVPA	Calculates standard deviation based on the entire population given as arguments.
STEYX	Returns the standard error of the predicted y-value for each x in the regression.
TDIST	Returns the student's t-distribution.
TINV	Returns the inverse of the student's t-distribution for the specified degrees of freedom.
TREND	Returns values along a linear trend.
TRIMMEAN	Returns the mean of the interior of a data set.
TTEST	Returns the probability associated with the student's t-test.
VARA	Estimates variance based on a sample.
VARP	Calculates variance based on the entire population.
VARPA	Calculates variance based on the entire population. In addition to numbers, text and logical values, such as TRUE and FALSE, are included in the calculation.
WEIBULL	Returns the Weibull distribution.
ZTEST	Returns the two-tailed P-value of a z-test.

Text Functions

CHAR	Returns the character specified by a number.
CLEAN	Removes all nonprintable characters from text.
CODE	Returns a numeric code from the first character in a text string.
CONCATENATE	Joins several text strings into one text string.
DOLLAR	Converts a number to text using Currency format, with the decimals rounded to the specified place.
EXACT	Compares two text strings and returns TRUE if they're exactly the same, and FALSE otherwise.
FIND	Finds one text string with another text string, and returns the number of the starting position of find_text, from the leftmost character of within_text.
FIXED	Rounds a number to a specified number of decimals, formats the number in decimal format using a period and commas, and returns the result as text.
LEFT	Returns the first character or characters in a text string.

LEN	Returns the number of characters in a text string.
LOWER	Converts all uppercase letters in a text string to lowercase.
MID	Returns a specific number of characters from a text string, starting at the position you specify.
PROPER	Capitalizes the first letter in a text string and any other letters in text that follow any character other than a letter.
REPLACE	Replaces a portion of a text string with a different text string based on the number of characters you specify.
REPLACEB	Replaces part of a text string with a different text string based on the number of bytes you specify.
REPT	Repeats text a given number of times.
RIGHT	Returns the last character or characters in a text string.
SEARCH	Returns the number of the character at which a specific character or text string is first found, reading from left to right. SEARCH is not case sensitive and can include wildcard characters.
SEARCHB	Returns the number of the character at which a specific character or text string is first found, reading from left to right.
SUBSTITUTE	Substitutes new_text for old_text in a text string.
T	Returns the text referred to by value.
TEXT	Converts a value to text in a specific number format.
TRIM	Removes all spaces from text except for single spaces between words.
UPPER	Converts text to uppercase.
VALUE	Converts a text string that represents a number to a number.

CHAPTER 2

Managing Your Business with Functions

An Overview

This chapter is specifically designed to breakout certain functions and apply those functions to everyday business. Although daily business may differ from individual to individual (and business to business), you'll find problems and situations common to most everyone. From creating forms for standardization, to presenting information graphically, and managing and viewing data quickly and efficiently, these are problems many face in day to day business activities. In addition to explanations of specific functions for lookup and reference, finances, and so on, the following topics are discussed in this chapter.

- Activity Ratios
- Applying a Named Range to Formulas
- Automating Projected Cash Flows
- Averaging Positive Numbers Only in a Range
- Building Custom Functions
- Cascading Schedules
- Channel Velocity
- Counting Unique Items in a List
- Coverage Ratios
- International Rate Converters
- Liquidity Ratios

- P&L—Direct Contribution
- Producing a Line Item Milestone Management Chart
- Profitability Ratios
- Ramping Up Production on a Single-Line Item
- Rate Exchange Tables
- Resource Pools
- Reverse Schedules
- Sell In Versus Sell Through
- Summing the Total Velocity
- Transposing Tables with Formulas (without Absolute Referencing)
- Using the EUROCONVERT Formula

Using Functions for Lookup and Reference, Math, and Trigonometry

VLOOKUP

VLOOKUP looks for a value in the leftmost column of a table and returns a value from the column number that you specify.

In Figure 2.1, VLOOKUP references cell C9 for the reference of Compu Check, then the data range F4:G7 is entered, followed by the column number 2 for which you want a value returned. The result is $189,844, the corresponding value to the product Compu Check.

MATCH

MATCH returns the position of an item in an array that matches a specified value and order or matches the position of an item.

In Figure 2.1, MATCH references cell C10 for the date reference of the record to match, then the data range C4:C7 is entered, followed by the match type—0 for record number and 1 for record order. The result of the record number is the second record down in the list.

OFFSET

The OFFSET function returns a reference to a range that is a specific number of rows and columns from a cell or range of cells.

In Figure 2.1, the OFFSET formula references the cell C4, 0 is the number or rows down from the cell reference, 2 is the number of columns over from the cell reference, 1 is the height, and 1 is the width that returns the result of the ISBN 2 columns over to the right.

SUMIF

The SUMIF function adds the cells specified by given criteria.

In Figure 2.1, the SUMIF function references the product range F4:F7, then the cell reference to sum up which is C15, and the sums of the range that matches the specified criteria in the range G4:G7. The result is the total dollars for the two Anti Virus Scan products of $8,041.

SUMIF with a Conditional Month

The SUMIF function adds the cells specified by given criteria. The MONTH function is a condition applied to the formula that finds the month specified in the condition.

In Figure 2.1, the SUM(IF(MONTH function references the month range of C4:C7 and then references the condition to apply in cell C17 which is the month number(3=March). The sum range is applied in the cell range G4:G7 and returns the result of $1,188. Note that this formula is used in the form of an array and must be activated by pressing Ctrl+Shft+Enter.

SUMIF with a Cell Reference Year Conditional and Month

The SUMIF function in this case adds the cells specified by given criteria. And the MONTH function is a condition applied to the formula that finds the month specified in the condition.

In Figure 2.1, the conditional SUMIF function, SUM(IF(YEAR(MONTH, applies a second condition in which to return a result. The year range of B4:B7 is applied and referenced to the year in cell C19. Think of the asterix as "and". The month condition in the range C4:C7 is applied from the previous formula and references cell D19 as the number 4 for April, the sum range is G4:G7. The total dollars is $4,021. Note that this formula is used in the form of an array and must be activated by pressing Ctrl+Shft+Enter.

SUBTOTAL

SUBTOTAL returns a subtotal from a list or database.

In Figure 2.1, the SUBTOTAL function returns the mathmatical function_num applied, note the numbers that correspond below. The function number in the example is 9 for sum, then the range is applied in cells G4:G7. The result of $199,073 is the sum of all the visible cells in the range. Use this when filtering a list. Here are a couple reasons to use the SUBTOTAL function instead of the functions themselves. Let's take a look at SUM, for example.

1. SUM ignores other SUBTOTAL functions when included in a reference. This is handy when you want to add up all the items in a column except their subtotals. Most people use a SUM that includes each of the subtotal figures, like =SUM(E15,E35). But, if you use the SUBTOTAL function for the subtotals in E15 and E35, then =SUBTOTAL(9,E5:E50) will total all the figures in the range except for E15 and E35. Using SUBTOTAL allows you to easily add a new section of items within the E5:E50 range without having to change the =SUBTOTAL(9,E5:E50) formula.

2. Ignores hidden rows when you've run a filter. Manually hiding rows will not work. This feature is not as useful. If you are running a filter, for example, it's much easier to use the SUBTOTAL command on the Data menu.

INDEX (Reference Form)

Based on the intersection of a particular row and column, INDEX returns the reference of the cell.

In Figure 2.1, the INDEX function returns the result of the record number from the range. The range is B4:B7, and the specified number is 3. The result is the third record down in the range—in this case, 1,999.

INDEX with a MATCH Condition

Where INDEX is based on the intersection of a particular row and column, this function returns the reference of the cell. MATCH returns the position of an item in an array that matches a specified value and order.

In Figure 2.1, the INDEX MATCH function returns the text result for the record corresponding to the ISBN number. The index looks through the table array of E3:F7, matches the cell reference ISBN number from C25, references the ISBN range, then matches the corresponding text record from the product column.

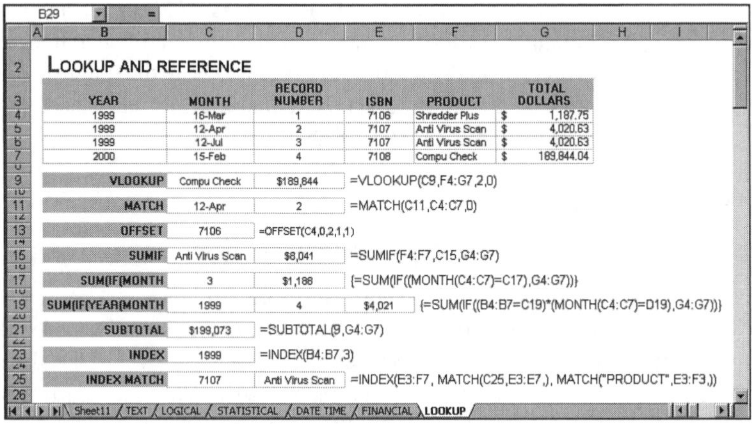

Figure 2.1

Common *LOOKUP* and *REFERENCE* functions used against lists.

Working with Date and Time

TODAY

TODAY returns the current date as a serial number. There are no arguments for this function.

The TODAY function is a powerful dynamic function that allows you to see the current day every time the workbook is opened. You could place the TODAY function in a cell on a report so that you always have the correct date. Notice the example in Figure 2.2, there are no arguments for this function.

NOW

Returns the current date and time in the form of a serial number with the NOW function. There are no arguments for this function.

The NOW function calculates the time the function was entered. This could be in the form of a year, month, day, hour, minute, or second. See the example in Figure 2.2.

EDATE

The EDATE function returns the value or serial number of the date you specified and the number of months before or after the specified date. Use EDATE to calculate the maturity date or date due that falls on the same day of the month as the date of issue.

The example in Figure 2.2 shows two EDATE examples with the maturity date occuring 1 and 2 months after the date of issue.

NETWORKDAYS

The NETWORKDAYS function returns the number of working days between two dates. Excludes weekends and specified holidays.

The NETWORKDAYS function allows you to find out the total number of working days between two dates excluding the weekends and holidays. This is an extremely important function when calculating schedules that have to be completed within specific time frames. Notice the structure of the example in Figure 2.2. The date value operates as text in quotes.

Figure 2.2

Common *DATE AND TIME* functions.

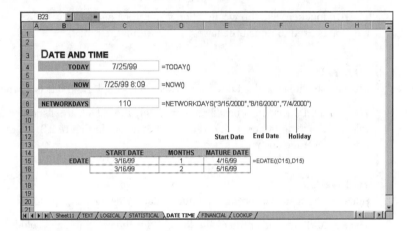

Computing Statistics

AVERAGE

AVERAGE returns the average of the arguments.

The AVERAGE function averages the numbers over a range or in the form of an array over several ranges. Figure 2.3 shows the AVERAGE function averaging the dollars from column E, "Total Dollars."

COUNTA

Use COUNTA to count the number of cells that are not empty and the values within the list of arguments.

The COUNTA function illustrated in Figure 2.3 shows the count over the range of cells to equal 5. Blank cells are not counted. (Use the COUNT function if you want to count blank cells as well.)

COUNTIF

The COUNTIF function counts the number of cells within a range that meets the given criteria.

COUNTIF is used over a range of cells and returns a numeric result based on logical criteria. The logical criteria in Figure 2.3 is in quotes, and counts all values in excess or greater than 10,000.

MAX

MAX returns the largest value in a set of values.

The MAX function can be used on numbers and dates. As you notice in Figure 2.3, the MAX function is used to return the largest date in a range of dates.

MIN

MIN returns the smallest number in a set of values with MIN.

The MIN function, like the MAX function, can return dates and values. In Figure 2.3, the MIN function is used to return the lowest value within the range.

STDEVA

STDEVA estimates standard deviation based on a sample, and it acts upon values.

The standard deviation is based on how widely the values are dispersed from the average value. The average value is referred to as the mean. In Figure 2.3, the standard deviation from the average count of units is 1.41.

FORECAST

FORECAST calculates or predicts a future value by using existing values.

The FORECAST function returns the forecast for the existing units sold in column F of Figure 2.3. The known y's and known_x's are in arrays, and the predicted value is achieved using linear regression.

Figure 2.3
Commonly used
STATISTICAL
functions.

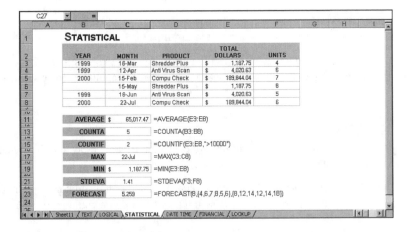

Generating Financial Results

CUMIPMT

Use CUMIPMT to return the cumulative interest on a loan between start and stop dates.

See Figure 2.4 for the setup and example. In the example, the functions formula is derived by using cell referencing. Where nper is number of periods, pv is present value, and type is the timing of the payment. See the bottom of Figure 2.4 for the Timing description.

CUMPRINC

CUMPRINC returns the cumulative principal amount between start and stop dates.

See Figure 2.4 for the setup and example. In the example, the functions formula is derived by using cell referencing. Where nper is number of periods, pv is present value, and type is the timing of the payment. See the bottom of Figure 2.4 for the Timing description.

IPMT

IPMT returns the interest payment for a period of time based on an investment with periodic constant payments and a constant interest rate.

See Figure 2.4 for the setup and example. In the example, the functions formula is derived by using cell referencing. Where nper is number of periods and pv is present value, per is the period for which you want to see what the interest payment would be, and type is the timing of the payment. See the bottom of Figure 2.4 for the Timing description.

FV

Return the future value of periodic payments and a constant interest rate by using the FV function.

See Figure 2.4 for the setup and example. In the example, the functions formula is derived by using cell referencing. The FV function is used primarily for finding the payments over a period of time to reach a specific goal or lump sum. Notice in Figure 2.4 that the deposit amount or present value is 1,000, the constant payments is 200, the nper is the number of periods, and type is the timing of the payment. See the bottom of Figure 2.4 for the Timing description.

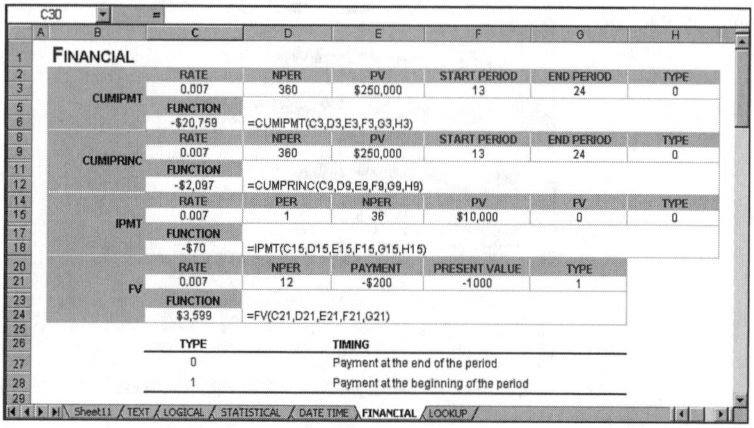

Figure 2.4

These common *FINANCIAL* functions are essential for managing your personal finances.

Producing Logical and Informational Data

IF

IF returns a value if one condition is true, and returns another value if the condition is false.

The IF function is used to compare logical tests and return text or numeric results. Notice in Figure 2.5, there are three IF examples. The first example in cell E4, is used to compare whether text in a cell equals the text of "Pass" in the formula, returns a text response based on the cell input in D4. The second example in cell F11 in Figure 2.5 compares whether or not a value is zero, and if so, returns zero or else adds two cells together. And the third example is a nested IF, which returns a text result based on a numeric condition being met, and if the numeric condition is less than the previous in the second, third, or fourth condition, the lower result is used.

ISNUMBER

The ISNUMBER function returns a value if the cell has a number.

The ISNUMBER example in Figure 2.5 is used to compare whether a numeric result is met in cell D20, if so, it returns a text response if the condition is met, and False if it's not.

ISBLANK

Return the value associated with the number of empty cells with the ISBLANK function.

ISBLANK returns a logical True or False result based on whether a cell has data in it. Combined with the SUM and IF functions, it can be used as a tracking function to return the result from a specified range based on the result of another range. The example in Figure 2.5 shows the function looking up how many dates are entered in a column and returns the actual page count from column D. In essence, it tracks the pages based on vertical and horizontal processes.

Figure 2.5

Common *LOGICAL* and information functions.

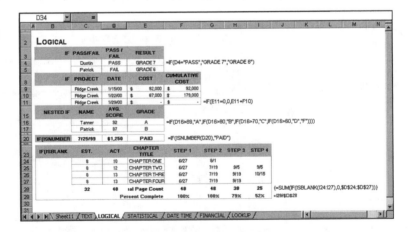

Working with Text

CONCATENATE

CONCATENATE joins several text strings into one text string.

CONCATENATE joins text. However, you'll most likely want the text separated, so the two examples in Figure 2.6 in cells E5 and E6 use a quote separater to apply text or space between the characters. The ampersand sign also adjoins text as an alternative to the CONCATENATE function.

PROPER

Capitalize the first letter in a text string and any other letters in text that follow any character other than a letter by using the PROPER function.

The PROPER function cleans text and applies uppercase to the first letter in a text string—referred to as initial caps. Notice the example in Figure 2.6.

UPPER

UPPER converts text to uppercase.

The UPPER function reverts all text within a cell to upper case. Notice the example in Figure 2.6. To do the opposite, use the LOWER function to convert all text to lowercase.

RIGHT

The RIGHT function returns the last character or characters in a text string.

The RIGHT function combined with the LEN and FIND functions can be used to extract text strings of any size. Where the cell referenced is C14, the RIGHT function looks for the text, and the LEN function counts the text in the right text string, minus the numeric position of the space in quotes using the FIND function.

MID

Use MID to return a specific number of characters from a text string, starting at the position you specify.

The MID function can be used to extract left names or characters combined with the FIND function. The MID function counts the characters starting with the first character, and the FIND function subtracts one character space from the space to return the left text string result as shown in cell D18 of Figure 2.6.

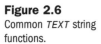

Figure 2.6

Common *TEXT* string functions.

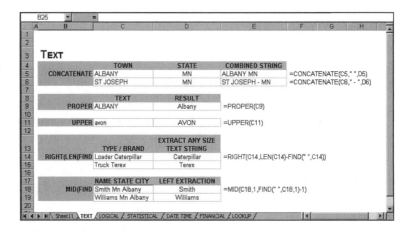

Important Tools for Any Business

There are situations common to many businesses. Take a look at how Excel functions can help you tackle most of them.

Sell In Versus Sell Through

Sell in versus sell through is the important factor when running your business if you sell goods into a distribution channel. In addition, if your products aren't revolving off the shelf, the retailer will ultimately pull the product and find a product that generates revenues for the store or chain. Pivot tables are great summaries of information for analyzing the marketplace and measuring product velocity per store, chain, sku, product type, and so on. However, you'll still need to view the product in a manner that allows you to see the product and the volume dollars per period that it is generating. Given this, you'll have to create a formula that shows velocity, or the rate at which the product is selling—which is viewed as a percentage. A conditional SUM formula is used in the following examples. The key is setup. Notice in Figure 2.7 that the conditional SUM formula in cell D4 is in the form of an array and looks up the date in cell D3 in the Date column in the In/Through table. The formula then looks up the product in cell C4 in the product column in the In/Through table. It returns the quantity for that date and product from the range D12 through D36, which is the sell in column. The same formula is applied to the sold through row (5), however the return is from column E, which is the sell through column. The array is activated by pressing Ctrl+Shft+Enter. The formula's syntax is as follows.

Channel Velocity

Channel velocity is the rate at which your products are selling through a channel, store, or marketplace. This can be measured in the form of a percentage. The velocity is based on the amount of time the product will remain in the channel or the life of the product—the total unit sales expected for the product and the weekly projected flow or sell through for the product. However simple the formula may be, the structure and having all the components in place is important. The formula just divides the actual sell through by the weekly average. If your sales are seasonal and you have fluctuating performance, as most products do, find the velocity by dividing by that particular week (see Figure 2.8).

Figure 2.7
Using a conditional *SUM* formula to set up sell in versus sell through.

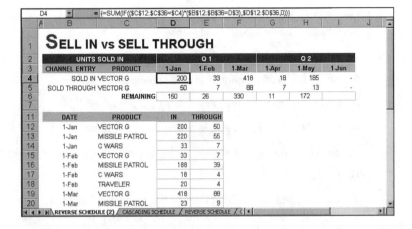

Figure 2.8
The velocity formula is the percentage sold through for the period of time—in this case, weeks.

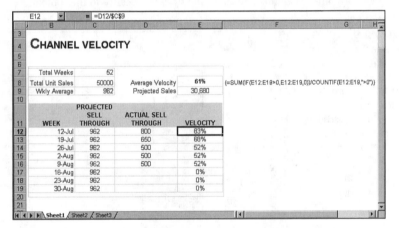

Cascading Schedules

If you sell multiple products into a distribution channel and have to accumulate the sell-in and sell-through numbers, you'll want to create a cascading schedule that reflects a product's performance. A cascading schedule gives you the information you need and helps you see when a product entered the channel and where its peak performance is. Many times, peak performance is seasonal, and if you sell toys, the winter holidays are going to be a big shot in the arm compared to July. Also, with a cascading schedule you can create charts from the information for quick access to the product's sales velocity and peak performance. You'll definitely need to have a list or database set up for extracting the information. Based on receiving the data and pumping the data into a data-warehouse, database, or an Excel spreadsheet, you can create a cascading schedule that extracts the information. (Pivot tables also work well for this. For more information about pivot tables and different ways to apply them, see "Sell In Versus Sell Through" previously in this chapter or see the book, *Special Edition Using Microsoft Excel 2000.)*

When creating a cascading schedule with ease, there are a couple of key elements. To create a cascading schedule follow these steps.

1. Sort the list or database by date in ascending order.

2. Select the product range and do not include the heading.

3. From the Data menu choose Filter then Advanced Filter.

4. Click No when Excel asks whether you want to include the row above the selection.

5. Select the option that shows Unique records only as shown in Figure 2.9.

6. Click OK.

7. Copy the unique records. Use the Select Visible Cells button found in the Commands tab of the Tools, Customize menu. See Figure 2.10. From categories choose Edit, under Commands select and drag the feature to the toolbar.

Figure 2.9
To create the cascading schedule, sort the list by ascending date, then filter the records by unique records only, giving you the cascading effect by order of occurrence.

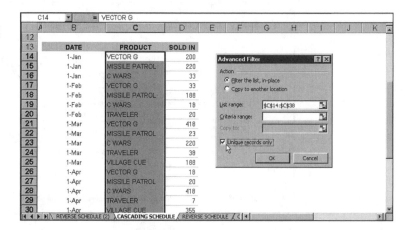

Figure 2.10
Select and copy visible cells only.

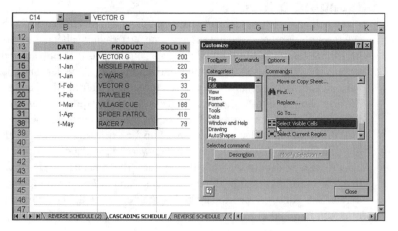

8. Paste the copied visible cells to a new location. This creates the foundation for the cascading schedule. Now that the order of occurrence is sorted by date, all you have to do is create the same conditional `SUM` formula shown previously in Figure 2.7. However, be sure the absolute referencing is as follows so you can create the formula once and drag it the length of your table. Notice the formula with absolute referencing in place in the formula bar in Figure 2.11.

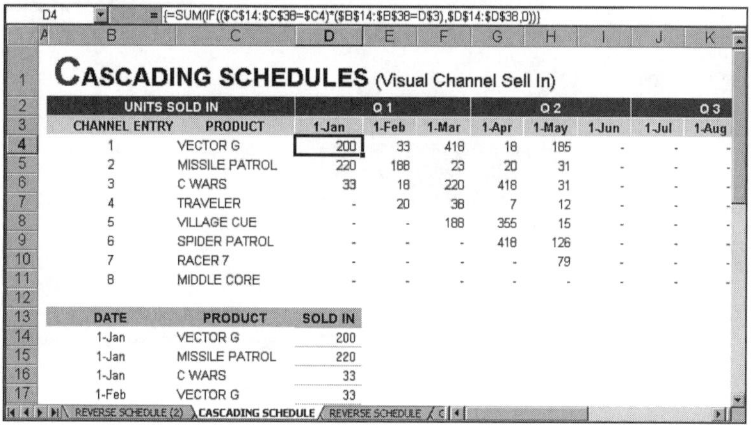

D4 = {=SUM(IF(($C$14:$C$38=$C4)*($B$14:$B$38=D$3),$D$14:$D$38,0))}

CASCADING SCHEDULES (Visual Channel Sell In)

UNITS SOLD IN		Q 1			Q 2			Q 3	
CHANNEL ENTRY	PRODUCT	1-Jan	1-Feb	1-Mar	1-Apr	1-May	1-Jun	1-Jul	1-Aug
1	VECTOR G	200	33	418	18	185	-	-	-
2	MISSILE PATROL	220	188	23	20	31	-	-	-
3	C WARS	33	18	220	418	31	-	-	-
4	TRAVELER	-	20	38	7	12	-	-	-
5	VILLAGE CUE	-	-	188	355	15	-	-	-
6	SPIDER PATROL	-	-	-	418	126	-	-	-
7	RACER 7	-	-	-	-	79	-	-	-
8	MIDDLE CORE	-	-	-	-	-	-	-	-

DATE	PRODUCT	SOLD IN
1-Jan	VECTOR G	200
1-Jan	MISSILE PATROL	220
1-Jan	C WARS	33
1-Feb	VECTOR G	33

Figure 2.11
The *CASCADING SCHEDULES* helps you visualize your channel sell in.

Reverse Schedules

Now that you've created a sell-in cascading schedule, you can easily create a reverse sell-through schedule that reflects the units sold through in order of occurrence. The key here is creating a channel entry number. Notice the channel entry number in Column B in Figure 2.12. All you have to do is sort the table by entry number in ascending or descending order. Because the formula is setup with the proper cell referencing, it always reflects the dates and products referenced.

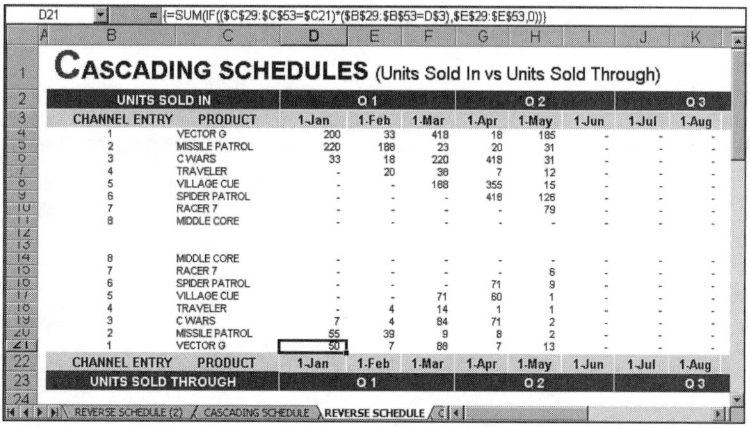

D21 = {=SUM(IF(($C$29:$C$53=$C21)*($B$29:$B$53=D$3),$E$29:$E$53,0))}

CASCADING SCHEDULES (Units Sold In vs Units Sold Through)

UNITS SOLD IN		Q 1			Q 2			Q 3	
CHANNEL ENTRY	PRODUCT	1-Jan	1-Feb	1-Mar	1-Apr	1-May	1-Jun	1-Jul	1-Aug
1	VECTOR G	200	33	418	18	185	-	-	-
2	MISSILE PATROL	220	188	23	20	31	-	-	-
3	C WARS	33	18	220	418	31	-	-	-
4	TRAVELER	-	20	38	7	12	-	-	-
5	VILLAGE CUE	-	-	188	355	15	-	-	-
6	SPIDER PATROL	-	-	-	418	126	-	-	-
7	RACER 7	-	-	-	-	79	-	-	-
8	MIDDLE CORE	-	-	-	-	-	-	-	-
8	MIDDLE CORE	-	-	-	-	-	-	-	-
7	RACER 7	-	-	-	-	6	-	-	-
6	SPIDER PATROL	-	-	-	71	9	-	-	-
5	VILLAGE CUE	-	-	71	60	1	-	-	-
4	TRAVELER	-	4	14	1	1	-	-	-
3	C WARS	7	4	84	71	2	-	-	-
2	MISSILE PATROL	55	39	9	8	2	-	-	-
1	VECTOR G	50	7	88	7	13	-	-	-
CHANNEL ENTRY	PRODUCT	1-Jan	1-Feb	1-Mar	1-Apr	1-May	1-Jun	1-Jul	1-Aug
UNITS SOLD THROUGH		Q 1			Q 2			Q 3	

Figure 2.12
Creating a *REVERSE SCHEDULE* reflecting sell through.

Summing the Total Velocity

Now use the velocity formula as shown in Figure 2.13 that reflects total percentage of sales for the month. Generally referred to as POS (Point of Sale).

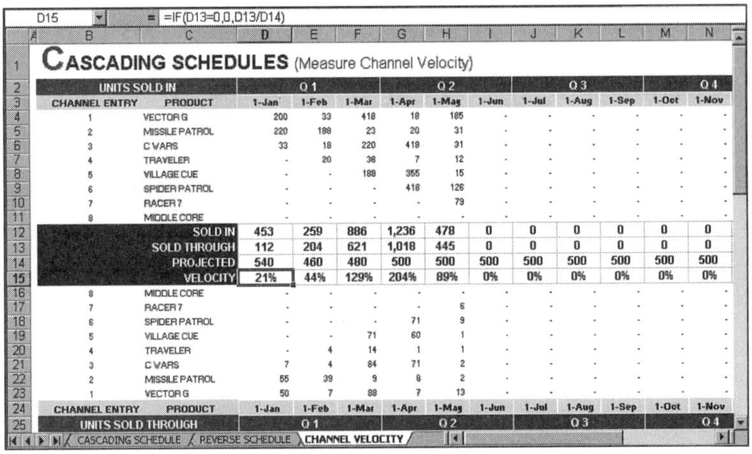

Figure 2.13

Insert the velocity between the schedules and divide the sold through number by the projected units sold in number.

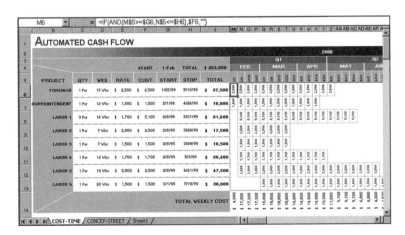

Automating Projected Cash Flows

Whether you're in business, finance, accounting, marketing, or production, at some point you're going to have to forecast project cash flows, units created, and so on. Here's an IF AND formula that moves units, people, or money over time. Notice the formula in Figure 2.14, =IF(AND(M$5>=$G6,N$5<=$H6),$F6,""). The formula basically says, if the corresponding week is greater than or equal to the start date and the next week is less than or equal to the stop date, then return the weekly cost in cell F6. In this example, conditional formatting is used to block off the timeline into boxes. (The example is also on the CD accompanying this book.) As you change the quantity, weeks, rates, or start date, the timeline automatically moves to correspond with your changes.

Figure 2.14

Create automated time-lines and cash flows with the combination of *IF* and *AND*.

Transposing Tables with Formulas (without Absolute Referencing)

There are many occasions when you'll have tables that reference lists of information and the formulas don't have absolute referencing. Now, in the likely event you'll have to view the information in a new format, you may have to spend countless hours applying an absolute reference to all the formulas—or you can use this undocumented trick. Select the region with the formulas as shown in Figure 2.15. From the Edit menu, select Replace. Under Find what type =. Under Replace with type ≤.

Figure 2.15
Select the region with the formulas to transpose the table.

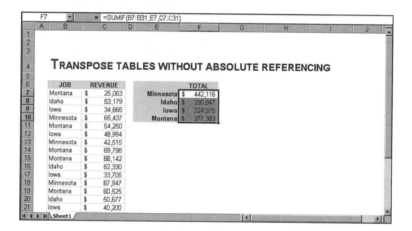

Select and copy the entire table to transpose the table as shown in Figure 2.16.

Figure 2.16
Copy the entire table to transpose the table.

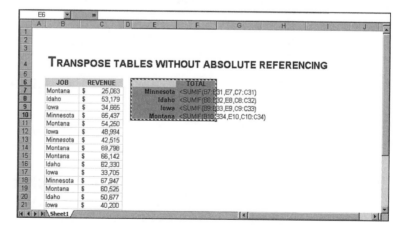

Select a cell or destination where you want the transposed table to be placed. Under the Edit menu choose Paste Special. From the Paste Special dialog box select Transpose. Now select the transposed formula cells as shown in Figure 2.17.

Figure 2.17
Select the formula cells in the transposed table to replace the < sign back to =.

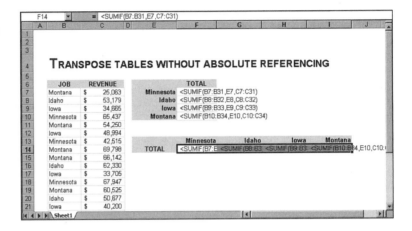

From the Edit menu, select Replace. Under Find what type <. Under Replace with type =. The transposed table now reflects the original referencing without using absolute as shown in Figure 2.18.

Figure 2.18
The result of replacing the < sign with the = sign reactivates the formula with the same referencing.

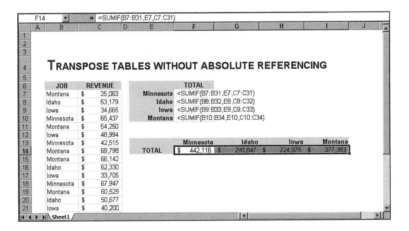

Averaging Positive Numbers Only in a Range

You'll often run into situations in which you'll have a range of numbers that you want to average. However, there will inevitably be times when not all the numbers are going to be positive. In that case, including the nonpositive numbers generates an inaccurate description of the average. What if you sell products globally and you have regions that sometimes select the product and other times they don't because it's not relevant to their culture?

When regions aren't able to sell the product, you would only want the average of the positive cells rather than an average that includes regions that have not selected it. Using the SUM, IF, and COUNTIF functions in the form of an array will average just the positive cells. Notice the example in Figure 2.19.

Figure 2.19

Average only positive cells for a more accurate average.

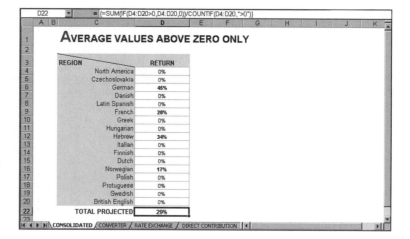

International Rate Converters

If you have to deal with international currency rates from countries around the world, it's good practice to build currency converter tables. You can create a database for each country or a database combining the countries and then extracting the country and currency and applying the rate against a US dollar table. The example in Figure 2.20 illustrates three countries with a fictitious currency rate along with the formula in the converter table to convert all currencies into US dollars.

NOTE The new Euro symbol first appeared in Excel 2000. It is unavailable in previous Excel versions. ▧

Figure 2.20

Use international currency converter tables to convert international dollars to US dollars.

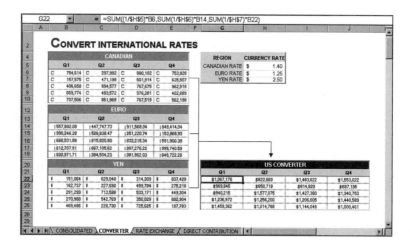

Rate Exchange Tables

When traveling abroad, at some point, you'll have to create an expense report. Creating a rate-exchange calculator by region is a quick and efficient way to handle your expense reports. Even though this is a simple formula, people continuously go the long way around to achieve the same result. Notice in Figure 2.21, =SUM(F7)*$G$5/$F$5 the region costs is to the left of the US converted column, if you have several regions in the calculator, apply the regions to the left of the US dollar as well.

Figure 2.21

A simple rate-exchange calculator can help you manage expense reports when traveling abroad.

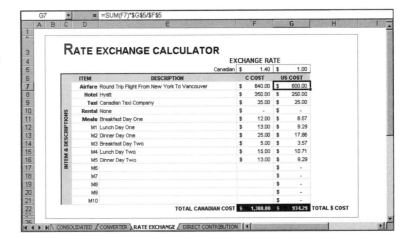

Using the EUROCONVERT Formula

The EUROCONVERT formula uses a fixed conversion rate from the European Union (EU). It converts a number to Euros, and can convert Euros from one Euro Member to another.

The EUROCONVERT formula can be used when dealing with international regions, however, it uses a fixed rate and you may want to apply your own formula that uses actual rates or current rates. The EUROCONVERT formula is a good tool for forecasting and applying assumptions. In Figure 2.22, the table represents the country, the country's basic unit currency, and the ISO code by the European Union (EU). The ISO code is the code Excel refers to when converting one rate to another. In Figure 2.22, the five examples show the EUROCONVERT function with and without the full precision and triangulation displayed. When full precision is true, then the triangulation is the number of decimals to round to.

NUMBER — This is the Euro currency to convert. The number also can be in the form of a cell reference.

SOURCE — The source is the three-letter ISO code that represents the basic unit currency for a particular country. The source is the current currency into which you want to convert.

TARGET	The target is the three-letter ISO code that represents the basic unit currency for a particular country that you want the source to convert to.
FULL_PRECISION	Full precision is the logical value of True or False that tells Excel how to round. If True, it then refers to the number for triangulation precision. If False, it defaults to two spaces.
TRIANGULATION PRECISION	Is the number of decimal digits to round to. It's activated if the Full Precision argument is True. If omitted, Excel does not round the Euro value.

Figure 2.22
Use the *EUROCONVERT* function to convert Euro currencies from one European Union to another.

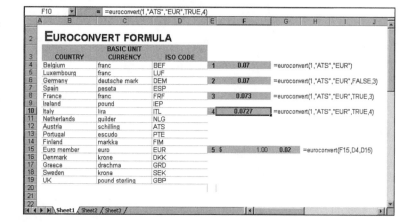

Applying a Named Range to Formulas

When you have ranges that you often refer to when using formulas, you may want to consider using a named range to represent the range. What does this mean? Let's say you have a range from A1:A100 that represents months in a year. You could apply a name to the range and call it Months. Now, when you write a formula, you can paste the named range in the formula to represent the range A1:A100. For example, in a SUMIF formula as shown in Figure 2.23, the formula in cell J6 shows the SUMIF formula using range referencing, while the formula in cell J8 is the same formula, however, named ranges are created to replace the cell ranges. To apply a named range follow these steps:

1. Select the range to which you want to apply a name.

2. From the Insert menu, select Name then Define.

3. Under Names in workbook, type the name of the range. If it's a couple of words, space the words using underscores.

4. Click Add.

5. Click OK.

Now, to paste the name into a formula, create the formula. When it comes time to apply the range, simply choose from the Insert menu, Name, and Paste. Select the name to insert and click OK.

Figure 2.23
Instead of using range referencing in formulas, apply named ranges to simplify the formula.

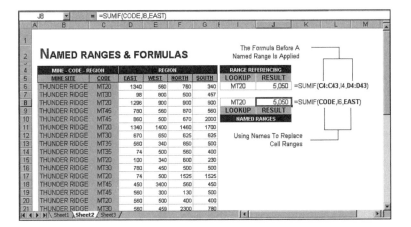

P&L—Direct Contribution

When managing your business, you're going to need a certain amount of return on every investment to remain profitable. By creating a simple P&L layout, with the right formulas combined on the P&L, you can effectively forecast each project's contribution-margin ratio to your business. It's also important to know where your breakeven points are for both total and monthly sales. Notice the example in Figure 2.24. There are six formulas that operate off each other and can effectively help you manage your projected return on investments. The key formulas and descriptions are:

Contribution Margin Ratio =IF(C12<>0,C19/C12,0) The contribution margin dollar divided by the Projected Sales.

Break Even Sales =IF(C4<>0,F25/F4,0) The Total Fixed Expenses divided by the Contribution Margin Ratio.

Monthly Breakeven Sales =IF(C11<>0,C5/C11,0) The Breakeven Sales dollar amount divided by Months. Months also can be described as the life of the product.

Contribution Margin =C12-SUM(C15:C18) The Projected Sales dollar amount divided by the sum of the Variable Expenses (Materials, Labor, Variable Overhead, Other).

Total Fixed Expenses =SUM(F11:F24) The sum of the total Fixed Expenses.

Profit During the Period =(C12-C5)*C4 The Projected Sales minus the Breakeven Sales times the Contribution Margin Ratio.

Figure 2.24
Establish a P&L to
understand direct
contribution and
breakeven sales.

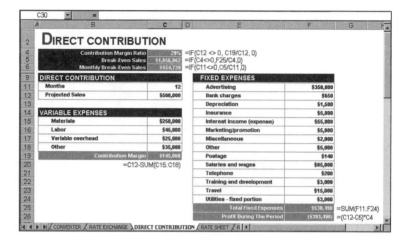

Financial Ratios

The following financial ratios give an overview of the financial ratio's description as well as
the formula description to create the ratio.

Current Ratio

The Current Ratio shows the ratio of current assets to current liabilities, as of the report date.

Gross Margin Percentage

Gross Margin Percentage indicates what percentage of each dollar of sales is left over after
paying the costs of sales amount for the period.

Days Sales in AR

Days Sales in AR shows how long it takes a business to collect receivables from its customers
for the period.

Allowance for Bad Debt As Percentage of AR

Allowance for Bad Debt as Percentage of AR shows what percentage of the accounts receivable
balance is considered uncollectable for the period.

Bad Debt As Percentage of Net Revenues

Bad Debt as Percentage of Net Revenues shows what percentage of revenue is considered
uncollectable for the period.

Inventory Turnover

Inventory Turnover shows how quickly a business sells its inventory by comparing the inventory
balance to the cost of goods sold expense for the period on an annualized basis.

Days Inventory

Days Inventory shows a ratio indicating how many days a business could continue selling using only its existing inventory as of the report date.

Net Sales to Inventory

Net Sales to Inventory shows the size of annual net sales relative to inventory for the period, on an annualized basis.

Days Purchases in AP

Days Purchases in AP indicates the size of the accounts payable relative to cost of sales for the period.

Net Sales to Working Capital

Net Sales to Working Capital indicates the size of annual net sales relative to working capital for the period on an annualized basis.

Total Assets to Net Sales

Total Assets to Net Sales shows how many dollars of assets are required to produce a dollar of sales for the period on an annualized basis.

Net Sales to AR

Net Sales to AR indicates the size of annual net sales relative to accounts receivable for the period on an annualized basis.

Net Sales to Net Fixed Assets

```
(Net Sales*Days in Year)/(Fixed Assets*Days in Period)
```

Net Sales to Net Fixed Assets shows the size of the annual net sales relative to the net fixed assets for the period on an annualized basis.

Net Sales to Total Assets

Net Sales to Total Assets shows the size of the annual net sales relative to total assets for the period on an annualized basis.

Net Sales to Net Worth

Net Sales to New Worth shows the size of the net sales relative to net worth (Total Assets minus Total Liabilities) for the period on an annualized basis.

Amortization and Depreciation Expense to Net Sales

Amortization and Depreciation Expense to Net Sales indicates what percentage of each dollar of sales pays noncash expenses, such as amortization expense of intangible assets such as copyrights and patents and depreciation expense of fixed assets for the period.

Gross Profit Percentage

Gross Profit Percentage indicates what percentage of each dollar of sales is left over after paying the cost of sales amount for the period.

Operating Expense As a Percent of Net Sales

Operating Expense as a Percent of Net Sales indicates what percentage of each sale goes to pay operating expenses for the period.

Return on Total Assets

Return on Total Assets indicates the size of net income after taxes relative to a company's total assets for the period on an annualized basis.

Return on Net Worth

Return of Net Worth indicates the size of net income after taxes relative to a company's net worth (Total Assets minus Total Liabilities) for the period on an annualized basis.

Return on Net Sales

Return on Net Sales indicates what percentage of sales ends up as profit for the period.

Income Before Tax to Net Worth

Indicates the size of net income before taxes relative to a company's net worth (Total Assets minus Total Liabilities) for the period on an annualized basis.

Income Before Tax to Total Assets

Income Before Tax to Total Assets indicates the size of net income before taxes relative to a company's total assets for the period on an annualized basis.

Retained Earning to Net Income

Retained Earning to Net Income indicates the size of the retained earning to net income for the period on an annualized basis.

Times Interest Earned

Times Interest Earned indicates the size of a company's interest expense relative to its operating profits for the period on an annualized basis.

Interest Expense to Net Sales

Interest Expense to Net Sales indicates what percentage of a company's net sales goes to pay interest expense on its debts for the period.

Current Liabilities to Net Worth

Current Liabilities to Net Worth indicates the size of a company's current liabilities relative to its net worth as of the day of the report.

Current Liabilities to Inventory

Current Liabilities to Inventory indicates the size of a company's current liabilities relative to its inventory as of the day of the report.

Accounts Payable to Net Sales

```
(Accounts Payable*Days in Period)/(Net Sales*Days in Year)
```

Accounts Payable to Net Sales indicates the size of a company's accounts payable relative to its sales revenue for the period on an annualized basis.

Total Liabilities to Net Worth

Total Liabilities to Net Worth indicates the size of a company's total liabilities relative to its net worth as of the report date.

Net Worth to Total Liabilities

Net Worth to Total Liabilities indicates the size of a company's total net worth relative to its total liabilities as of the report date.

Resource Pools

At times you'll have to schedule and manage resource pools. There are several ways to do this. This resource pool takes into account international employee rates converted to US dollar rates and applies the rates to a schedule that forecasts resource allocation over time, per employee. By using VLOOKUP to lookup the rate of the employee, the IF and AND functions as well as the SUBTOTAL function, you can create effective time-management tools for scheduling out people. First, establish a rate sheet. The example in Figure 2.25 shows the Canadian rates of the employees converted to US currency.

Figure 2.25

Establish the employee table from which to reference the dollar amount.

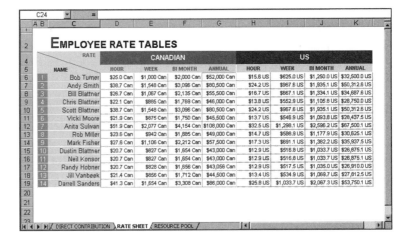

Establish the VLOOKUP formula as shown in Figure 2.26 to refer to the name on the Resource Pool Gantt chart worksheet: =VLOOKUP(C7,'RATE SHEET'!$C$6:$K$19,7,0). Where C7 refers to the employee in column C, the RATE SHEET range is C6:K19 and 7 is the seventh column over in the range.

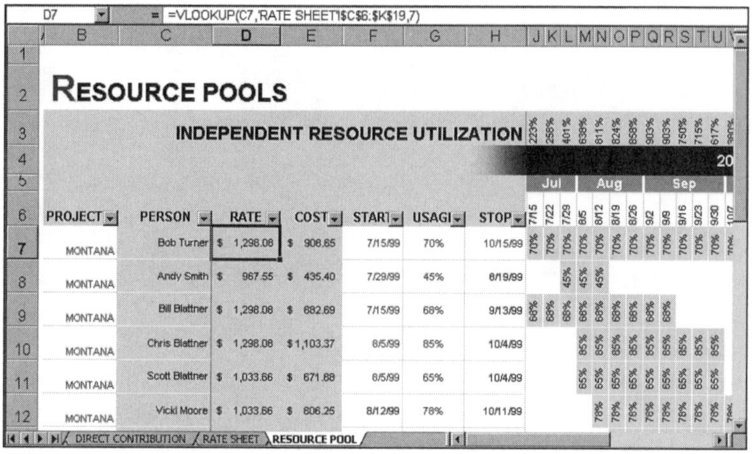

Figure 2.26
Establish *VLOOKUP* to lookup the employee rate.

Create the IF and AND dynamic Gantt chart formula =(IF(AND(J$6>=$F7,J$6<$H7),$G7,"")) as shown in Figure 2.27.

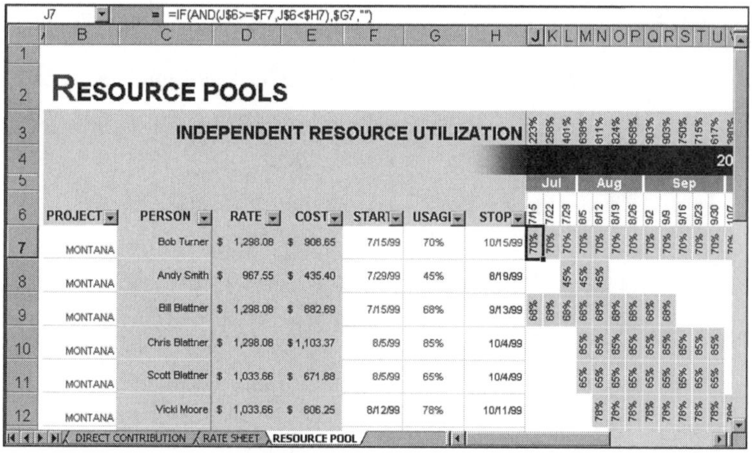

Figure 2.27
The dynamic Gantt chart formula will move and manage the percentage utilization over time.

Use the SUBTOTAL function above each week as shown in Figure 2.28. Now, when you apply filters above the names, you can pull up individual names and see their total resource allocation.

Figure 2.28
The *SUBTOTAL* function can be placed above the corresponding weeks to subtotal individuals when filtered.

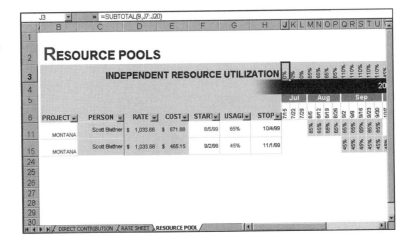

Building Custom Functions

There are times you may want to build your own custom function that does a calculation specific to your needs. For example, if you run a construction company and have several pieces of equipment with specific rates, you could apply the rates to the function and customize Excel to your needs, even nesting your own custom functions. You could establish your company's new rates at the beginning of the year and post the functions with syntax to all the estimators in the organization—then all they have to do is use the functions. To create this example—a custom function—follow these steps.

1. From the Visual Basic toolbar select the Visual Basic Editor command.

2. From the Insert menu choose Module. A new module opens.

3. In the first line of the module enter the following code, also shown as Module 1 code in Figure 2.29. Use the tab key to indent.

```
Function Cat769(hours, units)
    Cat769 = ((82.5 * hours) * Units)
End Function
```

4. Click Save.

5. Switch back to the worksheet and create a column heading for the syntax "Hours" starting in cell D7 and then "Units" in E7.

6. Type 1,250 in cell D8 and 5 in cell E8.

7. In cell F8 type the formula =Cat769(D8,E8). The return result is $515,625 as shown in Figure 2.30.

Figure 2.29
Create custom functions for your company to manage rates on equipment or sales prices.

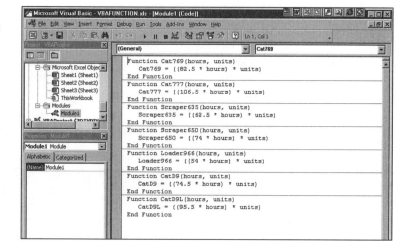

Figure 2.30
Custom functions using your company's rates can provide accuracy throughout the company.

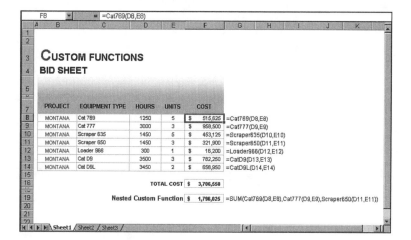

Producing a Line Item Milestone Management Chart

On many occasions you'll have to view multiple events on the same timeline. This can be achieved via one simple IF–AND statement nested several times. Notice the example in Figure 2.31, the original formula that would return one result for a date is: =IF(AND(X$7>=$B9,X$7<$C9),$P9,"")). However, what if you need several results on the same line item? All you have to do is nest the function and refer the start and stop dates to a table of dates. The nested function begins after the first return results $P9. It is

```
=IF(AND(X$7>=$B9,X$7<$C9),$P9,IF(AND(X$7>=$D9,X$7<$E9),$Q9,"")))
```

All seven nested functions would be

```
=IF(AND(X$7>=$B9,X$7<$C9),$P9,IF(AND(X$7>=$D9,X$7<$E9),$Q9,
➥IF(AND(X$7>=$F9,X$7<$G9),$R9,IF(AND(X$7>=$H9,X$7=$J9,X$7<$K9),$T9,IF(AND(X$7>=$
L9,X$7<$M9),$U9,
➥IF(AND(X$7>=$N9,X$7<$O9),$V9,"")))))))
```

Now, how do you return a conditional format that would highlight each result that's returned in a line item? Because conditional formats are limited to three conditions, you'll want to select the line range and from the conditional formatting dialog box, set the condition 1 to Cell Value Is - greater than - ="=" and then set the format as shown in Figure 2.32. This will highlight any cell that has a return result in the line item. You also can refer to the CD to review the structure of this table and formula.

Figure 2.31
Use the nested *IF-AND* function to return multiple results on a single line item.

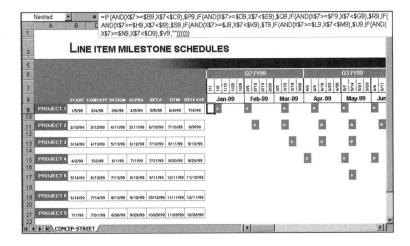

Figure 2.32
Set the conditional formatting to return any result that occurs on a line item.

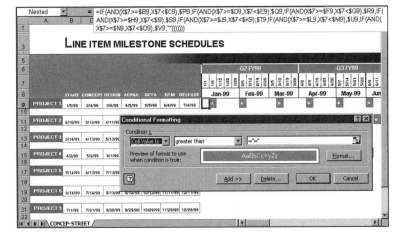

Ramping Up Production on a Single-Line Item

Quite often in the production world you'll have to move into production mode and the result is that it takes a few weeks before production is running smoothly at 100%. In this case, you'll have to ramp up the production. Here's a formula that ramps the production after 21 days by 25% in week 4, 50% in week 5, and 75% in week 6, before reaching 100% or full capacity. The formula is shown in Figure 2.33.

Because of the complexity of this setup, I would suggest referring to the CD. This example actually tells you when you need to start a project based on a completion date with the following variables: Weekly Average, Total Output or Units, and Capacity to Deliver per phase.

Figure 2.33
This formula operates off of a given completion date and three variables to tell you when to start production based on a six-week ramp up time to 100% production.

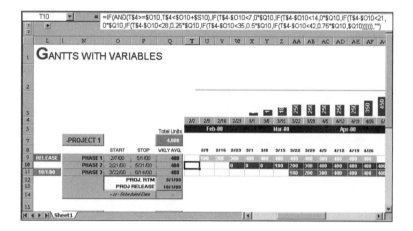

Counting Unique Items in a List

You can count unique items in a list with these two formulas. Yes, you could filter the list with unique items only, however, if your list is quite large, you'll still need to count the items. Notice Figure 2.34. The first array formula counts the unique items in a list with {=SUM(1/COUNTIF(D4:D10,D4:D10))}, however, if there is a blank cell the result is #DIV/0!. To circumvent this problem, the following formula will return the unique items in a list regardless of the blank cells.

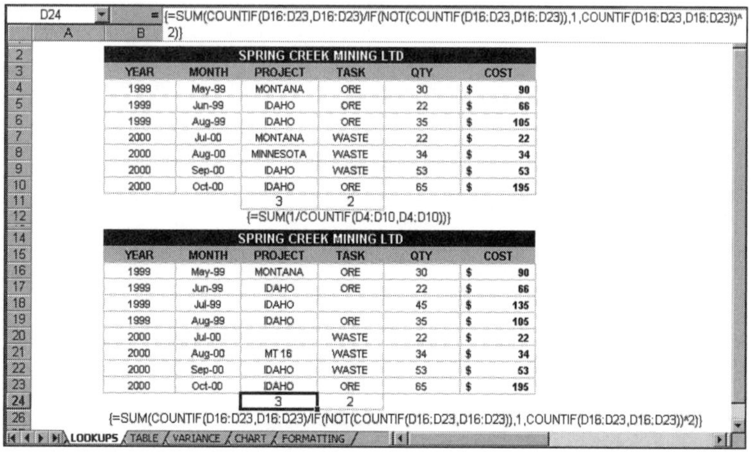

Figure 2.34
Return the number of unique items in a list with these two formulas.

Database- and List-Management Functions

Database Functions Overview

Database functions operate over ranges that can span more than one row or column. As with all functions, you can reference the database with a range name or with the cell references, either way works.

This chapter covers the following functions.

▶ DAVERAGE

▶ DCOUNT

▶ DCOUNTA

▶ DGET

▶ DMAX

▶ DMIN

▶ DPRODUCT

▶ DSTDEV

▶ DSTDEVP

▶ DSUM

▶ DVAR

▶ DVARP

▶ GETPIVOTDATA

General DFUNCTION Syntax

If you have large data stores or databases, DFUNCTIONS can be quite useful. The general syntax for the DFUNCTIONS is as follows:

`=DFUNCTION(database,field,criteria)`

- The *database* argument refers to the range encompassing the entire list or database.

- The *field* argument refers to a particular column in the list that contains the data that you want calculated. If you omit the *field* argument, the function operates on the entire list.

- The *criteria* argument specifies the basis on which you want the function to select particular cells. Another way to describe it is: Criteria is the specific requirements you set for the return. If you omit the *criteria* argument, the function operates on the entire range specified in the *field* argument.

> **N O T E** The **database range** can be a cell reference (Example 1a) or a named range (Example 2a) on all database functions.

    1a. `=DFUNCTION(C3:F17,field,criteria)`

    2a. `=DFUNCTION(database,field,criteria)`

The **field** can be the number of the column such as 3, meaning the third column in the list (Example 1b). It can be a cell reference such as C3 that contains the column heading that you want calculated (Example 2b). The field can also be the column heading's text, however the text must be enclosed in quotes, though it is not case sensitive (Example 3b).

    1b. `=DFUNCTION(Database,3,Criteria)`

    2b. `=DFUNCTION(Database,C3,Criteria)`

    3b. `=DFUNCTION(Database,"Column Heading Name",Criteria)`

The **criteria** is the range containing restrictions on which data should be included in the calculation. This means that you can specifically call out parameters, such as the sum of all numbers greater than 30, with the DSUM function. ▨

DAVERAGE

DAVERAGE indicates the average of the values that meet the specified criteria.

`=DAVERAGE(database,field,criteria)`

The DAVERAGE function averages the range of numbers that span over a range based on criteria you specify. The criteria is the range containing restrictions on which data should be included in the calculation. This means that you can specifically call out parameters, such as the sum of all numbers greater than 30, with the DSUM function. The DAVERAGE function counts the total number of entries and divides the total of the numbers by the number of entries.

When sampling data, populations, or analyzing sales data over large ranges, the DAVERAGE function quickly summarizes and returns the average. Notice the example in Figure 3.1. The field can be referenced as a column number, as shown in column 4. The 4 represents the number of columns starting from left to right. In the second example the field is referenced as a column heading "1999." The column heading is text and needs to be in quotes. The third example also references column 4, however, the criteria in range C21:C22 shows the criteria as all numbers that exceed 3,000 and less than 7,000.

Figure 3.1
The *DAVERAGE* function can be used to average columns or lists of data.

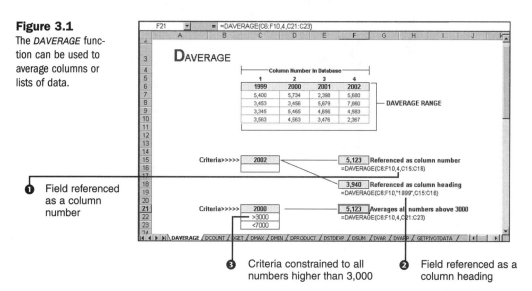

❶ Field referenced as a column number

❸ Criteria constrained to all numbers higher than 3,000

❷ Field referenced as a column heading

DCOUNT

DCOUNT counts the number of cells containing numbers that meet the specified criteria.

`=DCOUNT(database,field,criteria)`

The DCOUNT function tallies the number of cells containing numbers. Cells that contain text and blank cells are ignored. To include text cells, use DCOUNTA (see upcoming section). If you have a list or database, the database can be referenced as a cell reference or as a named range. The field is the number of the column in the database from left to right or the column heading in quotes (not case sensitive). The criteria is a range that contains the constraints the function operates from. For example, let's say you had a large database that had several blank cells as well as cells containing numbers, only some of which you were interested in. The criteria could specify to count all numbers having a value of more than 4,000 and less than 7,000, as shown in the third example in Figure 3.2. The criteria range is C20:C22, the field reference is left blank so that the function searches the entire list (C5:F9).

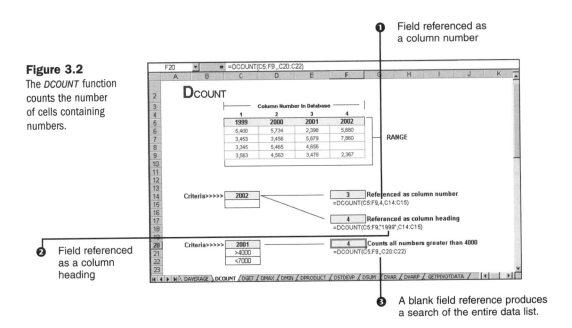

Figure 3.2
The *DCOUNT* function counts the number of cells containing numbers.

❶ Field referenced as a column number

❷ Field referenced as a column heading

❸ A blank field reference produces a search of the entire data list.

DCOUNTA

DCOUNTA counts nonblank cells containing numbers or text that meet the specified criteria.

`=DCOUNTA(database,field,criteria)`

The DCOUNTA function operates just as the DCOUNT function, however, it counts the number of cells containing numbers or text. If you have a database that has values stored as numbers and cells stored with text, you might need this function to count both storage types. The database is the cell reference range or named range of the database; and the field is referenced as the column number from left to right. The criteria is a range that is referenced and the function operates from the parameters set.

DGET

DGET returns a single value that meets the specified criteria.

`=DGET(database,field,criteria)`

The DGET function extracts a number within a database at two intersecting points. For example, if you have rate tables used in conjunction with a financial model, the DGET function can be used to apply rates based on the criteria in the criteria range. The database is the cell reference range or named range of the database; and the field is referenced as the column number from left to right.

The criteria is a range that is referenced and the function operates from the parameters set. Notice the example in Figure 3.3, the DGET formula looks up the field or Rate 2, and applies the criteria in B15:F16 to lookup Product C. Please note that if more than one value meets the specified criteria, DGET returns a #NUM! error.

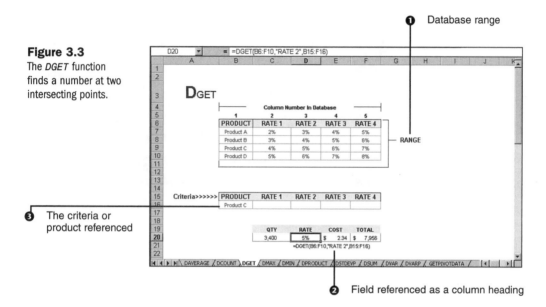

❶ Database range

Figure 3.3
The *DGET* function finds a number at two intersecting points.

❸ The criteria or product referenced

❷ Field referenced as a column heading

DMAX

DMAX extracts the highest value that meets the specified criteria.

```
=DMAX(database,field,criteria)
```

The DMAX function looks up the highest value in a range or database. The database is the cell reference range or named range of the database; and the field is referenced as the column number from left to right. The criteria is a range that is referenced and the function operates from the parameters set. The field can also be a cell reference. For example, notice the formula in Figure 3.4 that references the column heading Minnesota in cell F23. The criteria looks up the highest temperature less than 20 degrees. If you type a new column heading in the cell reference F23, the DMAX formula responds. The cell reference could be Minnesota or 1, meaning column one of the database, either way works. You can use cell references for the field in all Database functions. When you look at the figure, you'll notice that Minnesota in cell F23 is not case sensitive, however, the criteria headings are.

Database range

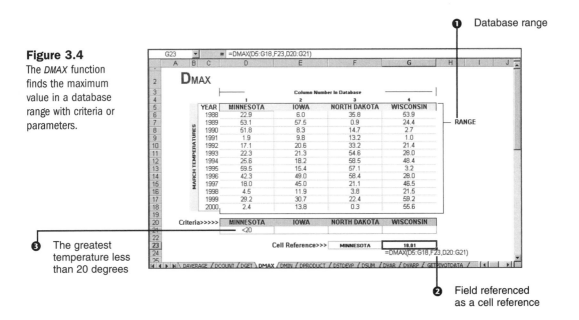

Figure 3.4
The *DMAX* function finds the maximum value in a database range with criteria or parameters.

RANGE

Field referenced as a cell reference

❸ The greatest temperature less than 20 degrees

DMIN

DMIN extracts the lowest value that meets the specified criteria.

`=DMIN(database,field,criteria)`

The DMIN function looks up the lowest value in a range or database. The database is the cell reference range or named range of the database and the field is referenced as the column number from left to right. The criteria is a range that is referenced and the function operates from the parameters set. The field can also be a cell reference. The DMIN function works the same way as the DMAX function. See DMAX for an example. See also the CD-ROM included with this book.

DPRODUCT

DPRODUCT returns the product of multiplying the values that meet the specified criteria.

`=DPRODUCT(database,field,criteria)`

The DPRODUCT function returns the product of multiplying the values that meet certain criteria you specify. In the syntax for this function, the database is the cell reference range or named range of the database; the field is referenced as the column number from left to right. The criteria is a range that is referenced and the function operates from the parameters set. The field can also be a cell reference. In Figure 3.5, the product is the multiplication of the cost and the markup. As well, the parameters are Unit 1 with a cost greater than two dollars and a markup less than 30%. The product is 2.88. Of course this is a simple example to illustrate parameters and the operation of the function.

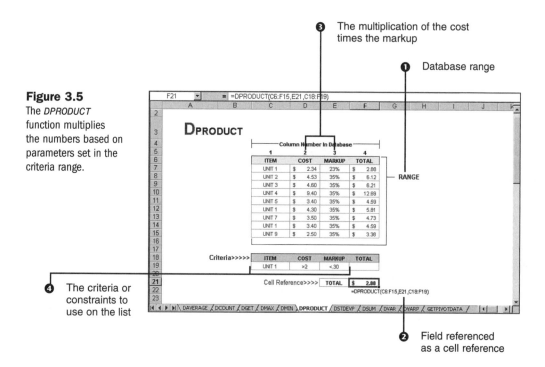

❸ The multiplication of the cost times the markup

❶ Database range

Figure 3.5
The *DPRODUCT* function multiplies the numbers based on parameters set in the criteria range.

❹ The criteria or constraints to use on the list

❷ Field referenced as a cell reference

DSTDEV

DSTDEV estimates the standard deviation of a population, based on a sample of selected entries from the database.

```
=DSTDEV(database,field,criteria)
```

The DSTDEV function estimates the deviation of a population based on entries in the list or database. The database in the syntax, shown previously, is the cell reference range or named range of the database, while the field is referenced as the column number from left to right. The criteria is a range that is referenced, and the function operates from the parameters set. The field also can be a cell reference. The standard deviation is actually a standard error amount based on an arithmetic mean formula. To view the actual formula on which the function is based, see the help file.

DSTDEVP

DSTDEVP returns the calculation of the standard deviation of a population, based on the sum of the whole population.

```
=DSTDEVP(database,field,criteria)
```

The DSTDEVP function calculates the standard deviation based on an entire population. The database is the cell reference range or named range of the database. In this syntax, the field is referenced as the column number from left to right. The criteria is a range that is referenced, and the function operates from the parameters set. The field can also be a cell reference.

In the example in Figure 3.6, the true standard deviation in the communities' population for the year 2001 is 1,233. Notice how the criteria takes into account a vertical range of towns the criteria calculates from. If the range were B13:B15, it would only include the populations of Avon and Albany in the year 2001.

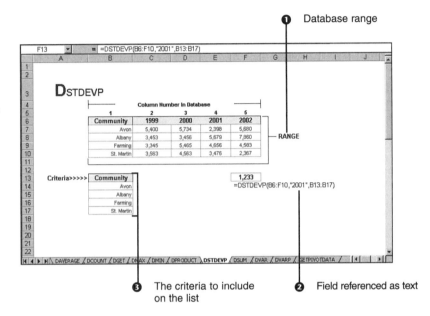

Figure 3.6
The *DSTDEVP* function calculates the true standard deviation of an entire population, in this case, all the communities in the year 2001.

① Database range

③ The criteria to include on the list

② Field referenced as text

DSUM

DSUM returns the total of the values that meet the specified criteria.

`=DSUM(database,field,criteria)`

The DSUM function operates much as the sum function except that it operates on a database with criteria. The database is the cell reference range or named range of the database, and the field is referenced as the column number from left to right. The criteria is a range that is referenced, and the function operates from the parameters set. The field can also be a cell reference. The criteria enable you to apply constraints, as shown in the example in Figure 3.7. Notice the criteria applies the sum of all sales for the cars greater than 1995 and less than 2000. The sum of sales dollars from 1996 through 1999 equals $2,034,572.

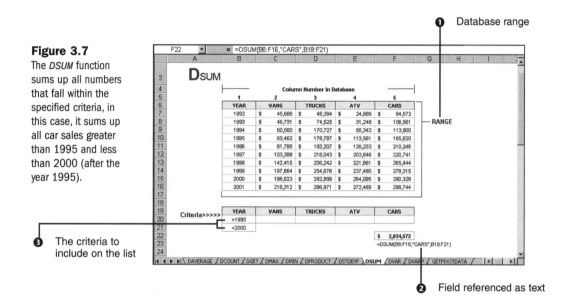

Figure 3.7
The *DSUM* function sums up all numbers that fall within the specified criteria, in this case, it sums up all car sales greater than 1995 and less than 2000 (after the year 1995).

❶ Database range

❷ Field referenced as text

❸ The criteria to include on the list

DVAR

DVAR estimates the variance of a sample population, based on the values that meet the specified criteria.

`=DVAR(database,field,criteria)`

The DVAR function provides the variance of a sample population. For this particular function's syntax, the database is the cell reference range or named range of the database; and the field is referenced as the column number from left to right. The criteria is a range that is referenced; and the function operates from the parameters set. The estimated variance of the sample database in Figure 3.8 shows the estimated variance in the Western regions. Notice how using the wildcard symbol allows you to extract variance against all Western regions from West, Southwest, Midwest, and Northwest. The wildcard symbol extracts all regions in the Western hemisphere. The result for the year 2000 Western hemisphere is $1,059,002.

Figure 3.8
The *DVAR* function returns an estimated variance of a sample population.

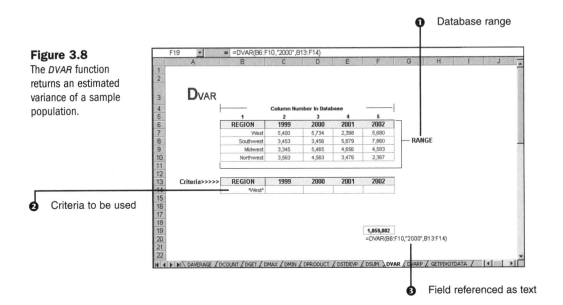

① Database range

② Criteria to be used

③ Field referenced as text

DVARP

DVARP returns the calculation of the true variance of an entire population, based on the values that meet the specified criteria.

=DVARP(database,field,criteria)

Whereas DVAR calculates the variance based only on a sample of the population, the DVARP function returns the true variance based on the entire population. In the syntax, there are three components: the database, the cell reference range or named range of the database; the field, referenced as the column number from left to right; and the criteria, a range that is referenced. The function operates from the parameters set. Notice in Figure 3.9, that the true variance of the entire population of the regions North and South is 5,051,679 for the year 2002. In this example, I've used wildcards to pull all information from the North and South for the year 2002 with an asterisk.

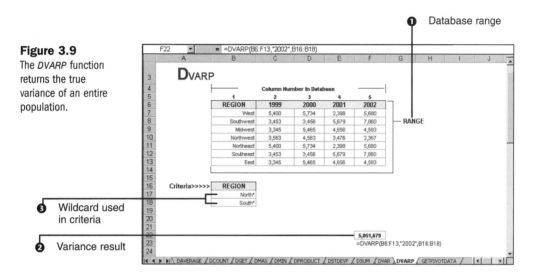

Figure 3.9
The *DVARP* function returns the true variance of an entire population.

GETPIVOTDATA

GETPIVOTDATA returns a value of data stored in a PivotTable.

`=GETPIVOTDATA(pivot_table,name)`

- The `pivot_table` argument refers to the pivot table that contains the data you want to retrieve. This can be a reference to any cell within the pivot table or a named range that refers to the pivot table.

- The *name* is the text string enclosed in double quotes or referenced as your lookup criteria.

The GETPIVOTDATA function can extract total sums from a pivot table or pull multiple sets of data and find the information at their intersecting points. For example, notice the pivot table in Figure 3.10. The months are shown down the left side and the years across the top. The formula to look up a grand total for the year 2000 is simply

`=GETPIVOTDATA(E4,"Sum of 2000")`

In this formula, E4 selects the entire PivotTable, and "Sum of 2000" in quotations is the column heading. To look up information at intersecting points, such as the sum of August for the year 2000, this is not case sensitive. The formula would read

`OK=GETPIVOTDATA(E4,"Aug Sum of Sales")`

Figure 3.10

The *GETPIVOTDATA* function can be used to extract total sums or to find the intersecting points of sets of data.

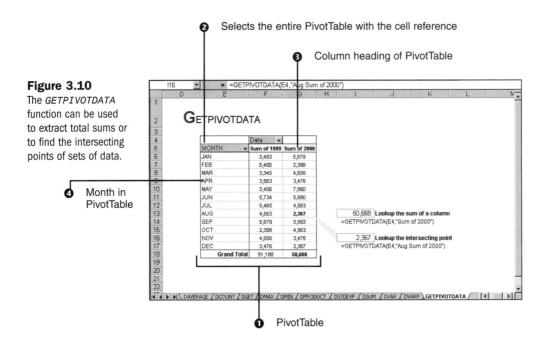

❷ Selects the entire PivotTable with the cell reference

❸ Column heading of PivotTable

❹ Month in PivotTable

❶ PivotTable

Date and Time Functions

Date and Time Functions Overview

Date and time functions are powerful functions that allow you to automate and manage information dealing with time elements. For example, if you have a daily report that goes out and you always want the report to include the day it was printed, you could manually enter the date into a cell or let Excel's date formula of TODAY() do it for you. The value of date and time formulas reaches much further than a simple date in a cell. It can also help you manage time by calling out due dates, weekends, holidays, or dates that are past due. You can find maturity dates, and create calculators that manage your bills and combine formulas to see workdays in the future.

Unlike most other numeric data, when you enter a date or a formula that calculates a date, in most cases, Excel will automatically display the result in an easily readable date format. The date is really a serial number representing the time elapsed since 12:00 AM, January 1, 1900. When you are comparing two dates, Excel is really looking at the serial numbers. Therefore, one date minus another date is really one serial number subtracted from another serial number, with the result converted back into a date format.

This chapter covers the following functions.

▶	DATE	▶	NOW
▶	DATEVALUE	▶	SECOND
▶	DAY	▶	TIME
▶	DAYS360	▶	TIMEVALUE
▶	EDATE	▶	TODAY
▶	EOMONTH	▶	WEEKDAY
▶	HOUR	▶	WEEKNUM
▶	MINUTE	▶	WORKDAY
▶	MONTH	▶	YEAR
▶	NETWORKDAYS	▶	YEARFRAC

DATE

DATE returns the DATE serial number.

`=DATE(year,month,day)`

The DATE function returns the date value of a given year, month, and day. Excel automatically formats this function in a date format, however, the date format is really a serial number that starts from the time 12:00 AM on January 1, 1900, and is formatted in the format of a date. Use the date function to convert serial numbers to dates or in conjunction with other formulas. Notice the examples in Figure 4.1.

YEAR	The serial number in Windows operating systems that falls between 1900 and the year 9999. For Macintosh, the number is 1904 to 9999.
MONTH	The serial number representing the month of the year from 1 to 12. If greater than 12, it adds that number to the first month in the year specified.
DAY	The serial number representing the day of the month. If that number is greater than 31, it adds the number of days to the first day in the month.

Figure 4.1
The *DATE* function returns the serial number of the year, month, and day, automatically converting the serial number to a date.

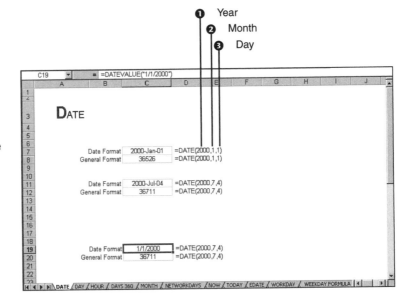

DATEVALUE

DATEVALUE converts date text to a DATEVALUE serial number.

`=DATEVALUE(date_text)`

The DATEVALUE function returns the function's serial number value from a text date. For example, the date value of the year 2000 would be: `=DATEVALUE("1/1/2000")` and the result would equal 36526 (days since 12:00 AM, January 1, 1900). The date value of Windows date systems is any date from 1/1/1900 to 12/31/9999. The date value of Macintosh systems is any date from 1/1/1904 to 12/31/9999. If you want Excel to calculate based on a starting date of 12:00 AM, January 1, 1904, in the Options dialog box from the Tools menu, change the date system of an Excel for Windows system to the 1904 date system in the calculation tab.

DATE_TEXT   The date value in the form of a serial number starting with the Windows date system number of 12:00 AM, January 1, 1900 to 12:00 PM, December 31, 9999.

DAY

DAY returns the corresponding day of the month serial number from 1 to 31.

=DAY(serial_number)

The DAY function can be used with a text reference of dates or used with a cell reference of days. Notice the two examples in Figure 4.2. The formula in cell B6 equals 1 because it is the first day of the month, and the formula in cell B9 equals 31 because it is the last day of the month. Any fictitious date that falls outside the range of 1 to 31 will default to 1 as shown in cell B10 for "Jan 45." You can also use the formula with cell referencing. The formula to the right in cell F6 references the date in E6 and returns the value of 1.

SERIAL NUMBER   The serial number is the date time code used by Microsoft Excel. You specify the serial number as text and Excel will automatically convert the serial number text to the day value.

❹ Used as cell referencing to a date

Figure 4.2
The *DAY* function returns the day serial number between 1 and 31 representing the day of the month.

❶ First day of the month

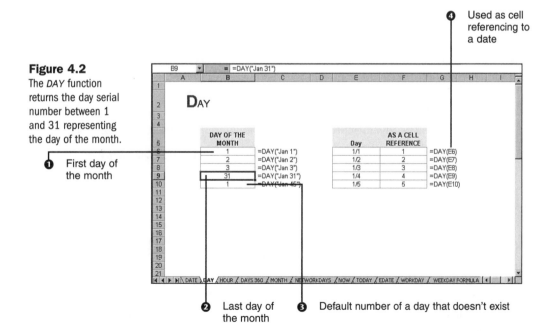

❷ Last day of the month   ❸ Default number of a day that doesn't exist

DAYS360

DAYS360 returns the number of days between two set dates based on a 360-day year.

=DAYS360(start_date,end_date)

The DAYS360 function is used primarily for accounting systems based on a 360-day year—if, for example, you calculate payments based on twelve 30-day months. Notice the example. In looking at Figure 4.3, you'll notice the DAYS360 function in cell D7 calculates the number of days between the start date of 3/16/2000 and 3/16/2005 to be 1800. This number divided by 30 gives you the number of payments. The second example builds the 30-day diviser into the formula as shown in D12. And last, you'll see that the DAYS360 function is used with text dates in cell D18, and that the dates are enclosed by quotes and are separated with a comma.

START AND END DATE   The start and end dates for which you want the number
                               of days returned between. If the end date is less than
                               the start date, the result is a negative number.

Figure 4.3
The *DAYS360*
formula operates
on a 360-day year
accounting system—
twelve 30-day months.

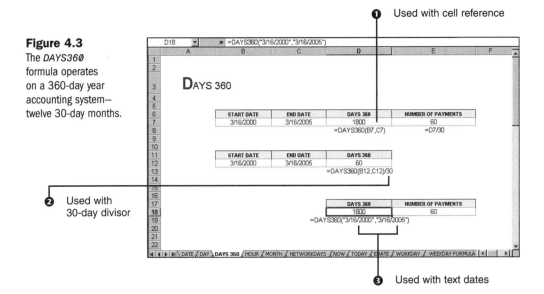

❶ Used with cell reference

❷ Used with
30-day divisor

❸ Used with text dates

EDATE

EDATE returns the value or serial number of the date specified by you and the number of months before or after the specified date. Use EDATE to calculate the maturity date or date due that falls on the same day of the month as the date of issue.

=EDATE(start_date,months)

The EDATE function is found in the Analysis Toolpak. If you don't see the EDATE function, you must first install the Analysis Toolpak and then enable the Toolpak under Add-Ins from the Tools menu. In Figure 4.4, the start date in cell B8 = 3/16/1999 and the number of months to maturity is in cell C8, thus the result would equal 4/16/1999. A –1 would result in the date 2/16/1999. The second example in cell D18 uses a text date entry and the months to maturity is 7, resulting in the date 10/16/1999. Note that because this function returns a serial number, you may have to apply a date format to the cell containing the formula.

START DATE   The start date to maturity.

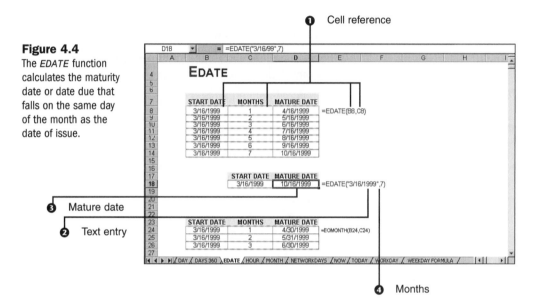

Figure 4.4
The *EDATE* function calculates the maturity date or date due that falls on the same day of the month as the date of issue.

EOMONTH

EOMONTH returns the calculated maturity dates or dates due that fall in the last day of the month.

=EOMONTH(start_date,months)

The EOMONTH function operates similar to the EDATE function and the syntax is the same, however, the calculation of the maturity date falls on the last day of the month. For example:

START DATE   The start date to maturity.

MONTHS   This is the number of months to maturity from the start date. If a negative number, it returns a past date.

For example:

=EOMONTH("3/16/99",1) results in a maturity date of 4/30/99

=EOMONTH("3/16/99",2) results in a maturity date of 5/31/99

=EOMONTH("3/16/99",3) results in a maturity date of 6/30/99

And so on.

HOUR

HOUR returns the hour as a serial number integer between 0 and 23.

=HOUR(serial_number)

The HOUR function returns the hour serial number between 0 and 23. Notice the example in Figure 4.5, the actual time is shown under the heading Actual Time and the HOUR function extracts the serial number between 0 and 23. The formula can be used with cell reference or with the serial number enclosed in parenthesis, as shown in the second example.

SERIAL NUMBER   The serial number is a number between 0 and 23 that represents a time of day. The serial number can be extracted from text in quotes or as a cell reference.

Figure 4.5
The *HOUR* function returns the hour of the day between 0 and 23.

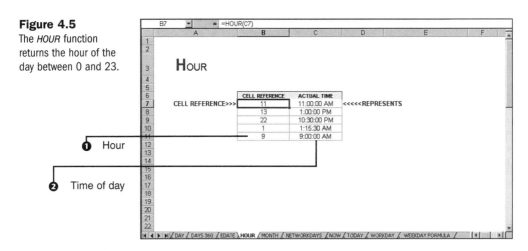

MINUTE

MINUTE returns the serial number that corresponds to the minute.

=MINUTE(serial_number)

The MINUTE function returns the value corresponding to a minute within an hour. For example, if you have a time of 5:30 in the MINUTE function as shown, =MINUTE("5:30 am"), the return result would equal 30.

SERIAL NUMBER   The serial number is a number between 0 and 59 that represents a time of day. The serial number can be extracted from text in quotes or as a cell reference.

MONTH

MONTH returns the corresponding serial number of the month between 1 and 12.

`=MONTH(serial_number)`

The MONTH function operates off the serial number or day of the year. For example, 1 equals the first day of the year and falls in January. You can use the MONTH formula with the serial number in parenthesis or as a cell reference. For example, the first example in Figure 4.6 shows the formula as =MONTH(C5) and returns 1 as the result of the first day of the year and falls in January. The second example in cell D10 uses the serial number and returns the result of 10. The 300th day of the year falls in October. The last example is used in the form of an array and sums up all costs in the month of February. The MONTH function combined with the SUM function can be a powerful tool when managing lists of information. See also, YEAR.

SERIAL NUMBER

The serial number is a number between 1 and 12 that represents a month in a year. The serial number can be extracted from text in quotes or as a cell reference.

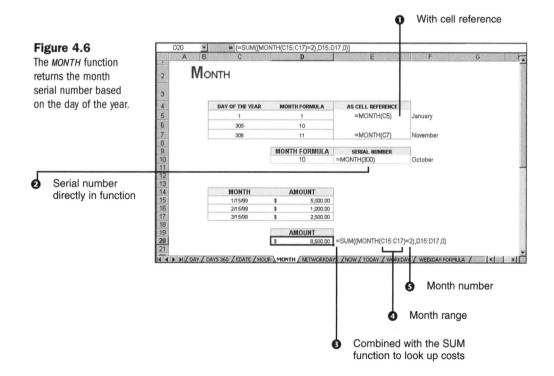

Figure 4.6
The *MONTH* function returns the month serial number based on the day of the year.

With cell reference

Serial number directly in function

Month number

Month range

Combined with the SUM function to look up costs

NETWORKDAYS

NETWORKDAYS returns the number of working days between two dates. Excludes weekends and specified holidays.

```
=NETWORKDAYS(start_date,end_date,holidays)
```

The NETWORKDAYS function allows you to find out the total number of working days between two dates excluding the weekends and holidays. This is an extremely important function when calculating schedules that have to be completed within specific time frames. Notice the example in Figure 4.7, the first example in cell C9 is used to calculate actual working days between two dates, the second example takes into account a third date, which is a holiday. The third example takes on several holidays that fall between two dates in the form of cell referencing a range of dates. If you exclude all holidays in a year, this would be the best approach, as well as using the start and stop dates with cell referencing. Notice how in the 4th and last example the structure is set up so you can apply a start date and an end date, and a range of holidays. The cell referencing will automatically adjust to your inputs.

START DATE	The date that represents the start date.
END DATE	The date that represents the end date.
HOLIDAYS	This is optional, however, you can use one or more holidays in the form of text in the formula or in a range of cells.

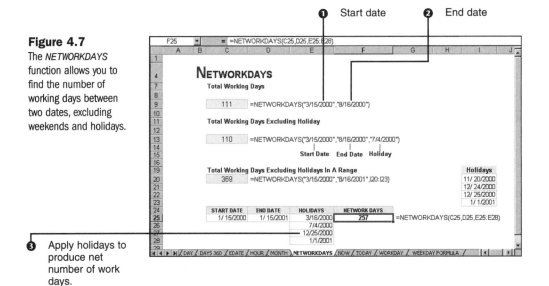

Figure 4.7

The *NETWORKDAYS* function allows you to find the number of working days between two dates, excluding weekends and holidays.

❸ Apply holidays to produce net number of work days.

NOW

NOW returns the current date and time in the form of a serial number. There are no arguments for this function.

`=NOW()`

The NOW function calculates the time the function was entered or when a worksheet is calculated. This function is not updated continuously on the worksheet. The NOW function will show the current time when a worksheet is printed, or the workbook is opened. The NOW function could be in the form of a year, month, day, hour, minute, or second. Notice the example in Figure 4.8. The time this formula was entered is calculated down to the second. The date value of Windows date systems is any date from 1/1/1900 to 12/31/9999. The date value of Macintosh systems is any date from 1/1/1904 to 12/31/9999. In the Options dialog box from the Tools menu, you can change the date system of an Excel for Windows system to the 1904 date system found on the calcualtion tab.

Figure 4.8
The NOW function returns the exact time the function was entered down to the second.

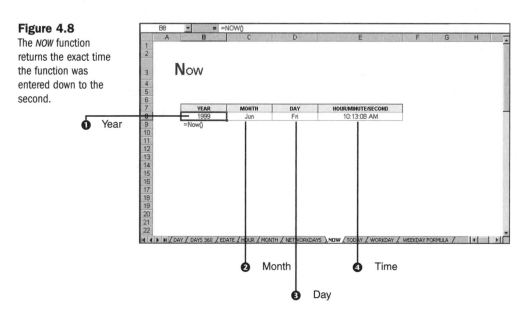

❶ Year

❷ Month

❸ Day

❹ Time

SECOND

SECOND returns the corresponding serial number of seconds as an integer between 0 and 59.

`=SECOND(serial_number)`

The SECOND function operates on serial numbers between 0 and 59. There are 60 seconds in a minute, so 30 equals 30 seconds. The function operates as follows: `=SECOND("8:25:30") =30`. The serial number for the SECOND function is the date and time code Microsoft Excel uses for date and time calculations.

TIME

TIME returns the corresponding serial number of time as a fraction between 0 and 0.99999999.

`=TIME(hour,minute,second)`

The TIME function returns the serial number of the time. The hour can be any number between 0 and 23. The minute can be any minute between 0 and 59. The second can be any number between 0 and 59. The serial number is the number associated with the 1900 date system. For example, `=TIME(8,30,25)` would return the serial number .35446 and Excel automatically formats this in the date format of 8:30 AM. The date and value of Windows date systems is any date from 1/1/1900 to 12/31/9999. The date value of Macintosh systems is any date from 1/1/1904 to 12/31/9999. In the Options dialog box from the Tools menu, you can change the date system of an Excel for Windows system to the 1904 date system found on the calculation tab. If a user wishes to derive a time from other time figures (either in cells, or in quotes), they will need to use other time functions to convert those time figures into their serial counterparts...

`=TIME(HOUR(B4),MINUTE(B6),SECOND(B5)).`

HOUR	The number between 0 and 23 that represents the hour.
MINUTE	The number between 0 and 59 that represents the minute of the hour.
SECOND	The second between 0 and 59 that represents the second of the minute.

TIMEVALUE

Returns the serial number represented by text as time.

`=TIMEVALUE(time_text)`

The TIMEVALUE function is similar to the TIME function in that it returns the serial number of time as a decimal or fraction between 0 and 0.99999999. However, the TIMEVALUE function converts time text to a serial number. For example, `=TIMEVALUE("8:30 AM")` returns the serial number value of .35417. If you include a date in the `time_text` argument, the date will have no bearing on the result. Also, `=TIMEVALUE("4/3/99 8:30 AM")` would return a value of .35417.

TIME TEXT	The text string that gives the time in any Excel time format.

TODAY

TODAY returns the current date as a serial number. There are no arguments for this function.

`=TODAY()`

The TODAY function is a powerful dynamic function that allows you to see the current day every time the workbook is opened, calculated, or printed. You could place the TODAY function in a cell on a report so you always have the current day posted on the report, or, you could use the TODAY function to calculate the total days you have left to complete a project or pay a bill. Notice the examples in Figure 4.9—the first example shows the TODAY function in cell D6 and the completion date of the project is 7/16/1999 in cell C6. Because the TODAY function always displays the current day, it can keep a running tab on how many days are left. The second example shows bill payments, where today is the current date, the bills have different due dates, and the days left keep a running log on how many days until the bill comes due. A conditional format highlights and warns bills coming due in less than 10 days in addition to bills that are past due.

Figure 4.9
The *TODAY* function can operate as a time management tool as shown in both examples.

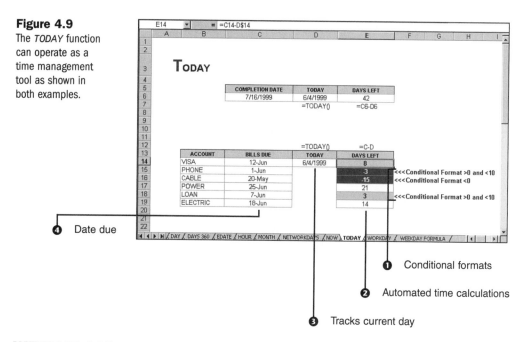

- ❹ Date due
- ❶ Conditional formats
- ❷ Automated time calculations
- ❸ Tracks current day

WEEKDAY

WEEKDAY returns the corresponding day of the week as a serial number.

```
=WEEKDAY(serial_number,return_type)
```

The WEEKDAY function is another function that can be a powerful tool when combined with other functions. It returns the number corresponding to the day of the week between 1 and 7, where the first day of the week is Sunday and the seventh day is Saturday. If your date format is 1/1/00 and you're planning your work schedule, you can simply type in the cell, =WEEKDAY("1/1/00"), or reference a cell as shown in Figure 4.10. Notice the second example uses the IF function. This formula guarantees that any date in the future will land on a workday. For example, let's say you're planning to deliver certain materials to a vendor on multiple dates in the future, you could use this formula to always guarantee a weekday result. The actual day appears on Saturday in cell C22, however, the guaranteed formula kicks it to Friday. If the day landed on Sunday, the formula would kick it to Monday.

SERIAL NUMBER The serial number is the date time code used by Microsoft Excel. You can specify the serial number as text and Excel will automatically convert the serial number text to the day value, or you can apply the day value.

RETURN TYPE This number determines the type of return value. 1 or omitted, returns 1 (Sun) through 7 (Sat) or 2 returns 1 (Mon) through 7 (Sun) or 3 returns 0 (Mon) through 6 (Sun).

Figure 4.10
The *WEEKDAY* function allows you to determine a date's day of the week with a result between 1 and 7 with the first day equal to Sunday.

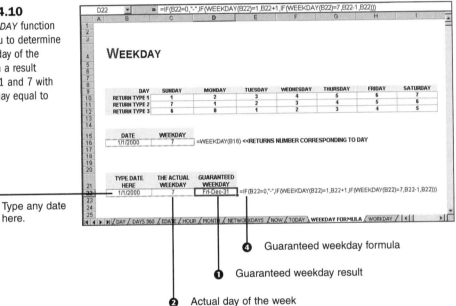

❸ Type any date here.

❹ Guaranteed weekday formula

❶ Guaranteed weekday result

❷ Actual day of the week

WEEKNUM

WEEKNUM returns a number of where the week falls numerically within a year.

`=WEEKNUM(serial_number,return_type)`

The WEEKNUM function is found in the Analysis Toolpak. If you don't see the WEEKNUM function, you must first install the Analysis Toolpak and then enable the Toolpak under Add-Ins from the Tools menu. In this instance, the formula `=WEEKNUM("12/25/00",1)` returns the week number 52, and the formula `=WEEKNUM("1/1/00",1)` returns the week number 1.

SERIAL NUMBER The serial number date within the week.

RETURN TYPE This number determines the type of return value. 1 begins the week on Sunday and 2 begins the week on Monday. The weekdays are numbered 1 through 7.

WORKDAY

WORKDAY returns a date that is indicated by the number of working days including holidays.

`=WORKDAY(serial_number,return_type)`

The WORKDAY function is found in the Analysis Toolpak. If you don't see the WEEKNUM function, you must first install the Analysis Toolpak and then enable the Toolpak under Add-Ins from the Tools menu. Notice in the example in Figure 4.11, the start date is indicated in cell B12; 11/15/2000 and the number of workdays for the project is 100, if you have 5 holidays in the range D12:D16, what's the final date the project will complete on? The result is the date value of 4/6/2001. The WORKDAY function is good for scheduling events and invoices.

START DATE	The start date.
DAYS	The number of non-weekend and non-holiday workdays available before or after the start date.
HOLIDAYS	One or more dates that will be included in the formula but excluded in the days available.

Figure 4.11
The *WORKDAY* function is good for scheduling dates in the future when a start date is known as well as the number of workdays.

❶ Project start date

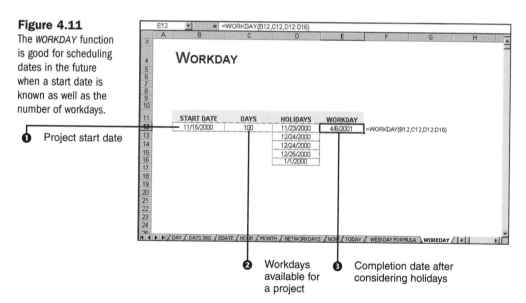

❷ Workdays available for a project

❸ Completion date after considering holidays

YEAR

YEAR returns the corresponding year as a serial number in the form of an integer.

`=YEAR(serial_number)`

The YEAR function returns the date time code between the numbers 1900 and 9999. The serial number is the code that Excel uses for date and time calculations. The date and value of Windows date systems is any date from 1/1/1900 to 12/31/9999. The date value of Macintosh systems is any date from 1/1/1904 to 12/31/9999. In the Options dialog box from the Tools menu, you can change the date system of an Excel for Windows system to the 1904 date system found on the calcualtion tab. The year value of =YEAR("1/1/2000") results in 2000. The serial number of =YEAR(0.007) results in 1900, if you're using the 1904 date system, the the same year value of =YEAR(0.007) results in 1904.

SERIAL NUMBER	The serial number is the date time code used by Microsoft Excel. You can specify the serial number as text and Excel will automatically convert the serial number text to the year value, or you can apply the year value.

YEARFRAC

YEARFRAC calculates the fraction of the year between two dates.

=YEARFRAC(start_Date,end_Date,basis)

The YEARFRAC function is found in the Analysis Toolpak. If you don't see the YEARFRAC function, you must first install the Analysis Toolpak and then enable the Toolpak under Add-Ins from the Tools menu. The YEARFRAC functions is primarily used when your looking for an entire year's benefits or obligations to assign to a term.

START DATE	The start date.
END DATE	The end date.
BASIS	The type of day count basis to use. 0=Or omitted US(NASD)30/360, 1=Actual/actual, 2=Actual/360, 3=Actual/365, 4=European 30/360.

CHAPTER 5

Engineering Functions

Engineering Functions Overview

Engineering functions are built-in formulas that allow you to apply engineering analysis against statistical and logical information. Each one of the examples in this chapter has an accompanying figure to help illustrate the usage of the function.

The following functions will be discussed in this chapter.

▶ BESSELI	▶ ERFC	▶ IMLOG10
▶ BESSELJ	▶ GESTEP	▶ IMLOG2
▶ BESSELK	▶ HEX2BIN	▶ IMPOWER
▶ BESSELY	▶ HEX2DEC	▶ IMPRODUCT
▶ BIN2DEC	▶ HEX2OCT	▶ IMREAL
▶ BIN2HEX	▶ IMABS	▶ IMSIN
▶ BIN2OCT	▶ IMAGINARY	▶ IMSQRT
▶ COMPLEX	▶ IMARGUMENT	▶ IMSUB
▶ CONVERT	▶ IMCONJUGATE	▶ IMSUM
▶ DEC2BIN	▶ IMCOS	▶ OCT2BIN
▶ DEC2HEX	▶ IMDIV	▶ OCT2DEC
▶ DEC2OCT	▶ IMEXP	▶ OCT2HEX
▶ DELTA	▶ IMLN	▶ SQRTPI
▶ ERF		

BESSELI

The `BESSELI` function returns the `BESSEL` function in modified form for imaginary arguments.

`=BESSELI(x,n)`

The `BESSELI` function is found only if the Analysis Toolpak is installed. In addition it must be turned on in the Add-Ins from the Tools menu. Both X and N must be numeric and greater than zero. Notice the example in Figure 5.1. Where the value is 2 and the integer is 1, the `BESSELI` function results in 1.5906.

X	The value to evaluate the function.
N	The order of the `BESSEL` function. Truncated if not an integer.

The n-th order modified `BESSEL` function of the variable x is

$$I_n(x) = (i)^{-n} J_n(ix)$$

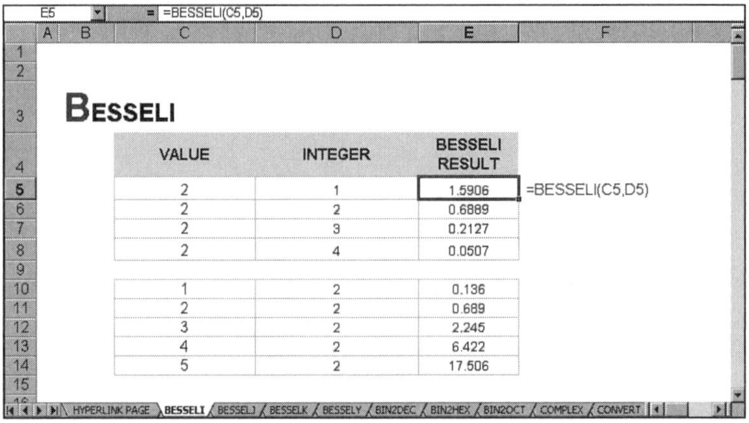

E5 =BESSELI(C5,D5)

BESSELI

VALUE	INTEGER	BESSELI RESULT
2	1	1.5906
2	2	0.6889
2	3	0.2127
2	4	0.0507
1	2	0.136
2	2	0.689
3	2	2.245
4	2	6.422
5	2	17.506

Figure 5.1
The *BESSELI* function returns the modified *BESSEL* function for imaginary arguments.

BESSELJ

This `BESSELJ` function returns the actual `BESSEL` function. X is the value of at which to evaluate the function. Y is the order of the `BESSEL` function.

`=BESSELJ(x,n)`

The `BESSELJ` function is found only if the Analysis Toolpak is installed. In addition it must be turned on in the Add-Ins from the Tools menu. Both X and N must be numeric and greater than zero. Notice the example in Figure 5.2. Where the value is is 2 and the integer is 1, the `BESSELJ` function results in 0.5767.

X	The value to evaluate the function.
N	The order of the `BESSEL` function. Truncated if not an integer.

The n-th order BESSEL function of the variable x is

$$J_n(x) = \sum_{k=0}^{\infty} \frac{(-1)^k}{k!\,\Gamma(n+k+1)} \left(\frac{x}{2}\right)^{n+2k}$$

where

$$\Gamma(n+k+1) = \int_0^{\infty} e^{-x} x^{n+k} \, dx$$

is the GAMMA function.

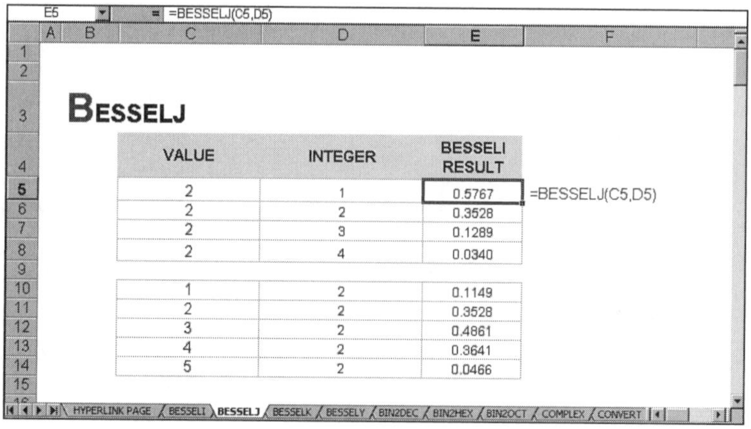

VALUE	INTEGER	BESSELI RESULT
2	1	0.5767
2	2	0.3528
2	3	0.1289
2	4	0.0340
1	2	0.1149
2	2	0.3528
3	2	0.4861
4	2	0.3641
5	2	0.0466

Figure 5.2
The *BESSELJ* function returns the actual *BESSEL* function.

BESSELK

The BESSELK function returns the BESSEL function in modified form for imaginary arguments.

```
=BESSELK(x,n)
```

The BESSELK function is found only if the Analysis Toolpak is installed. In addition it must be turned on in the Add-Ins from the Tools menu. Both X and N must be numeric and greater than zero. Notice the example in Figure 5.3. Where the value is is 2 and the integer is 1, the BESSELK function results in 0.1399.

X	The value to evaluate the function.
N	The order of the BESSEL function. Truncated if not an integer.

The n-th order modified BESSEL function of the variable x is

$$K_n(x) = \frac{p}{2} i^{n+1} [J_n(ix) + iY_n(ix)]$$

where Jn and Yn are the J and Y BESSEL functions.

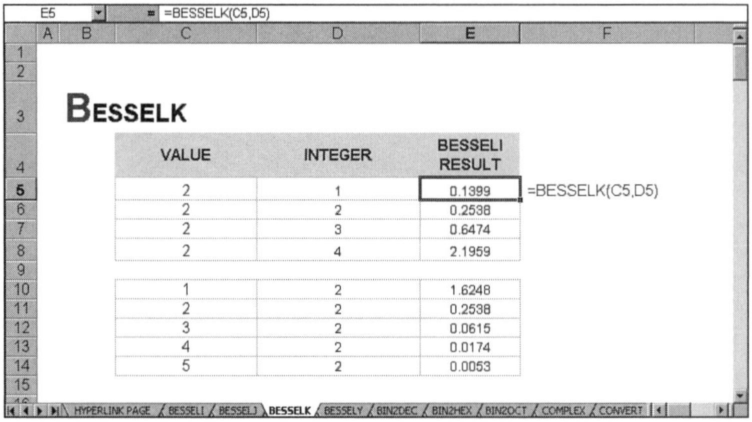

Figure 5.3
The *BESSELK* function returns the modified *BESSEL* function for imaginary arguments.

		E5		= =BESSELK(C5,D5)		
	A	B	C	D	E	F
1						
2						
3			**BESSELK**			
4			VALUE	INTEGER	BESSELI RESULT	
5			2	1	0.1399	=BESSELK(C5,D5)
6			2	2	0.2538	
7			2	3	0.6474	
8			2	4	2.1959	
9						
10			1	2	1.6248	
11			2	2	0.2538	
12			3	2	0.0615	
13			4	2	0.0174	
14			5	2	0.0053	
15						

HYPERLINK PAGE / BESSELI / BESSELJ \ BESSELK / BESSELY / BIN2DEC / BIN2HEX / BIN2OCT / COMPLEX / CONVERT

BESSELY

The BESSELY function returns the BESSEL function, also known as the Weber or Neumann function. X is the value at which to evaluate the function. N is the order of the function.

=BESSELY(x,n)

The BESSELY function is found only if the Analysis Toolpak is installed. In addition it must be turned on in the Add-Ins from the Tools menu. Both X and N must be numeric and greater than zero. Notice the example in Figure 5.4.

X   The value to evaluate the function.

N   The order of the BESSEL function. Truncated if not an integer.

The n-th order BESSEL function of the variable x is

$$Y_n(x) = \lim_{v \to n} \frac{J_v(x)\cos(v\,\pi) - J_{-v}(x)}{\sin(v\,\pi)}$$

where

$$\mathrm{ERF}(z) = \frac{2}{\sqrt{\pi}} \int_0^z e^{-t^2} dt$$

Figure 5.4
BESSELY returns the *BESSEL* function and is also known as the Neumann or Weber function.

VALUE	INTEGER	BESSELI RESULT
2	1	-0.1070
2	2	-0.6174
2	3	-1.1278
2	4	-2.7659
1	2	-1.6507
2	2	-0.6174
3	2	-0.1604
4	2	0.2159
5	2	0.3677

E5 = =BESSELY(C5,D5)

BESSELY

=BESSELY(C5,D5)

BIN2DEC

The BIN2DEC function converts a binary number to decimal form.

`=BIN2DEC(number)`

The BIN2DEC function is found only if the Analysis Toolpak is installed. In addition it must be turned on in the Add-Ins from the Tools menu. The number cannot be more than 10 characters. Notice the example in Figure 5.5. Where the Binary Number is 10000010 and the conversion to a decimal results in 130.0000.

NUMBER   The binary number to convert. The most significant number is the sign bit. The remaining 9 bits are magnitude bits.

Figure 5.5
Use the *BIN2DEC* function to convert a binary number to a decimal. The binary number cannot be more than 10 characters.

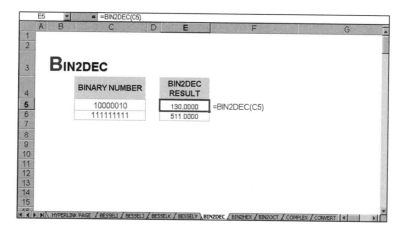

E5 = =BIN2DEC(C5)

BIN2DEC

BINARY NUMBER	BIN2DEC RESULT
10000010	130.0000
111111111	511.0000

=BIN2DEC(C5)

BIN2HEX

Convert a binary number to hexadecimal with the BIN2HEX function.

```
=BIN2HEX(number,places)
```

The BIN2HEX function is found only if the Analysis Toolpak is installed. In addition it must be turned on in the Add-Ins from the Tools menu. The number cannot be more than 10 characters. The sign bit being the most significant, the remaining 9 bits are magnitude bits. Notice the example in Figure 5.6. Where the Binary Number is 10000010 and the Places is 3, the conversion to a hexadecimal results in 082.

NUMBER	The binary number to convert.
PLACES	The number of characters to use. If omitted, the function uses the minimum number of characters needed. Use when you want to pad the result with leading zeros.

Figure 5.6
This function converts a binary number to a hexadecimal. The binary number cannot be more than 10 characters.

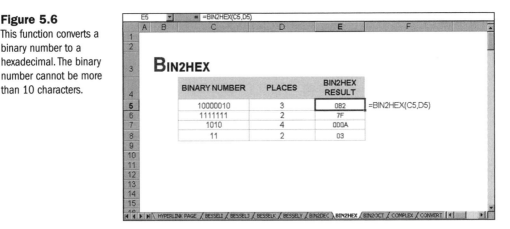

BIN2OCT

BIN2OCT converts a binary number to octal.

```
=BIN2OCT(number,places)
```

The BIN2OCT function is found only if the Analysis Toolpak is installed. In addition it must be turned on in the Add-Ins from the Tools menu. The binary number cannot be more than 10 characters. The sign bit being the most significant, the remaining 9 bits are magnitude bits. Negatives are represented using Two's complement notation. Notice the example in Figure 5.7, where the Binary Number is 10000010 and the Places is 3, the conversion to an Octal results in 202.

NUMBER	The binary number to convert.
PLACES	The number of characters to use. If omitted, the function uses the minimum number of characters needed. Use when you want to pad the result with leading zeros to achieve uniformity.

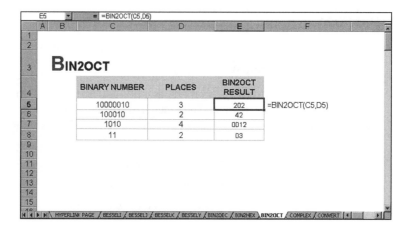

Figure 5.7
BIN2OCT converts a binary number to an octal. The binary number cannot be more than 10 characters.

COMPLEX

Use the COMPLEX function to convert real and imaginary coefficients into a complex number of the form x + yi or x + yj.

=COMPLEX(real_num,I_num,suffix)

The COMPLEX function is found only if the Analysis Toolpak is installed. In addition it must be turned on in the Add-Ins from the Tools menu. Lowercase "i" and "j" must be used for the suffix argument in order for the function to work. In addition the suffixes must match. Notice the example in Figure 5.8, where the Real Imaginary Coefficient is 3 and the Imaginary Coefficient is 4, the result is 3+4i.

REAL_NUM	The real coefficient of the complex number.
I_NUM	The imaginary coefficient of the complex number.
SUFFIX	The suffix for the imaginary component. If omitted, it's assumed to be "i."

Figure 5.8
Converts real and imaginary coefficients into a complex number.

E5	=COMPLEX(C5,D5)			
	B	C	D	E	F

COMPLEX

REAL IMAGINARY COEFFICIENTS	IMAGINARY COEFFICIENT	COMPLEX RESULT	
3	4	3+4i	=COMPLEX(C5,D5)
2	4	2+4i	
0	1	i	
1	0	1	

CONVERT

CONVERT interprets data from one measurement system to another.

=CONVERT(number,from_unit,to_unit)

The CONVERT function is found only if the Analysis Toolpak is installed. In addition it must be turned on in the Add-Ins from the Tools menu. Notice the conversion examples and how the formula is structured in Figure 5.9. The conversion tables in Tables 5.1 and 5.2 show the conversion text that must be used to convert units of measure.

NUMBER	The number to convert.
FROM_UNIT	Measurement unit to convert from.
TO_UNIT	Measurement unit to convert to.

Table 5.1 Conversion Table

Unit Type	From Unit to Unit
Weight and Mass	
Gram	"g"
Slug	"sg"
Pound mass	"lbm"
U	"u"
Distance	
Meter	"m"
Statute mile	"mi"
Nautical mile	"Nmi"
Inch	"in"
Foot	"ft"
Yard	"yd"
Angstrom	"ang"
Pica(1/72 in.)	"Pica"
Time	
Year	"y"
Day	"day"
Hour	"hr"
Minute	"mn"
Second	"sec"

Table 5.1   Conversion Table

Unit Type	From Unit to Unit
Pressure	
Pascal	"Pa"
Atmosphere	"atm"
Mm of Mercury	"mmHG"
Force	
Newton	"N"
Dyne	"dyn"
Pound force	"lbf"
Energy	
Joule	"j"
Erg	"e"
Thermodynamic calorie	"c"
IT calorie	"cal"
Electron volt	"eV"
Horsepower hour	"HPh"
Watt-hour	"Wh"
Foot-pound	"flb"
BTU	"BTU"
Power	
Horsepower	"HP"
Watt	"W"
Magnetism	
Telsa	"T"
Gauss	"ga"
Temperature	
Degree Celsius	"C"
Degree Fahrenheit	"F"
Degree Kelvin	"K"

continues

Table 5.1 Continued

Unit Type	From Unit to Unit
Liquid Measure	
Teaspoon	"tsp"
Tablespoon	"tbs"
Fluid ounce	"oz"
Cup	"cup"
Pint	"pt"
Quart	"qt"
Gallon	"gal"
Liter	"l"

Table 5.2 Additional Conversions

Prefix	Multiplier	Abbreviation
Exa	1E+18	"E"
peta	1E+15	"P"
tera	1E+12	"T"
giga	1E+09	"G"
mega	1E+06	"M"
Kilo	1E+03	"k"
hecto	1E+02	"h"
dekao	1E+01	"e"
deci	1E-01	"d"
centi	1E-02	"c"
milli	1E-03	"m"
micro	1E-06	"u"
nano	1E-09	"n"
pico	1E-12	"p"
femto	1E-15	"f"
atto	1E-18	"a"

Figure 5.9
Converts measurement units from one unit to another.

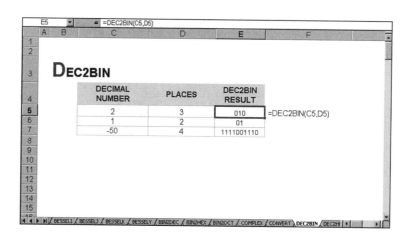

DEC2BIN

The DEC2BIN function converts decimal numbers to binary.

```
=DEC2BIN(number,places)
```

DEC2BIN is found only if the Analysis Toolpak is installed. In addition it must be turned on in the Add-Ins from the Tools menu. The number cannot be more than 10 characters. The sign bit being the most significant, the remaining 9 bits are magnitude bits. Negatives are represented using Two's complement notation. Notice the example in Figure 5.10. Where the Decimal Number is 2 and the Places is 3, the conversion to a binary results in 010.

NUMBER	The number to convert. Cannot be less than –512 or greater than 511.
PLACES	The number of characters to use. If places is omitted it uses the least characters necessary. If the value is not an integer, the value is truncated. Use when you want to pad the result with leading zeros to achieve uniformity.

Figure 5.10
Converts decimals to binary numbers.

DEC2HEX

Convert decimal numbers to hexadecimal with the DEC2HEX function.

=DEC2HEX(number,places)

The DEC2HEX function is found only if the Analysis Toolpak is installed. In addition it must be turned on in the Add-Ins from the Tools menu. The number returned is a 10 character hexadecimal number. The sign bit being the most significant, the remaining 39 bits are magnitude bits. Negatives are represented using Two's complement notation. Notice the example in Figure 5.11. Where the Binary Number is 10000010 and the Places is 3, the conversion to Octal results in 202.

NUMBER   The number to convert.

PLACES   The number of characters to use. If the value is not an integer, the value is truncated. Use when you want to pad the result with leading zeros to achieve uniformity.

Figure 5.11
Converting decimal numbers to hexadecimal numbers.

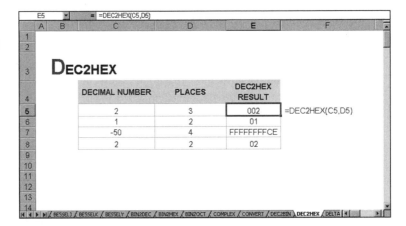

DELTA

DELTA tests whether numbers or values are equal with a number result—sometimes referred to as Kronecker.

=DELTA(number1,number2)

The DELTA function is found only if the Analysis Toolpak is installed. In addition it must be turned on in the Add-Ins from the Tools menu. If the first number is 1 and the second number is 2, the result is 0. However if the first number 1 and the second number is 1 the result is 1. Similar to a True or False logical test except the return is a number instead of a text result. Notice the example in Figure 5.12.

NUMBER 1   The first number.

NUMBER 2   The second number. If omitted, assumes 0.

Figure 5.12
DELTA tests whether two numbers are equal with a numeric result.

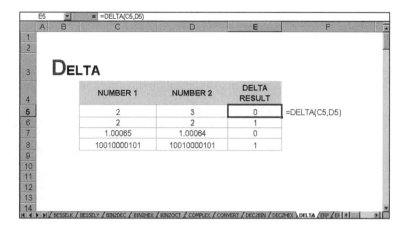

	NUMBER 1	NUMBER 2	DELTA RESULT	
	2	3	0	=DELTA(C5,D5)
	2	2	1	
	1.00065	1.00064	0	
	10010000101	10010000101	1	

ERF

Use the ERF function to return the integrated error function between a lower and upper limit.

`=ERF(lower_limit,upper_limit)`

The ERF function is found only if the Analysis-Toolpak is installed. In addition it must be turned on in the Add-Ins from the Tools menu. Notice the example in Figure 5.13. The lower-bound limit in the first example is 2 and the upper-bound limit is 3. The error result is .0047.

LOWER LIMIT   The numeric lower-bound for integrating the function.

UPPER LIMIT   The numeric upper-bound for integrating the function.

The equations are as follows:

$$\text{ERF}(z) = \frac{2}{\sqrt{\pi}} \int_0^z e^{-t^2} dt$$

$$\text{ERF}(a,b) = \frac{2}{\sqrt{\pi}} \int_a^b e^{-t^2} dt = \text{ERF}(b) - \text{ERF}(a)$$

Figure 5.13
Returns the integrated error function for upper and lower-bound limits.

ERF

	LOWER LIMIT	UPPER LIMIT	ERF RESULT	
	2	3	0.0047	=ERF(C5,D5)
	2	2	0.0000	
	2	10	0.0047	
	7		-1.0000	

ERFC

ERFC returns a complementary ERF function integrated between x and infinity. X is the lower-bound for integrating ERF.

`=ERFC(x)`

The ERFC function is found only if the Analysis Toolpak is installed. In addition it must be turned on in the Add-Ins from the Tools menu. Notice the example in Figure 5.14.

X   The numeric lower-bound for integrating the ERF.

The equation is as follows:

$$\mathrm{ERFC}(x) = \frac{2}{\sqrt{\pi}} \int_{x}^{\infty} e^{-t^2}\,dt = 1 - \mathrm{ERF}(x)$$

Figure 5.14
Returns a complementary *ERFC* function integrated between *x* and infinity—x is the lower-bound for integrating *ERFC*.

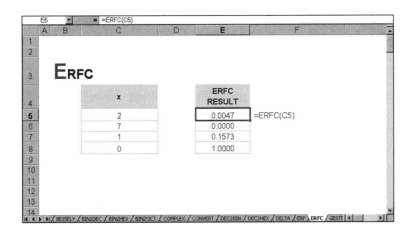

GESTEP

The GESTEP function returns the value of 1 if the number is greater than or equal to a specified step value, otherwise 0.

`=GESTEP(number,step)`

The GESTEP function is found only if the Analysis Toolpak is installed. In addition it must be turned on in the Add-Ins from the Tools menu. Notice the example in Figure 5.15. Where the number is equal to or greater than the step, the result is 1. Otherwise the result is zero. You can use this to sum up only those values that exceed the step value.

NUMBER   The number to test against the step value.

STEP   The step value is the threshold value the number is tested upon. If the value for step is omitted, it assumes zero.

Figure 5.15
Returns the value of 1
if the number is greater
than or equal to the
step, otherwise 0.

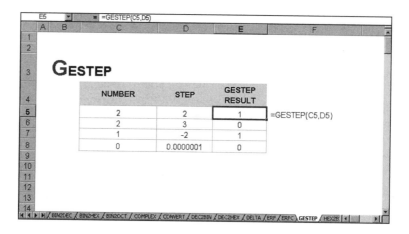

HEX2BIN

Convert hexadecimal numbers to binary with the HEX2BIN function.

=HEX2BIN(number,places)

HEX2BIN is found only if the Analysis Toolpak is installed. In addition it must be turned on in the Add-Ins from the Tools menu. Notice the example in Figure 5.16. The binary number is converted to a hexadecimal and then the HEX2BIN function converts the hexadecimal back to a binary number. The number cannot be more than 10 characters. The sign bit being the most significant, the remaining 9 bits are magnitude bits. Negatives are represented using Two's complement notation.

NUMBER   The number to convert. Cannot be less than –512 or greater than 511.

PLACES   The number of characters to use. If places is omitted it uses the least characters necessary. If the value is not an integer, the value is truncated. Use when you want to pad the result with leading zeros to achieve uniformity.

Figure 5.16
Converts hexadecimal
numbers to binary
numbers.

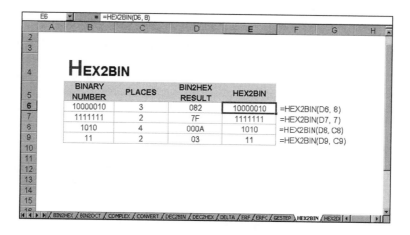

HEX2DEC

HEX2DEC converts hexadecimal numbers to decimal.

=HEX2DEC(number)

The HEX2DEC function is found only if the Analysis Toolpak is installed. In addition it must be turned on in the Add-Ins from the Tools menu. Notice the example in Figure 5.17. The binary number is converted to a hexadecimal and then the HEX2DEC function converts the hexadecimal back to a decimal number. The number cannot be more than 10 characters. The sign bit being the most significant, the remaining 39 bits are magnitude bits. Negatives are represented using Two's complement notation.

NUMBER   The hexadecimal number to convert.

Figure 5.17
Converts hexadecimal numbers to decimal.

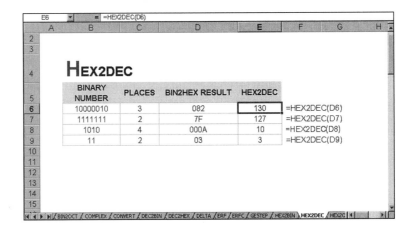

HEX2OCT

Use the HEX2OCT function to convert hexadecimal numbers to octal.

=HEX2OCT(number)

The HEX2OCT function is found only if the Analysis Toolpak is installed. In addition it must be turned on in the Add-Ins from the Tools menu. Notice the example in Figure 5.18. The binary number is converted to a hexadecimal and then the HEX2OCT function converts the hexadecimal to an octal. The binary number cannot be more than 10 characters. The sign bit being the most significant, the remaining 39 bits are magnitude bits. Negatives are represented using Two's complement notation.

NUMBER   The binary number to convert.

PLACES   The number of characters to use. If places is omitted it uses the least characters necessary. If the value is not an integer, the value is truncated. Use when you want to pad the result with leading zeros to achieve uniformity.

Figure 5.18

Converts hexadecimal numbers to octal.

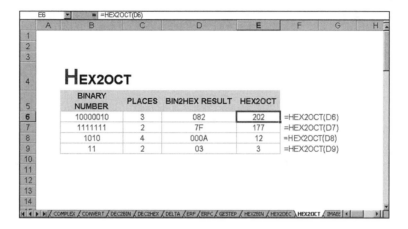

IMABS

Use the IMABS function to return the absolute value (modulus) of a complex number in x+yi or x+yj text format.

=IMABS(inumber)

The IMABS function is found only if the Analysis Toolpak is installed. In addition it must be turned on in the Add-Ins from the Tools menu. Notice the imaginary number in Figure 5.19. By using cell referencing the imaginary number is converted to an absolute value.

INUMBER   The complex number to convert to an absolute value.

The absolute value of a complex number is

$$\text{IMABS}(z) = |z| = \sqrt{x^2 + y^2}$$

where

$$z = x + yi$$

Figure 5.19
Returns the absolute value of a complex number.

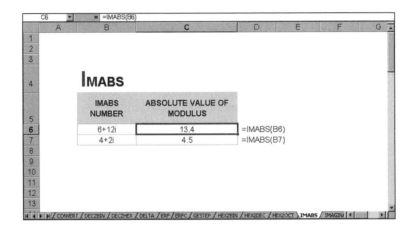

IMAGINARY

IMAGINARY returns the coefficient of a complex number in x+yi or x+yj text format.

=Imaginary(inumber)

The IMAGINARY function is found only if the Analysis Toolpak is installed. In addition it must be turned on in the Add-Ins from the Tools menu. Notice the example in Figure 5.20. The complex numbers are converted to the imaginary coefficients by using cell referencing.

INUMBER   The complex number to convert to an imaginary coefficient.

Figure 5.20
Converts complex numbers to imaginary coefficients.

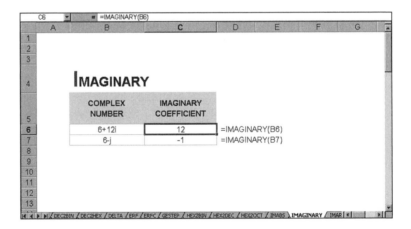

IMARGUMENT

The IMARGUMENT function RETURNS the theta argument, an angle expressed in radians.

`=IMARGUMENT(inumber)`

IMARGUMENT is found only if the Analysis Toolpak is installed. In addition it must be turned on in the Add-Ins from the Tools menu. In Figure 5.21, the complex number expressed as radians is the argument theta result of 0.927 for 3+4i.

INUMBER   The complex number to convert to the argument theta.

Returns the theta argument and angle expressed in radians such that:

The IMARGUMENT calculation is as follows:

$$\text{IMARGUMENT}(z) = \tan^{-1}\left(\frac{y}{x}\right) = \theta$$

where

$\theta \in]-\pi; \pi]$ and

$z = x + yi$

Figure 5.21
Returns the theta argument and angle expressed in radians.

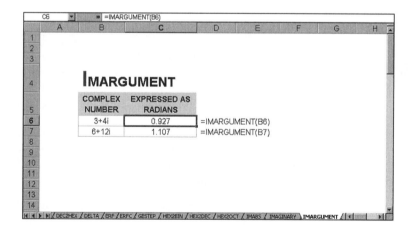

IMCONJUGATE

Returns the complex conjugate of a complex number in x+yi or x+yj text format with the INCONJUGATE function.

`=IMCONJUGATE(inumber)`

IMCONJUGATE is found only if the Analysis Toolpak is installed. In addition it must be turned on in the Add-Ins from the Tools menu. Where the complex number in Figure 5.22 is 3+4i, the complex conjugate results in 3-4i.

INUMBER   The complex number you want converted to the complex conjugate.

Where the formula is:

IMCONJUGATE ("3+4i") equals 3 - 4i

Figure 5.22
Returns the complex conjugate of a complex number in *x+yi* or *x+yj* text format.

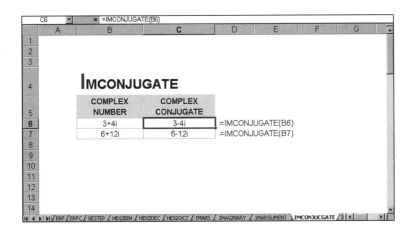

IMCOS

IMCOS returns the cosine of a complex number x+yi or x+yj in text format.

=IMCOS(inumber)

The IMCOS function is found only if the Analysis Toolpak is installed. In addition it must be turned on in the Add-Ins from the Tools menu. The IMCOS function returns the cosine of the complex number as shown in Figure 5.23.

INUMBER   The complex number to convert to the cosine.

Where the cosine of the complex number is:

$$\cos(x + yi) = \cos(x)\cosh(y) - \sin(x)\sinh(y)i$$

See the COMPLEX function earlier in this chapter for obtaining the complex number of real and imaginary coefficients.

Figure 5.23
Returns the cosine of a complex number $x+yi$ or $x+yj$ in text format.

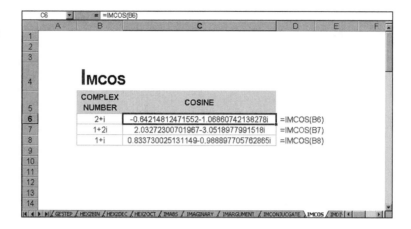

IMDIV

IMDIV returns the quotient of complex numbers in x+yi or x+yj text format.

=IMDIV(inumber1,inumber2)

The IMDIV function is found only if the Analysis Toolpak is installed. In addition it must be turned on in the Add-Ins from the Tools menu. The quotient of the complex number in the first example in Figure 5.24 is .4-0.2i.

INUMBER 1   The complex numerator/dividend.

INUMBER 2   The complex denominator/divisor.

The quotient of the two complex numbers:

$$\text{IMDIV}(z_1, z_2) = \frac{(a+bi)}{(c+di)} = \frac{(ac+bd)+(bc-ad)i}{c^2+d^2}$$

See the COMPLEX function earlier in this chapter for obtaining the complex number of real and imaginary coefficients.

Figure 5.24
Returns the cosine of a
complex number $x+yi$
or $x+yj$ in text format.

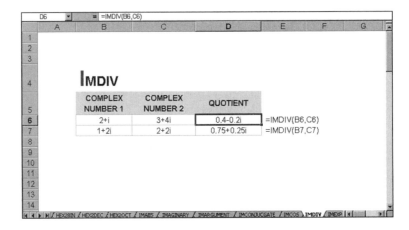

IMEXP

IMEXP returns the exponential of complex numbers x+yi or x+yj in text format.

=IMEXP(inumber)

The IMEXP function is found only if the Analysis Toolpak is installed. In addition it must be turned on in the Add-Ins from the Tools menu. The example in Figure 5.25 shows the exponentials of the complex numbers.

INUMBER   The complex number you want the exponential for.

The exponential of the complex number:

$$IMEXP(z) = e^{(x+yi)} = e^x e^{yi} = e^x(\cos y + i \sin y)$$

See the COMPLEX function earlier in this chapter for obtaining the complex number of real and imaginary coefficients.

Figure 5.25
Returns the exponential
of complex numbers
$x+yi$ or $x+yj$ in text
format.

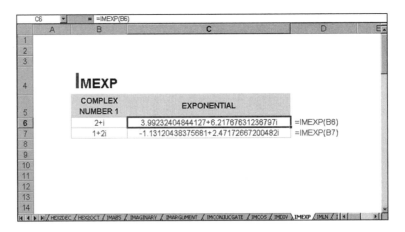

IMLN

Return the natural logarithm of a complex number in x+yi or x+yj text format with the IMLN function.

`=IMLN(inumber)`

The IMLN function is found only if the Analysis Toolpak is installed. In addition it must be turned on in the Add-Ins from the Tools menu. The example in Figure 5.26 shows the Natural Logarithm of the complex numbers.

INUMBER   The complex number you want the logarithm for.

The natural logarithm for the complex number is

$$\ln(x + yi) = \ln \sqrt{x^2 + y^2} + i \tan^{-1}\left(\frac{y}{x}\right)$$

where

$$\theta \in \left]-\pi; \pi\right]$$

See the COMPLEX function earlier in this chapter for obtaining the complex number of real and imaginary coefficients.

Figure 5.26
Returns the natural logarithm of complex numbers x+yi or x+yj in text format.

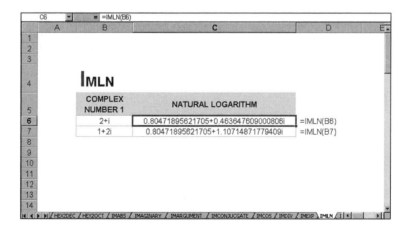

IMLOG10

IMLOG10 returns the common logarithm (Base 10) of a complex number in x+yi or x+yj text format.

`=IMLOG10(inumber)`

The IMLOG10 function is found only if the Analysis Toolpak is installed. In addition it must be turned on in the Add-Ins from the Tools menu. The example in Figure 5.27 shows the common Logarithm (Base 10) of the complex numbers.

INUMBER   The complex number for which you want the common logarithm (Base10).

Calculated from the natural logarithm as follows:

$$\log_{10}(x + yi) = (\log_{10} e)\ln(x + yi)$$

See the COMPLEX function earlier in this chapter for obtaining the complex number of real and imaginary coefficients.

Figure 5.27
Returns the common logarithm (Base 10) of complex numbers $x+yi$ or $x+yj$ in text format.

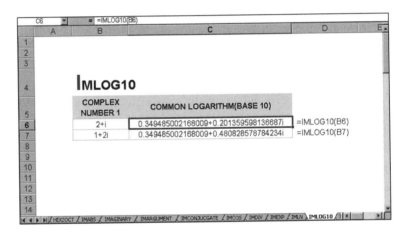

IMLOG2

IMLOG2 returns the Base 2 logarithm of a complex number in x+yi or x+yj text format.

=IMLOG2(inumber)

The IMLOG2 function is found only if the Analysis Toolpak is installed. In addition it must be turned on in the Add-Ins from the Tools menu. The example in Figure 5.28 shows the common Logarithm (Base 2) of the complex numbers.

INUMBER   The complex number for which you want the common logarithm (Base2).

Calculated from the natural logarithm as follows:

$$\log_2(x + yi) = (\log_2 e)\ln(x + yi)$$

See the COMPLEX function earlier in this chapter for obtaining the complex number of real and imaginary coefficients.

Figure 5.28
Returns the Base 2 logarithm of complex numbers in $x+yi$ or $x+yj$ in text format.

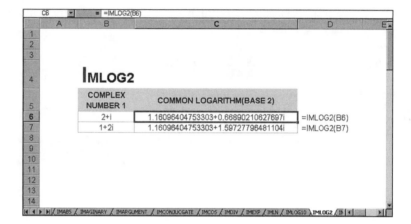

IMPOWER

Returns a complex number raised to a power in x+yi or x+yj text format with IMPOWER.

```
=IMPOWER(inumber,number)
```

The IMPOWER function is found only if the Analysis Toolpak is installed. In addition it must be turned on in the Add-Ins from the Tools menu. The example in Figure 5.29 shows the complex numbers with the powers to raise the numbers to and the result.

INUMBER	The complex number to raise to a power.
NUMBER	The power to raise the complex number to.

Where the number being raised to the power is calculated as follows:

$$(x + yi)^n = r^n e^{in\theta} = r^n \cos n\theta + ir^n \sin n\theta$$

where

$$r = \sqrt{x^2 + y^2}$$

and

$$r = \sqrt{x^2 + y^2}$$

and:

$$\theta = \tan^{-1}\left(\frac{y}{x}\right)$$

See the COMPLEX function earlier in this chapter for obtaining the complex number of real and imaginary coefficients.

Figure 5.29
Returns a complex number raised to a power in x+yi or x+yj text format.

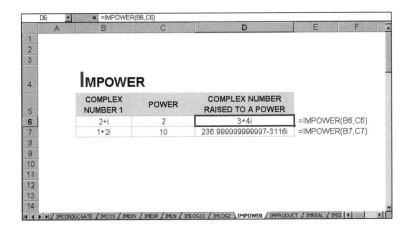

IMPRODUCT

IMPRODUCT returns the product from 2 to 29 complex numbers in x+yi or x+yj text format.

=IMPRODUCT(inumber1,inumber2,...)

The IMPRODUCT function is found only if the Analysis Toolpak is installed. In addition it must be turned on in the Add-Ins from the Tools menu. The example in Figure 5.30 shows the complex numbers and their products. You can use from 1 to 29 complex numbers

INUMBER 1,2, ...   1 to 29 complex numbers to multiply.

The product of two complex numbers:

$$(a + bi)(c + di) = (ac - bd) + (ad + bc)i$$

See the COMPLEX function earlier in this chapter for obtaining the complex number of real and imaginary coefficients.

Figure 5.30
Returns the product from 2 to 29 in complex numbers *x+yi* or *x+yj* text format.

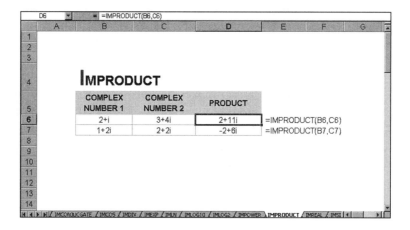

IMREAL

IMREAL returns the real coefficient of a complex number in x+yi or x+yj text format.

=IMREAL(inumber)

The IMREAL function is found only if the Analysis Toolpak is installed. In addition it must be turned on in the Add-Ins from the Tools menu. The example in Figure 5.31 shows the complex numbers and their real coefficients.

INUMBER   The complex number to convert to the real coefficient.

See the COMPLEX function earlier in this chapter for obtaining the complex number of real and imaginary coefficients.

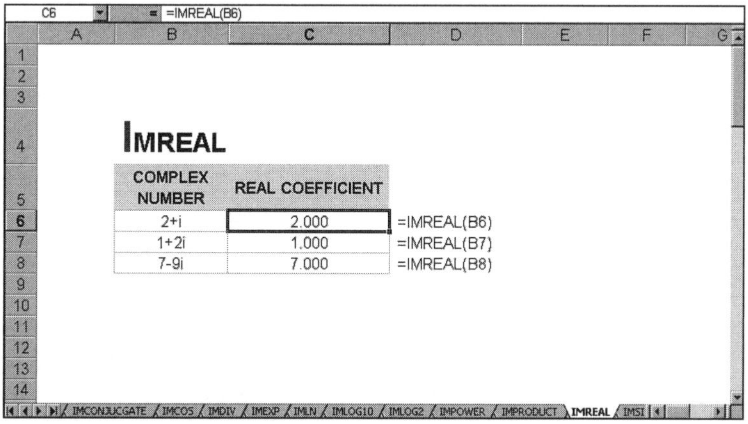

Figure 5.31
Returns real coefficients of complex numbers *x+yi* or *x+yj* in text format.

IMSIN

IMSIN returns the sine of complex numbers x+yi or x+yj in text format.

=IMSIN(inumber)

The IMSIN function is found only if the Analysis Toolpak is installed. In addition it must be turned on in the Add-Ins from the Tools menu. The example in Figure 5.32 shows the complex numbers converted to the sine of the complex number.

INUMBER   The complex number to convert to its sine.

Where the sine of the complex number is:

$$\sin\left(x + yi\right) = \sin\left(x\right)\cosh\left(y\right) - \cos\left(x\right)\sinh\left(y\right)i$$

See the COMPLEX function earlier in this chapter for obtaining the complex number of real and imaginary coefficients.

Figure 5.32
Returns the sine of complex numbers x+yi or x+yj in text format.

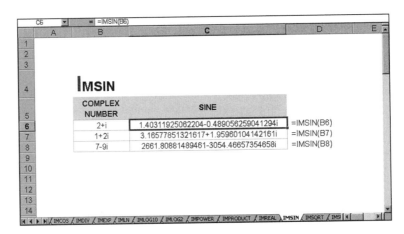

IMSQRT

Returns the square root of a complex number in x+yi or x+yj text format.

=IMSQRT(inumber)

The IMSQRT function is found only if the Analysis Toolpak is installed. In addition it must be turned on in the Add-Ins from the Tools menu. The example in Figure 5.33 shows the complex numbers converted converted to their square roots.

INUMBER   The complex number you wanted the square root of.

Where the square root of a complex number is as follows:

$$\sqrt{x + yi} = \sqrt{r}\cos\left(\frac{\theta}{2}\right) + i\sqrt{r}\,\sin\left(\frac{\theta}{2}\right)$$

where

$$r = \sqrt{x^2 + y^2}$$

and

$$\theta = \tan^{-1}\left(\frac{y}{x}\right)$$

and:
$$\theta \in \,]-\pi; \pi]$$

See the COMPLEX function earlier in this chapter for obtaining the complex number of real and imaginary coefficients.

Figure 5.33
Returns the square root of complex numbers x+yi or x+yj in text format.

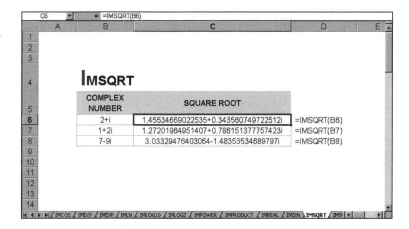

IMSUB

Returns the difference of two complex numbers in x+yi or x+yj text format with IMSUB.

=IMSUB(inumber1,inumber2)

The IMSUB function is found only if the Analysis Toolpak is installed. In addition it must be turned on in the Add-Ins from the Tools menu. The example in Figure 5.34 shows the difference when two complex numbers are subtracted.

INUMBER 1   The complex number to subtract from Inumber 2.

INUMBER 2   The complex number to subtract from Inumber 1.

Where the difference between two complex numbers is:

$$(a+bi)-(c+di)=(a-c)+(b-d)i$$

See the COMPLEX function earlier in this chapter for obtaining the complex number of real and imaginary coefficients.

Figure 5.34
Returns the difference of two complex numbers $x+yi$ or $x+yj$ in text format.

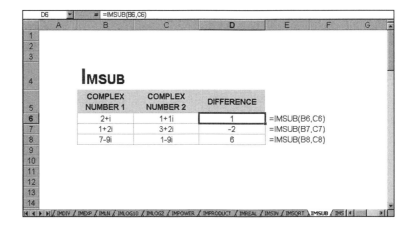

IMSUM

IMSUM returns the sum of two complex numbers x+yi or x+yj in text format.

=IMSUM(inumber1,inumber2,...)

The IMSUM function is found only if the Analysis Toolpak is installed. In addition it must be turned on in the Add-Ins from the Tools menu. The example in Figure 5.35 shows the sum of 1-29 complex numbers when added together.

INUMBER 1   The complex number to add to inumber 1–29.

Where the addition or sum of two complex numbers are:

$$(a+bi)+(c+di)=(a+c)+(b+d)i$$

See the COMPLEX function earlier in this chapter for obtaining the complex number of real and imaginary coefficients.

Figure 5.35
Returns the sum of two complex numbers $x+yi$ or $x+yj$ in text format.

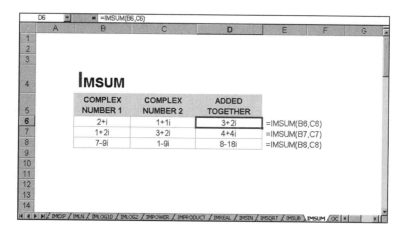

OCT2BIN

Converts an octal number to binary with the OCT2BIN function.

```
=OCT2BIN(number,places)
```

The OCT2BIN function is found only if the Analysis Toolpak is installed. In addition it must be turned on in the Add-Ins from the Tools menu. The number cannot be more than 10 characters. The sign bit being the most significant, the remaining 29 bits are magnitude bits. Negatives are represented using Two's complement notation. Notice the example in Figure 5.36. Where the Binary Number is 10000010 and the Places is 3, the conversion to a Octal results in 202, and the conversion back to the binary results in 10000010.

NUMBER	The number in which to convert. If the number is negative it ignores the places and returns 10-character binary. The number cannot be greater than 777 and less than or equal to 7777777000.
PLACES	The number of characters to use.

Figure 5.36
Converts an octal number to binary number.

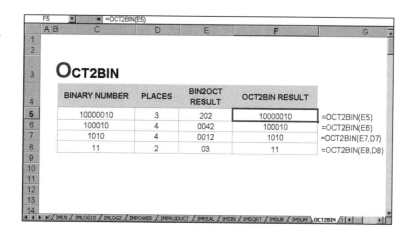

OCT2DEC

OCT2DEC converts an octal number to decimal.

`=OCT2DEC(number)`

The OCT2DEC function is found only if the Analysis Toolpak is installed. In addition it must be turned on in the Add-Ins from the Tools menu. The number cannot be more than 10 characters. The sign bit being the most significant, the remaining 29 bits are magnitude bits. Negatives are represented using Two's complement notation. Notice the example in Figure 5.37. Where the Binary Number is 10000010 and the Places is 3, the conversion to an octal results in 202, and the conversion from an octal to the decimal is 130 in cell F5.

NUMBER   The octal number to convert.

Figure 5.37
Converts an octal
number to decimal.

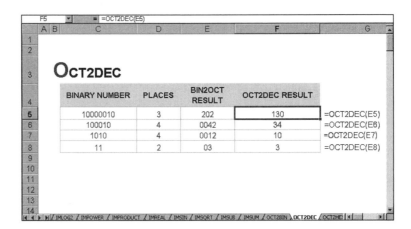

OCT2HEX

Use the OCT2HEX function to convert an octal number to hexadecimal.

`=OCT2HEX(number,places)`

The OCT2HEX function is found only if the Analysis Toolpak is installed. In addition it must be turned on in the Add-Ins from the Tools menu. The number cannot be more than 10 characters. The sign bit being the most significant, the remaining 29 bits are magnitude bits. Negatives are represented using Two's complement notation. Notice the example in Figure 5.38. Where the Binary Number is 10000010 and the Places is 3, the conversion to an octal results in 202. The conversion from an octal to the hexadecimal is 82 in cell F5.

NUMBER   The octal number to convert to a hexadecimal.

PLACES   The number of characters to use.

Figure 5.38
Converts an octal
number to hexadecimal.

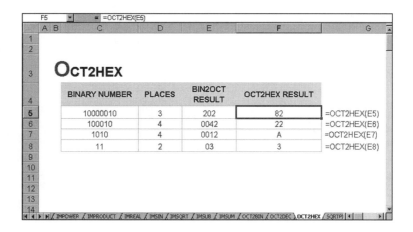

CHAPTER 6

Financial Functions

Financial Functions Overview

Financial functions can be used to calculate house mortgage payments, annuities, accrued interest, and just about any other financial calculation for which you may need to calculate future, present, or past values. Excel has more than 50 financial functions that can operate independently or can be combined with other functions for a more customized situation. The financial functions are also accompanied by descriptions of the syntax. This helps in understanding the function as a whole. Because most of these functions are used with cell referencing in the workbooks, you can refer to the CD and put numbers, dates, and rates in the corresponding cells and the formula calculates the outcome for you. You should take note that when creating functions to return date results, you may have to format the result in a date format. If the return is in digit format, simply change the cell format from the Format menu.

The following functions are discussed in this chapter.

▶ ACCRINT	▶ DDB	▶ MIRR	▶ PV
▶ ACCRINTM	▶ DISC	▶ NOMINAL	▶ RATE
▶ AMORDEGRC	▶ DOLLARDE	▶ NPER	▶ RECEIVED
▶ AMORLINC	▶ DOLLARFR	▶ NPV	▶ SLN
▶ COUPDAYBS	▶ DURATION	▶ ODDFPRICE	▶ SYD
▶ COUPDAYS	▶ EFFECT	▶ ODDFYIELD	▶ TBILLEQ
▶ COUPDAYSNC	▶ FV	▶ ODDLPRICE	▶ TBILLPRICE
▶ COUPNCD	▶ FVSCHEDULE	▶ ODDLYIELD	▶ TBILLYIELD
▶ COUPNUM	▶ INTRATE	▶ PMT	▶ VDB
▶ COUPPCD	▶ IPMT	▶ PPMT	▶ XIRR
▶ CUMIPMT	▶ IRR	▶ PRICE	▶ XNPV
▶ CUMPRINC	▶ ISPMT	▶ PRICEDISC	▶ YIELD
▶ DB	▶ MDURATION	▶ PRICEMAT	▶ YIELDDISC
			▶ YIELDMAT

ACCRINT

ACCRINT returns accrued interest for securities that pay periodic interest.

`=ACCRINT(issue,first_interest,settlement,rate,par,frequency,basis)`

The ACCRINT function is found only if the Analysis Toolpak is installed. It must be turned on using the Add-Ins command on the Tools menu. Notice the example in Figure 6.1. The example is setup with cell referencing so that you can make adjustments to dates, percentages, par values, and so on. By using cell referencing instead of applying the dates in the formula, your formula becomes more flexible.

ISSUE	The date of the security issue.
FIRST INTEREST	The first interest date of the security.
SETTLEMENT	The security settlement date is the date the security is traded to the buyer after the issue date.
RATE	The annual coupon rate of the security.
PAR	The securities par value. If you omit par, ACCRINT uses the default of $1,000.
FREQUENCY	The number of payments per year. Quarterly is 4, semiannually is 2, and annually is 1.
BASIS	The day count basis to use. If omitted, the function uses 0. Refer to Figure 6.1 for a list of choices.

The ACCRINT formula is calculated as:

$$ACCRINT = par \times \frac{rate}{frequency} \times \sum_{i=1}^{NC} \frac{A_i}{NL_i}$$

Figure 6.1
The *ACCRINT* function returns the interest for a security that pays interest periodically.

❶ The function built with cell referencing

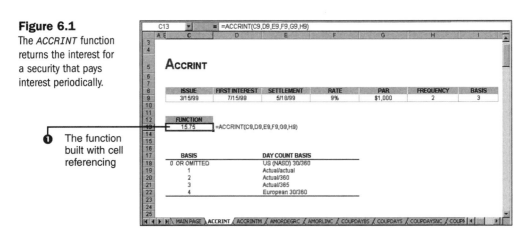

ACCRINTM

ACCRINTM returns accrued interest for securities that pay interest at the maturity date.

=ACCRINTM(issue,maturity,rate,par,basis)

The ACCRINTM function is found only if the Analysis Toolpak is installed. In addition, it must be turned on in the Add-Ins command from the Tools menu. Notice the example in Figure 6.2. The example is setup with cell referencing so that you can make adjustments to dates, percentages, par values, and so on. By using cell referencing instead of applying the dates in the formula, your formula becomes more flexible.

ISSUE   The date of the security issue.

MATURITY   The date the security matures.

RATE   The securities annual coupon rate.

PAR   The securities par value. If you omit par, ACCRINT uses the default of $1,000.

BASIS   The day count basis to use. If omitted, the function uses 0. See Figure 6.2 for a list of choices.

The ACCRINTM formula can be calculated with:

$$ACCRINTM = par \times rate \times \frac{A}{D}$$

Figure 6.2
The *ACCRINTM* function returns the accrued interest for the security that pays interest at maturity.

❶ Another function built with cell referencing

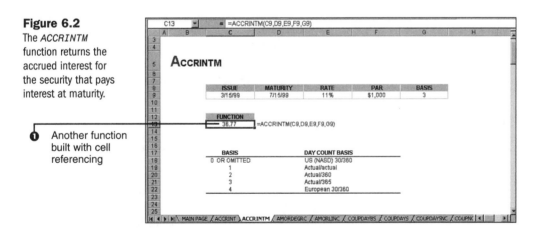

AMORDEGRC

AMORDEGRC returns the depreciation for each accounting period within the formula.

=AMORDEGRC(cost,date_purchased,first_period,salvage,period,rate,basis)

The AMORDEGRC function is provided for the French accounting system. If an asset is purchased within the middle of the accounting period, the prorated depreciation is taken into account. The AMORDEGRC function is found only if the Analysis Toolpak is installed. It must be turned on using the Add-Ins command from the Tools menu. Notice the example in Figure 6.3, where the depreciation on a machine cost of $36,234 with a 15% rate of depreciation is $11,857. By using cell referencing instead of applying the dates in the formula, your formula becomes more flexible.

COST	The cost of the asset.
DATE_PURCHASED	The date the asset was purchased.
FIRST_PERIOD	The date at the end of the first period.
SALVAGE	The salvage value of the asset at the end of the asset life.
PERIOD	The period of depreciation.
RATE	The rate of the asset depreciation.
BASIS	The year basis to use.

Figure 6.3
AMORDEGRC returns the depreciation for each accounting period within the formula.

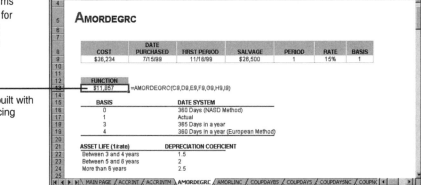

❶ A function built with cell referencing

AMORLINC

AMORLINC returns the depreciation for each accounting period.

`=AMORLINC(cost,date_purchased,first_period,salvage,period,rate,basis)`

The AMORLINC function is provided for the French accounting system. If an asset is purchased within the middle of the accounting period, the prorated depreciation is taken into account. The AMORLINC function is found only if the Analysis Toolpak is installed. It must be turned on using the Add-Ins command from the Tools menu. Notice the example in Figure 6.4. The depreciation on the cost of the the $36,234 machine at the end of the first period is $5,435 with a 15% rate of depreciation. By using cell referencing instead of applying the dates in the formula, your formula becomes more flexible.

COST	The cost of the asset.
DATE_PURCHASED	The date the asset was purchased.
FIRST_PERIOD	The date at the end of the first period.

SALVAGE	The salvage value of the asset at the end of the asset life.
PERIOD	The period of depreciation.
RATE	The rate of the asset depreciation.
BASIS	The year basis to use.

Figure 6.4
The *AMORLINC* function returns the depreciation of an asset for each accounting period.

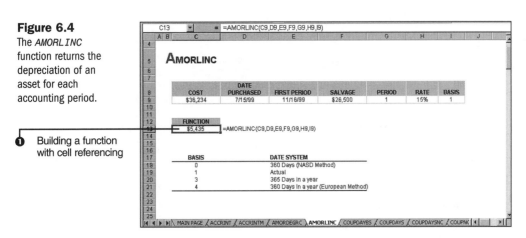

❶ Building a function with cell referencing

COUPDAYBS

COUPDAYBS returns the number of days from the beginning of the period to the coupon-period settlement date.

=COUPDAYBS(settlement,maturity,frequency,basis)

The COUPDAYBS function is found only if the Analysis Toolpak is installed. It must be turned on using the <u>A</u>dd-Ins command from the <u>T</u>ools menu. Notice in Figure 6.5, the bond settlement date (the date a buyer purchases a coupon such as a bond) is 5/15/1999 and the maturity date (the date the bond expires) is 7/15/2000. The frequency is semiannual and the basis is Actual/actual. And the number of days between the coupon day and the settlement is 120. By using cell referencing instead of applying the dates in the formula, your formula becomes more flexible.

SETTLEMENT	The security's settlement date. This is the date after the issue date when the security is traded to the buyer.
MATURITY	The security's maturity date. The date when the security expires.
FREQUENCY	The number of payments per year—Annual = 1; Semiannual = 2; Quarterly = 4.
BASIS	The day count basis to use. If omitted, 0 is used. See additional choices in Figure 6.5.

Figure 6.5
The *COUPDAYBS*
function returns the
number of days from
the start date of the
coupon period to the
settlement.

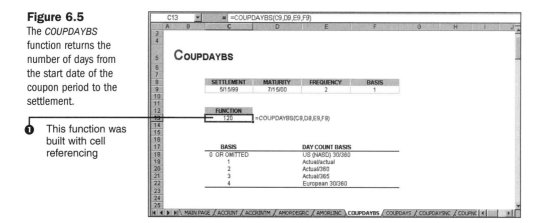

❶ This function was
built with cell
referencing

COUPDAYS

COUPDAYS returns the number of days in the period that contains the coupon period settlement date.

=COUPDAYS(settlement,maturity,frequency,basis)

The COUPDAYS function is found only if the Analysis Toolpak is installed. It must be turned on using the Add-Ins command from the Tools menu. In Figure 6.6 you'll see that the bond settlement date (the date a buyer purchases a coupon such as a bond) is 5/15/1999, and the maturity date (the date the bond expires) is 7/15/2000. The frequency is semianual and the basis is Actual/actual. The number of days between the coupon day and the settlement is 181. By using cell referencing instead of applying the dates in the formula, your formula becomes more flexible.

SETTLEMENT   The security's settlement date. This is the date after the issue date when the security is traded to the buyer.

MATURITY   The security's maturity date. The date when the security expires.

FREQUENCY   The number of payments per year—Annual = 1; Semiannual = 2; Quarterly = 4.

BASIS   The day count basis to use. If omitted, 0 is used. See additional choices in Figure 6.6.

Figure 6.6
COUPDAYS returns the
number of days in the
period that contains
the coupon period
settlement date.

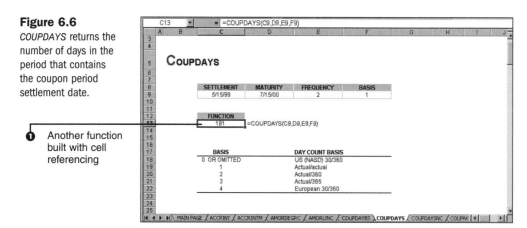

❶ Another function
built with cell
referencing

COUPDAYSNC

COUPDAYSNC returns the number of days between the settlement date to the next coupon date.

=COUPDAYSNC(settlement,maturity,frequency,basis)

The COUPDAYSNC function is found only if the Analysis Toolpak is installed. It must be turned on using the Add-Ins command from the Tools menu. Notice Figure 6.7. The bond settlement date (the date a buyer purchases a coupon such as a bond) is 5/15/1999 and the maturity date (the date the bond expires) is 7/15/2001. The frequency is semiannual and the basis is Actual/actual. The number of days from the coupon settlement date to the next coupon date is 61. By using cell referencing instead of applying the dates in the formula, your formula becomes more flexible.

SETTLEMENT	The security's settlement date. This is the date after the issue date when the security is traded to the buyer.
MATURITY	The security's maturity date. The date when the security expires.
FREQUENCY	The number of payments per year— Annual = 1; Semiannual = 2; Quarterly = 4.
BASIS	The day count basis to use. If omitted, 0 is used. See additional choices in Figure 6.7.

Figure 6.7
The *COUPDAYSNC* function returns the number of days between the settlement date to the next coupon date.

❶ The function resulting from cell referencing

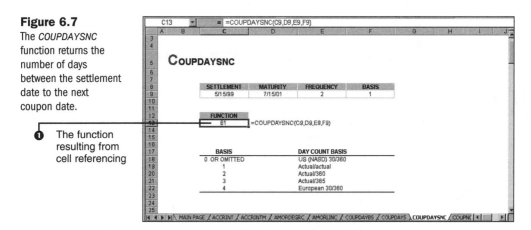

COUPNCD

COUPNCD returns the number that represents the next coupon date after the settlement date.

=COUPNCD(settlement,maturity,frequency,basis)

The COUPNCD function is found only if the Analysis Toolpak is installed. It must be turned on using the Add-Ins command from the Tools menu. The cell in which the function is in must also be in a date format. In Figure 6.8, the bond settlement date (the date a buyer purchases a coupon such as a bond) is 5/15/1999 and the maturity date (the date the bond expires) is 9/15/2000. The frequency is semiannual and the basis is Actual/actual. The next coupon date after the settlement date is 9/15/1999. By using cell referencing instead of applying the dates in the formula, your formula becomes more flexible.

SETTLEMENT	The security's settlement date. This is the date after the issue date when the security is traded to the buyer.
MATURITY	The security's maturity date. The date when the security expires.
FREQUENCY	The number of payments per year—Annual = 1; Semiannual = 2; Quarterly = 4.
BASIS	The day count basis to use. If omitted, 0 is used. See additional choices in Figure 6.8.

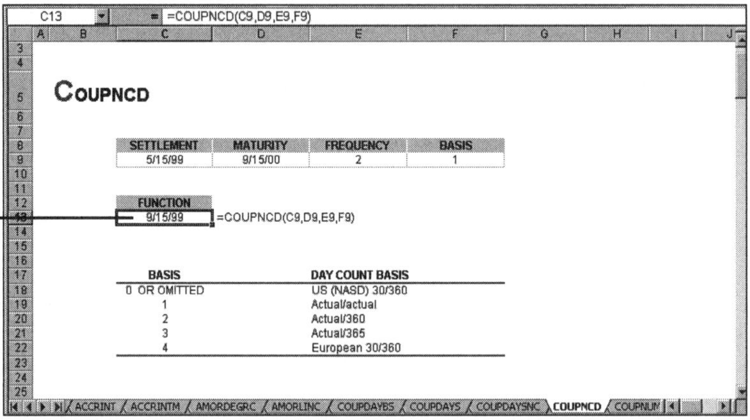

Figure 6.8

COUPNCD returns the number of the next coupon date after the settlement date.

① The function built with cell referencing

COUPNUM

COUPNUM returns the total number of coupons to be paid between the settlement and maturity dates, rounded up to the nearest whole coupon.

=COUPNUM(settlement,maturity,frequency,basis)

The COUPNUM function is found only if the Analysis Toolpak is installed. It must be turned on using the Add-Ins command from the Tools menu. When you look at Figure 6.9, you'll see that the bond settlement date (the date a buyer purchases a coupon such as a bond) is 5/15/1999 and the maturity date (the date the bond expires) is 9/15/2000. The frequency is semiannual and the basis is Actual/actual. The total number of coupons payable between the settlement and maturity date is 3. By using cell referencing instead of applying the dates in the formula, you give your formula greater flexibility.

SETTLEMENT	The security's settlement date. This is the date after the issue date when the security is traded to the buyer.
MATURITY	The security's maturity date. The date when the security expires.
FREQUENCY	The number of payments per year—Annual = 1; Semiannual = 2; Quarterly = 4.
BASIS	The day count basis to use.

Figure 6.9
The *COUPNUM* function returns the total number of coupons payable between the settlement and maturity date, rounded up to the nearest whole coupon.

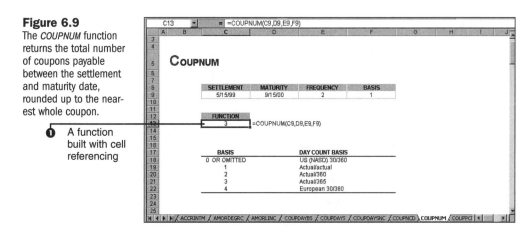

❶ A function built with cell referencing

COUPPCD

COUPPCD returns the number of the previous coupon date before the settlement date.

=COUPPCD(settlement,maturity,frequency,basis)

The COUPPCD function is found only in the Analysis Toolpak. It must be turned on using the Add-Ins command from the Tools menu. The cell in which the function is in must also be in a date format. Take a look at Figure 6.10. The bond settlement date (the date a buyer purchases a coupon such as a bond) is 5/15/1999 and the maturity date (the date the bond expires) is 9/15/2000. The frequency is semiannual and the basis is Actual/actual, and the number of the previous coupon date before the settlement date is 3/15/1999. By using cell referencing instead of applying the dates in the formula, you can manage your formula with greater flexibility.

SETTLEMENT	The security's settlement date. This is the date after the issue date when the security is traded to the buyer.
MATURITY	The security's maturity date. The date when the security expires.
FREQUENCY	The number of payments per year—Annual = 1; Semiannual = 2; Quarterly = 4.
BASIS	The day count basis to use.

Figure 6.10
COUPPCD returns the number of the previous coupon date before the settlement date.

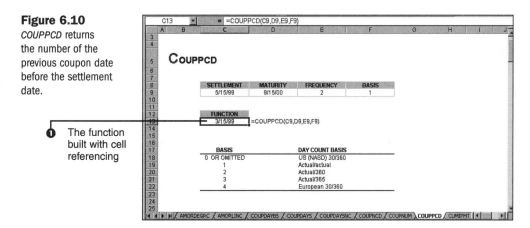

❶ The function built with cell referencing

CUMIPMT

CUMIPMT returns the cumulative interest on a loan between start and stop dates.

=CUMIPMT(rate,nper,pv,start_period,end_period,type)

The CUMIPMT function is found only in the Analysis Toolpak. It must be turned on using the Add-Ins command from the Tools menu. As you'll see in Figure 6.11, the rate is 7% on the loan, the number of payments on a 30-year mortgage is 360, and the present value of the loan is $250,000. The cumulative interest for the second year of the loan starts with 13 and ends with 24 (number in months). The type is 0 (payment at the end of the period). The cumulative interest on the loan for the second year of the mortgage is $20,759.

RATE	The interest rate of the loan.
NPER	The number of payment periods.
PV	The present value of the loan.
START_PERIOD	The first payment period. Payment periods start with one.
END_PERIOD	The last period in the calculation.
TYPE	The payment timing.

Figure 6.11
Use *CUMIPMT* to return the cumulative interest on a loan between start and stop dates.

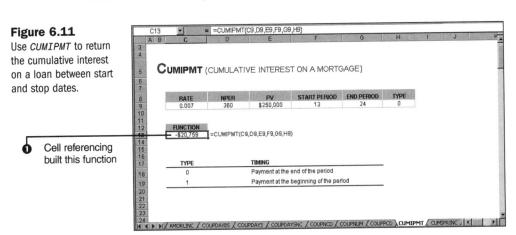

① Cell referencing built this function

CUMPRINC

CUMPRINC returns the cumulative principal amount between start and stop dates on a loan or mortgage.

=CUMPRINC(rate,nper,pv,start_period,end_period,type)

The CUMPRINC function is found only if the Analysis Toolpak is installed. It must be turned on using the Add-Ins command from the Tools menu. When you look at Figure 6.12, you'll see that in this example, the rate is 7% on the loan. The number of payments on a 30-year mortgage is 360. The present value of the loan is $250,000. The cumulative interest for the second year of the loan starts with 13 and ends with 24 (number in months). The type is 0 (payment at the end of the period). The cumulative principal on the loan for the second year of the mortgage is $2,097. You should note that both the interest rate and the number of periods should be using the same unit of measurement. The example uses months.

RATE	The interest rate of the loan.
NPER	The number of payment periods.
PV	The present value of the loan.
START_PERIOD	The first payment period. Payment periods start with one.
END_PERIOD	The last period in the calculation.
TYPE	The payment timing.

Figure 6.12
CUMPRINC returns the cumulative principal amount between start and stop dates on a loan or mortgage.

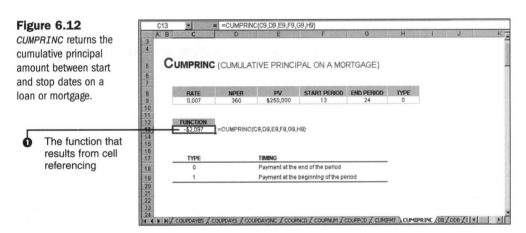

❶ The function that results from cell referencing

DB

DB returns the asset depreciation for a period using the fixed declining balance method.

`=DB(cost,salvage,life,period,month)`

Let's say you purchase a machine that cost $900,000, and has a lifespan of 5 years. The salvage value is $100,000. Figure 6.13 shows the depreciation over 5 years using the DB function.

COST	Asset's initial cost.
SALVAGE	The value at the end of the depreciation.
LIFE	The number of periods over which to depreciate the asset.
PERIOD	The period over which the depreciation is calculated. The period must use the same number as `Life`.
MONTH	The number of months in the first year. If omitted, Excel assumes 12.

Figure 6.13
DB returns the asset depreciation for a period using the fixed-declining balance method.

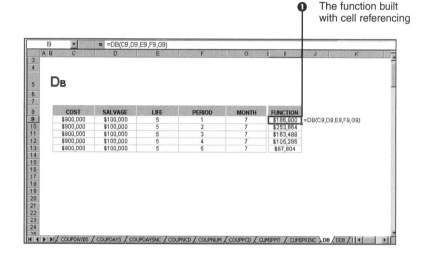

The function built with cell referencing

DDB

DDB returns the asset depreciation for a period using the double-declining balance method, or another method specified by you.

=DDB(cost,salvage,life,period,factor)

The double-declining method is highest in the first period and decreases in successive periods. If you purchase a machine that cost $5,000 and has a lifetime of 4 years, the salvage value of the machine is $1,250. Figure 6.14 shows the depreciation over 4 years using the DDB function (double-declining method). The double-declining balance method calculates depreciation at an accelerated rate. The depreciation is highest in the first period and decreases in successive periods thereafter.

COST	Asset's initial cost.
SALVAGE	The value at the end of the depreciation.
LIFE	The number of periods over which to depreciate the asset.
PERIOD	The period over which the depreciation is calculated. The period must use the same number as Life.
FACTOR	Is the rate in which the balance declines. If Factor is omitted, it is assumed to be 2, the double-declining method as explained previously.

① This function is a result of cell referencing

Figure 6.14
The *DDB* function returns the asset depreciation for a period using the double-declining balance method, or another method specified by you.

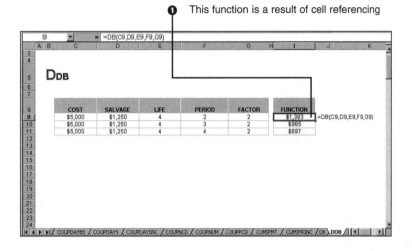

DISC

DISC returns the security discount rate.

=DISC(settlement,maturity,pr,redemption,basis)

The DISC function is found only if the Analysis Toolpak is installed. It must be turned on using the Add-Ins command from the Tools menu. You'll notice in Figure 6.15 the bond settlement date (the date a buyer purchases a coupon such as a bond) is 5/15/1999 and the maturity date (the date the bond expires) is 11/15/1999. The security price per $100 face value is $95. The redemption value is $100. And the basis is Actual/360. The bond discount rate equals 9.92%. By using cell referencing instead of applying the dates in the formula, your formula becomes more flexible.

SETTLEMENT   The security's settlement date. This is the date after the issue date when the security is traded to the buyer.

MATURITY   The security's maturity date—the date when the security expires.

PR   The security price per $100 face value.

REDEMPTION   The security redemption value per $100 face value.

BASIS   The day count basis to use.

Figure 6.15
The *DISC* function returns the security discount rate.

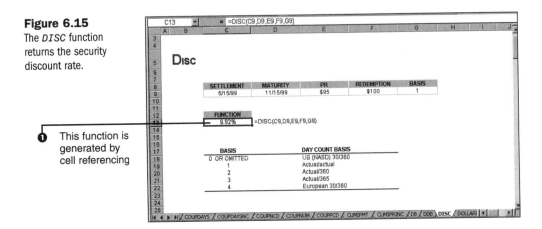

❶ This function is generated by cell referencing

DOLLARDE

DOLLARDE converts a fraction dollar price into a decimal dollar price.

=DOLLARDE(fractional_dollar,fraction)

The DOLLARDE function converts the dollar price expressed as a fraction of a dollar. This function is found only if the Analysis Toolpak is installed. It must be turned on using the Add-Ins command from the Tools menu.

FRACTIONAL_DOLLAR   Is the number expressed as a fraction?

FRACTION   Is the integer in the denominator of the fraction to be used?

For example: =DOLLARDE(1.35,6) returns the result 1.58.

DOLLARFR

DOLLARFR converts a decimal dollar price into a fraction dollar price.

=DOLLARFR(decimal_dollar,fraction)

The DOLLARFR function converts the dollar price expressed as a decimal to a dollar price expressed as a fraction. The DOLLARDE function is found only if the Analysis Toolpak is installed. It must be turned on using the Add-Ins command from the Tools menu.

DECIMAL_DOLLAR   A decimal number.

FRACTION   The integer in the denominator of the fraction to be used.

For example: =DOLLARFR (1.35,6) returns the result 1.21.

DURATION

DURATION returns the Macauley duration for an assumed par value.

=DURATION(settlement,maturity,coupon,yield,frequency,basis)

Notice that in Figure 6.16 the bond settlement date (the date a buyer purchases a coupon such as a bond) is 5/15/1999 and the maturity date (the date the bond expires) is 7/13/2007. The securities annual coupon rate is 8.7%. The securities annual yield is 9.2%. The frequency is semiannual and the basis is Actual/actual. The weighted average equals 5.89 years. By using cell referencing instead of applying the dates in the formula, your formula becomes more flexible.

SETTLEMENT	The security's settlement date. This is the date after the issue date when the security is traded to the buyer.
MATURITY	The security's maturity date. The date when the security expires.
COUPON	The security's annual coupon rate.
YIELD	The security's annual yield.
FREQUENCY	The number of payments per year—Annual = 1; Semiannual = 2; Quarterly = 4.
BASIS	The day count basis to use.

Figure 6.16
The *DURATION* method is the weighted average of the present value of the cash flows and is used as a measure of a bond's price response to changes in the yield.

❶ The function built with cell referencing

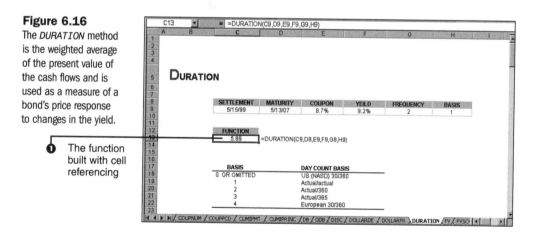

EFFECT

EFFECT returns the effective interest rate annually. This is based on the nominal annual interest rate and the number of compounding periods per year.

=EFFECT(nominal_rate,npery)

The EFFECT function is found only if the Analysis Toolpak is installed. It must be turned on using the Add-Ins command from the Tools menu.

| NOMINAL_RATE | The nominal interest rate. |
| NPERY | The number of compounding periods per year. |

For example: =EFFECT(6.25%,4) returns the result 6.40%.

FV

FV returns the future value of periodic constant payments and a constant interest rate.

=FV(rate,nper,pmt,pv,type)

The FV function is used primarily for finding the payments over a period of time to reach a specific goal or lump sum. As you should notice in Figure 6.17, the deposit amount or present value is $1,000, the interest earned is 7%, and the you plan on depositing $200 per month over the period of the annuity of 12 months at the beginning of each period. The value or worth at the end of the annuity is $3,599.

RATE	The interest rate per period.
NPER	The number of payment periods in an annuity.
PMT	The payment made per period. Typically containing principal and interest and does not change over the life of the loan.
PV	The present value that a series of payments is worth right now. If omitted, Excel assumes zero.
TYPE	The timing of the payment. When the payments are due.

Figure 6.17
FV returns the future value of periodic payments and a constant interest rate.

❶ The FV function built with cell referencing

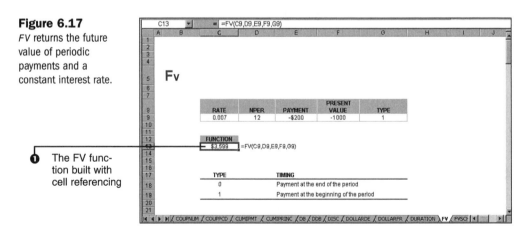

FVSCHEDULE

FVSCHEDULE returns the future value of a principal amount after applying several, or a series of compound interest rates.

=FVSCHEDULE(principal,schedule)

The FVSCHEDULE function returns the future value of a principal amount after applying several, or a series of compound interest rates. This function is found only if the Analysis Toolpak is installed. It must be turned on using the Add-Ins command from the Tools menu. Figure 6.18 demonstrates that the compound interest rates applied to the principal's present value is 7, 8, and 9%.

PRINCIPAL   The present value or deposited amount.

SCHEDULE   The array (series) of interest rates to apply.

Figure 6.18
FVSCHEDULE returns the future value of a principal amount after applying several, or a series of compound interest rates.

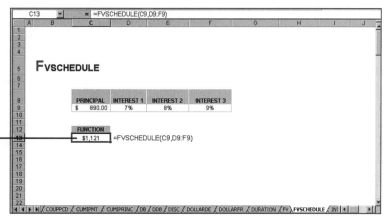

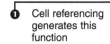
❶ Cell referencing generates this function

INTRATE

INTRATE returns the interest rate of a security that's fully invested.

=INTRATE(settlement,maturity,investment,redemption,basis)

The INTRATE function is found only if the Analysis Toolpak is installed. It must be turned on using the Add-Ins command from the Tools menu. In Figure 6.19 the settlement date is 5/15/1999. The maturity date is 9/15/1999. The investment is $500,000, and the redemption value of the bond is $524,000. With a day count basis of Actual/360, the interest rate for this fully invested security is 14%.

SETTLEMENT   The security's settlement date. This is the date after the issue date when the security is traded to the buyer.

MATURITY   The security's maturity date. The date when the security expires.

INVESTMENT	The amount invested in the security.
REDEMPTION	The amount to be received at maturity.
BASIS	The day count basis to use.

INTRATE is calculated as follows:

$$INTRATE = \frac{redemption - investment}{investment} \times \frac{B}{DIM}$$

Figure 6.19
The *INTRATE* function returns the interest rate of a security that's fully invested.

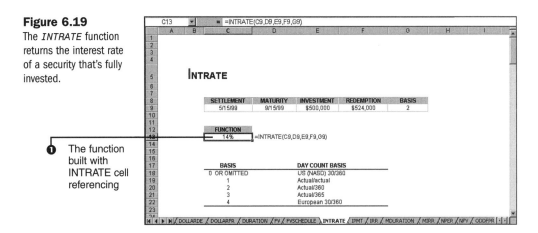

❶ The function built with INTRATE cell referencing

IPMT

IPMT returns the interest payment for a period of time based on an investment with periodic constant payments and a constant interest rate.

=IPMT(rate,per,nper,pv,fv,type)

The IPMT function returns an interest payment over a period of time. As shown in Figure 6.20, the interest rate per period is 7%. Period 1 is the period in which to find the payment when spread out over a total of 36 payments. The present value or lump sum amount that the future payments is worth right now is $10,000. As you see, the future value of the loan in this case is 0 and the payment is at the end of each period. So the interest payment for the first period of the loan in the example equals $70.

RATE	The interest rate per period.
PER	The period for which you want to find the interest. This must be in the range of 1 to Nper.
NPER	The number of payment periods in an annuity.
PV	The present value that a series of payments is worth right now. If omitted, Excel assumes zero.
FV	The future value or cash balance you want to attain upon the last payment.
TYPE	The timing of the payment. When the payments are due.

Figure 6.20
Use *IPMT* to determine the interest payment for a period of time based on an investment with periodic constant payments and a constant interest rate.

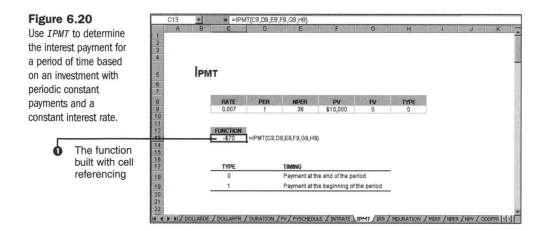

❶ The function built with cell referencing

IRR

IRR returns the internal rate of return for a series of cash flows represented by numbers in the form of values.

```
=IRR(values,irr,guess)
```

The IRR function is used to determine the internal rate of return for a series of cashflows. The cashflows can vary and do not have to be equal, however, they must occur at equal intervals. See also, NPV. Figure 6.21 shows that the investment in the business is $100,000. The series of cash flows you expect to receive within the next five years, or return on investment is $20,000, $30,000, $35,000, $40,000, and $45,000. Based on the 5-year cash return, the ROI is 18%. The ROI after 3 years is –7%. The breakeven point falls between years 3 and 4.

VALUES	The values must contain one positive and one negative value to calculate the internal rate of return.
IRR	The order of cash flows is determined by the order of values, so be sure to enter your payment and income values in the proper sequence.
GUESS	This is the number you guess is close to the IRR.

Figure 6.21
IRR generates the internal rate of return for cash flows in a series represented by numbers in the form of values.

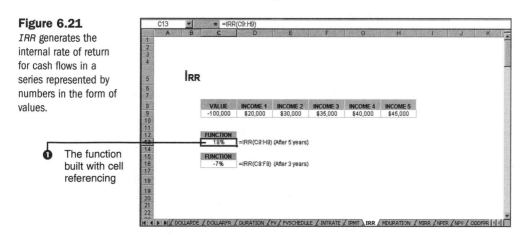

❶ The function built with cell referencing

ISPMT

ISPMT calculates the interest paid during a defined period of an investment. This function was provided originally for compatibility with the Lotus 1-2-3 spreadsheet program.

`=ISPMT(rate,per,nper,pv)`

The units used must be consistent with Rate and Nper. Let's say, for example, you make monthly payments on a five-year loan at an annual interest rate of 12%, use 12%/12 for Rate and 5*12 for Nper. If you make annual payments on the same loan, use 12% for Rate and 5 for Nper.

RATE	The interest rate for the investment.
PER	The period in which you want to find the interest. This must be between 1 and Nper.
NPER	The total number of payments in the period of an investment.
PV	The present value of the investment.

MDURATION

MDURATION returns the modified duration of a security with a par value assumed of $100.

`=MDURATION(settlement,maturity,coupon,yield,frequency,basis)`

The MDURATION function is found only if the Analysis Toolpak is installed. It must be turned on using the Add-Ins command from the Tools menu. Figure 6.22 shows that the settlement date is 5/15/1999 and the maturity date is 9/15/2004. The coupon's rate is 7.8% and the yield of the coupon is 9.2%. You'll also see that the frequency is semiannual and the basis is Actual/actual. This means that the modified duration equals 4.18.

SETTLEMENT	The security's settlement date. This is the date after the issue date when the security is traded to the buyer.
MATURITY	The security's maturity date—when the security expires.
COUPON	The security's annual coupon rate.
YIELD	The security's annual yield.
FREQUENCY	The number of payments per year—Annual = 1; Semiannual = 2; Quarterly = 4.
BASIS	The day count basis to use.

The modified duration is calculated as follows:

$$\text{MDURATION} = \frac{\text{DURATION}}{1 + \left(\dfrac{\text{Market yield}}{\text{Coupon payments per year}} \right)}$$

Figure 6.22
The *MDURATION* function returns the modified duration of a security with a par value assumed of $100.

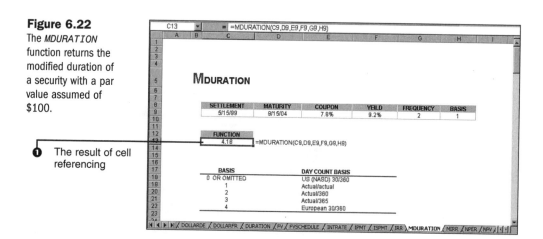

❶ The result of cell referencing

MIRR

MIRR returns a modified internal rate of return for several periodic cash flows.

```
=MIRR(values,finance_rate,reinvest_rate)
```

Consider the following example in Figure 6.23. You purchased a restaurant with an initial borrowing of $230,000 at 8.1%; your returns for the following five years were respectively $35,000, $36,000, $57,000, $76,000, and $87,000. You reinvest the profits over the five years, earning an annual return of 12.8%. Your modified rate of return after 5 years is 8.98%. (The difference between this function and IRR is mainly that MIRR takes into account finance and reinvestment interest.)

VALUES	The array of numbers or reference to cells represented by payments (negative values), and income (positive values).
FINANCE_RATE	The interest rate paid on the money used in the cash flows.
REINVEST_RATE	The interest rate received on the cash flows as they are reinvested.

MIRR can be calculated as:

$$\left(\frac{-\text{NPV}(rrate, values[positive]) * (1 + rrate)^n}{\text{NPV}(frate, values[negative]) * (1 + frate)} \right)^{\frac{1}{n-1}} - 1$$

Figure 6.23
Use *MIRR* to determine the modified internal rate of return for several periodic cash flows.

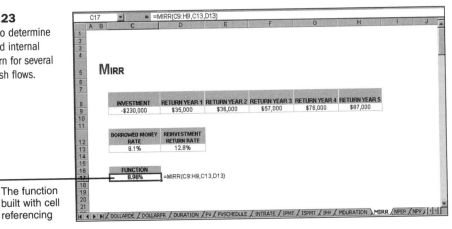

① The function built with cell referencing

NOMINAL

NOMINAL returns the nominal annual interest rate given an effective rate and the total number of compounding periods for the year.

=NOMINAL(effective_rate,npery)

The NOMINAL function is found only if the Analysis Toolpak is installed. It must be turned on using the Add-Ins command from the Tools menu.

EFFECT_RATE   The effective interest rate.

NPERY   The number of coumpounding periods over the year.

NOMINAL is calculated as follows:

$$EFFECT = \left(1 + \frac{Nominal\_rate}{Npery}\right)^{Npery} - 1$$

Note the following example:

For example: =NOMINAL(6.2%,4) would return the result of .060%.

NPER

NPER returns the total number of periods for an investment. This is based on a periodic constant payment and a constant interest rate.

=NPER(rate,pmt,pv,fv,type)

Notice the example in Figure 6.24. The interest rate is 3%, the payment per period is $350. The current present value is $11,500. The future value of the loan, or the amount you want to attain after the last payment is zero (the loan is paid off). And the payment type is zero (at the end of the period). The number of periods (NPER) to payoff the loan would equal 23. Note that not specifying a value for FV will result in a negative number of periods.

RATE   The interest rate per period.

PMT   The payment made per period and cannot change over the life of the loan or annuity (typically is the principal and interest).

PV   The present value that a series of payments is worth right now. If omitted, Excel assumes zero.

FV   The future value or cash balance you want to attain upon the last payment.

TYPE   The payment timing—when the payments are due.

Figure 6.24
Use the *NPER* function to return the total number of periods for an investment. This is based on periodic constant payment and a constant interest rate.

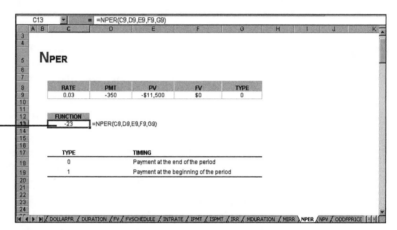

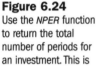

❶ The function built with cell referencing

NPV

NPV calculates the net present value of an investment with the discount rate and several future payments and income.

```
=NPV(rate,value1,value2,...)
```

The NPV function provides the net present value with the future incomes based on the current discount rate. For example, let's say you invested $35,000 in a business and you expect to receive over the next 4 years a return of $7,000, $13,000, $15,000, and $18,000. With an annual discount rate of 9%, the net present value of the investment would be $6,145, as shown in Figure 6.25.

RATE   The discount rate over the entire period.

VALUE   1-29 arguments representing the payments and income.

NPV can be calculated as:

$$NPV = \sum_{i=1}^{n} \frac{values_i}{(1+rate)^i}$$

Figure 6.25

NPV calculates the net present value of an investment with the discount rate and several future payments and income.

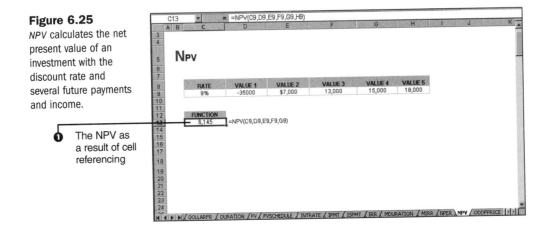

❶ The NPV as a result of cell referencing

ODDFPRICE

ODDFPRICE returns the value of a security based on a per $100 face value and an odd (short or long) first period.

=ODDFPRICE(settlement,maturity,issue,first_coupon,rate,yield,redemption,frequency, basis)

The ODDFPRICE function returns the security's price per $100 face value of a security with an odd (long or short) first period. For example, take a look at Figure 6.26. You'll see that the settlement date is 11/11/1996 and the maturity date is 3/1/2011. The issue date is 10/15/1996 with the first coupon date being 3/1/1997. The securities interest rate is 9.3%. The yield is 7.8% and the redemption value is $100 with the frequency set semiannually. The basis is Actual/actual. You'll also see that the price per $100 face value of the security is $113. The ODDFPRICE function is found only if the Analysis Toolpak is installed. It must be turned on using the Add-Ins command from the Tools menu.

SETTLEMENT	The security's settlement date. This is the date after the issue date when the security is traded to the buyer.
MATURITY	The security's maturity date—the date when the security expires.
ISSUE	The security's actual issue date.
FIRST_COUPON	The date of the security's first coupon.
RATE	The interest rate of the security.
YIELD	The annual yield of the security.
REDEMPTION	The redemption value of the security per $100 face value.
FREQUENCY	The number of payments per year—Annual = 1; Semiannual = 2; Quarterly = 4.
BASIS	The day count basis to use.

The odd short first coupon is calculated as:

$$ODDFPRICE = \left[\frac{redemption}{\left(1 + \frac{yld}{frequency}\right)^{\left(N-1+\frac{DSC}{E}\right)}} \right] + \left[\frac{100 \times \frac{rate}{frequency} \times \frac{DFC}{E}}{\left(1 + \frac{yld}{frequency}\right)^{\frac{DSC}{E}}} \right]$$

$$+ \left[\sum_{k=2}^{N} \frac{100 \times \frac{rate}{frequency}}{\left(1 + \frac{yld}{frequency}\right)^{\left(k-1+\frac{DSC}{E}\right)}} \right]$$

$$- \left[100 \times \frac{rate}{frequency} \times \frac{A}{E} \right]$$

The odd long first coupon can be determined using:

$$ODDFPRICE = \left[\frac{redemption}{\left(1 + \frac{yld}{frequency}\right)^{\left(N+N_q+\frac{DSC}{E}\right)}} \right]$$

$$+ \left[\frac{100 \times \frac{rate}{frequency} \times \left[\sum_{i=1}^{NC} \frac{DC_i}{NL_i} \right]}{\left(1 + \frac{yld}{frequency}\right)^{\left(N_q+\frac{DSC}{E}\right)}} \right]$$

$$+ \left[\sum_{k=2}^{N} \frac{100 \times \frac{rate}{frequency}}{\left(1 + \frac{yld}{frequency}\right)^{\left(k-N_q+\frac{DSC}{E}\right)}} \right]$$

$$- \left[100 \times \frac{rate}{frequency} \times \sum_{i=1}^{NC} \frac{A_i}{NL_i} \right]$$

Figure 6.26
To return the value of a security based on a per $100 face value and an odd (short or long) first period you should use the *ODDFPRICE* function.

❶ The function built with cell referencing

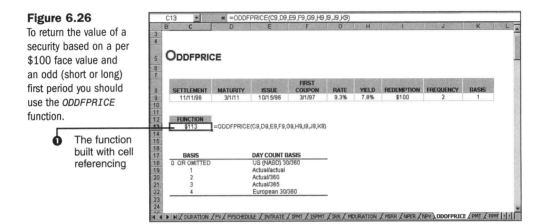

ODDFYIELD

ODDFYIELD returns the security yield with an odd first period.

=ODDFYIELD(settlement,maturity,issue,first_coupon,pr,yield,redemption,frequency,basis)

The ODDFYIELD function is found only if the Analysis Toolpak is installed. It must be turned on using the Add-Ins command from the Tools menu.

SETTLEMENT	The security's settlement date. This is the date after the issue date when the security is traded to the buyer.
MATURITY	The security's maturity date—the date when the security expires.
ISSUE	The security's actual issue date.
FIRST_COUPON	The date of the security's first coupon.
PR	The price of the security.
YIELD	The annual yield of the security.
REDEMPTION	The redemption value of the security per $100 face value.
FREQUENCY	The number of payments per year—Annual = 1; Semiannual = 2; Quarterly = 4.
BASIS	The day count basis to use.

ODDLPRICE

ODDLPRICE returns the per $100 face value of a security having an odd last coupon period.

=ODDLPRICE(settlement,maturity,last_interest,rate,yield,redemption,frequency,basis)

The ODDLPRICE function is used to return the price per $100 face value with an odd last period. As with many other functions, it is found only if the Analysis Toolpak is installed. You must turn it on using the Add-Ins command from the Tools menu.

SETTLEMENT	The security's settlement date. This is the date after the issue date when the security is traded to the buyer.
MATURITY	The security's maturity date—the date when the security expires.
LAST_INTEREST	The last security coupon date.
YIELD	The annual yield of the security.
ReEDEMPTION	The redemption value of the security per $100 face value.
FREQUENCY	The number of payments per year—Annual = 1; Semiannual = 2; Quarterly = 4.
BASIS	The day count basis to use.

ODDLYIELD

ODDLYIELD returns the security yield that has an odd last period.

=ODDLYIELD(settlement,maturity,last_interest,rate,pr,redemption,frequency,basis)

Using the ODDLYIELD function returns the yield of a security with an odd last period. The ODDLYIELD function is found only if the Analysis Toolpak is installed. It must be turned on using the Add-Ins command from the Tools menu.

SETTLEMENT	The security's settlement date. This is the date after the issue date when the security is traded to the buyer.
MATURITY	The security's maturity date—the date when the security expires.
LAST_INTEREST	The last security coupon date.
RATE	The interest rate of the security.
PR	The price of the security.
REDEMPTION	The redemption value of the security per $100 face value.
FREQUENCY	The number of payments per year—Annual = 1; Semiannual = 2; Quarterly = 4.
BASIS	The day count basis to use.

ODDLYIELD is calculated as follows:

$$ODDLYIELD = \left| \frac{\left(redemption + \left(\left(\sum_{i=1}^{NC}\frac{DC_i}{NL_i}\right) \times \frac{100 \times rate}{frequency}\right)\right) - \left(par + \left(\left(\sum_{i=1}^{NC}\frac{A_i}{NL_i}\right) \times \frac{100 \times rate}{frequency}\right)\right)}{par + \left(\left(\sum_{i=1}^{NC}\frac{A_i}{NL_i}\right) \times \frac{100 \times rate}{frequency}\right)} \right|$$
$$\times \left[\frac{frequency}{\left(\sum_{i=1}^{NC}\frac{DSC_i}{NL_i}\right)} \right]$$

PMT

PMT calculates the loan payment for a loan based on constant payments and constant interest rates.

`=PMT(rate,nper,pv,fv,type)`

The PMT function is used to calculate a loan payment based on a constant interest rate. If you take a look at Figure 6.27, you'll notice that the rate on the loan is 12% and the total number of payments is 36 (3 years). The present value of the loan or principal amount is -17,900 and the future value of the loan after it's paid off is 0. As indicated in the Type column, the payment timing is 1 or at the beginning of the period.

RATE   The interest rate of the loan.

NPER   The number of total payments.

PV   The present value or the principal amount.

FV   The future value or cash balance you want to attain upon the last payment— for a loan it would be zero.

TYPE   The payment timing—when the payments are due.

Figure 6.27
Calculate the loan payment for a loan based on constant payments and constant interest rates using the *PMT* function.

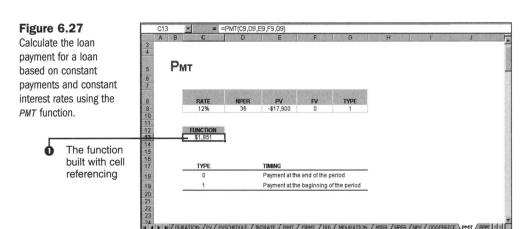

❶ The function built with cell referencing

PPMT

PPMT returns the principal payment for a period of an investment based on periodic constant payments and a constant interest rate.

`=PPMT(rate,per,nper,pv,fv,type)`

The PPMT function is used to calculate a principal payment based on a constant interest rate and constant payments for a set period. As you see in Figure 6.28, the rate of the loan is 12%. The period is 4 or the fourth month, and the total number of payments is 36 (3 years). The principal amount of the loan is -$17,900. The future value after the loan is paid off would be 0, and the type or timing is 1 (at the beginning of the period).

RATE	The interest rate of the loan.
PER	The period for which you want a return on what the principal amount is. It must be between 1 and Nper.
NPER	The number of total payments.
PV	The present value or the principal amount.
FV	The future value or cash balance you want to attain upon the last payment. For a loan it would be zero.
TYPE	The payment timing—when the payments are due.

Figure 6.28
Using the *PPMT* returns the principal payment for a period of an investment based on periodic constant payments and a constant interest rate.

❶ Build this function with cell referencing

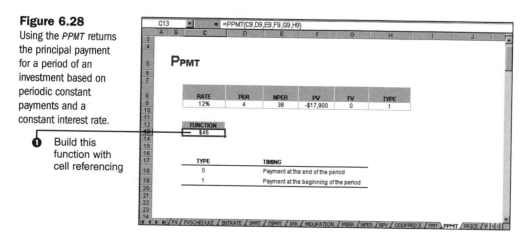

PRICE

PRICE returns the value of a security based on price per $100 face value and periodic interest payments.

=PRICE(settlement,maturity,rate,yield,redemption,frequency,basis)

The PRICE function returns the value of the security based on the price per $100 face value of the security with periodic interest payments. Figure 6.29 shows the settlement date is 11/11/1999. The maturity date is 3/1/2011, and the annual coupon rate is 5.9%. The annual yield of the security is 6.8% and the redemption is $100. With seminannual frequency, the basis is Actual/actual resulting in the value of the security being $93. The PRICE function is found only if the Analysis Toolpak is installed. It must be turned on using the Add-Ins command from the Tools menu.

SETTLEMENT	The security's settlement date. This is the date after the issue date when the security is traded to the buyer.
MATURITY	The security's maturity date—the date when the security expires.
RATE	The annual coupon rate of the security.
YIELD	The annual yield of the security.

REDEMPTION | The redemption value of the security per $100 face value.

FREQUENCY | The number of payments per year—Annual = 1; Semiannual = 2; Quarterly = 4.

BASIS | The day count basis to use.

PRICE is calculated as follows:

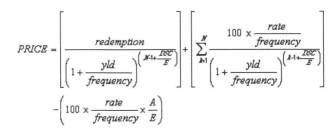

$$PRICE = \left[\cfrac{redemption}{\left(1 + \cfrac{yld}{frequency}\right)^{\left(N-1+\frac{DSC}{E}\right)}} \right] + \left[\sum_{k=1}^{N} \cfrac{100 \times \cfrac{rate}{frequency}}{\left(1 + \cfrac{yld}{frequency}\right)^{\left(k-1+\frac{DSC}{E}\right)}} \right] - \left(100 \times \frac{rate}{frequency} \times \frac{A}{E}\right)$$

Figure 6.29
Return the value of a
security based on price
per $100 face value
and periodic interest
payments with the
PRICE function.

❶ Generate
the function
results with
cell referencing

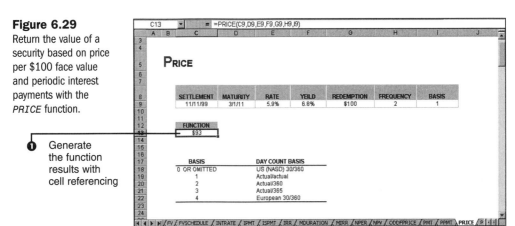

PRICEDISC

PRICEDISC returns the value of a discounted security based on a price per $100 face value.

=PRICEDISC(settlement,maturity,discount,redemption,basis)

The PRICEDISC function returns the value of a discounted security based on a $100 face value. The PRICEDISC function is found only if the Analysis Toolpak is installed. It must be turned on using the Add-Ins command from the Tools menu. As you'll notice in Figure 6.30, the settlement date of the security is 11/11/1999 and the security's maturity date is 12/15/1999. With a discount rate of 5.3%, the redemption value of the security is $100 per face value. The day count basis is Actual/actual.

SETTLEMENT | The security's settlement date. This is the date after the issue date when the security is traded to the buyer.

MATURITY | The security's maturity date—the date when the security expires.

DISCOUNT	The discount rate of the security.
REDEMPTION	The redemption value of the security per $100 face value.
BASIS	The day count basis to use.

PRICEDISC is calculated as follows:

$$PRICEDISC = redemption - discount \times redemption \times \frac{DSM}{B}$$

Figure 6.30
*PRICEDISC returns
the value of a
discounted security
based on a price per
$100 face value.*

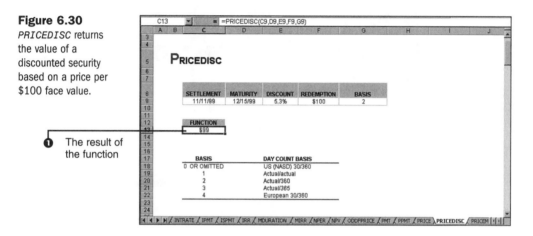

❶ The result of
the function

PRICEMAT

PRICEMAT returns the value of a security that pays interest at maturity and price per $100 face value.

`=PRICEMAT(settlement,maturity,issue,rate,yield,basis)`

The PRICEMAT function returns the price per $100 face value that pays the interest at the maturity of the security. The PRICEMAT function is found only if the Analysis Toolpak is installed. It must be turned on using the Add-Ins command from the Tools menu. Notice in Figure 6.31 that the settlement date is 10/11/1999. The maturity date is 12/15/1999. The issue date is 7/16/1999. The annual rate is 7.2% and the annual yield is 7.2%. As you see, the basis is 4 (European 30/360).

SETTLEMENT	The security's settlement date. This is the date after the issue date when the security is traded to the buyer.
MATURITY	The security's maturity date—the date when the security expires.
ISSUE	The issue date of the security.
RATE	The annual coupon rate of the security.
YIELD	The annual yield of the security.
BASIS	The day count basis to use.

PRICEMAT is calculated as follows:

$$PRICEMAT = \frac{100 + (\frac{DIM}{B} \times rate \times 100)}{1 + (\frac{DSM}{B} \times yld)} - \left(\frac{A}{B} \times rate \times 100\right)$$

Figure 6.31
Returns the value of
a security that pays
interest at maturity
and price per $100
face value by using the
PRICEMAT function.

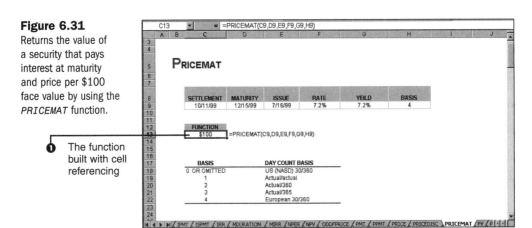

❶ The function
built with cell
referencing

PV

Based on an investment, PV returns the present value.

`=PV(rate,nper,pmt,fv,type)`

The PV function returns the present value of an investment. For example, on a car loan, the present value is the amount of the loan to the lender. Figure 6.32 presents a PV example. If you can afford monthly payments of $500 a month, and can get a loan for 5.8%, what amount could you afford on a 3-year loan? The formula `=PV(C9/12,D9*12,E9)` would result in a total loan amount over 3 years of $$16,485.

RATE   The interest rate of the loan. If the annual interest rate is 6% and you make monthly payments, the interest rate is 6%/12 =.50%.

NPER   The number of total payments—12 months per year at 2 years would be 12*2 =24.

PMT   The payment made each period. It must remain constant. Typically, it includes principal and interest.

FV   The future value or cash balance you want to attain upon the last payment. For a loan it would be zero. For a future amount you want to attain with payments, it would be the total goal amount.

TYPE   The payment timing—when the payments are due.

PV is calculated as follows:

$$pv*(1+rate)^{nper} + pmt(1+rate*type)*$$
$$\left(\frac{(1+rate)^{nper}-1}{rate}\right) + fv = 0$$

Figure 6.32
Based on an investment, *PV* returns the present value. For example, the total amount you could afford for a car loan.

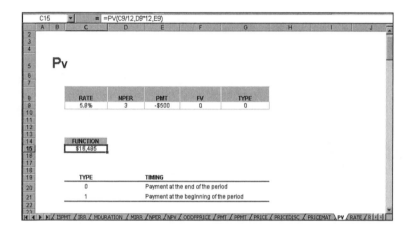

RATE

RATE returns per period the interest of an annuity.

`=RATE(nper,pmt,pv,fv,type,guess)`

The RATE function returns the interest on an annuity per period. The RATE function is calculated by iterations and can have many solutions. If results of RATE do not converge within .00000001 after a total of 20 iterations, the result returns #NUM. Notice the example in Figure 6.33. The number of periods is 48 (a 4-year loan), the payment is $200 a month, and the present value of the loan is $8,000. The monthly rate is .77%. Multiply the rate times 12 for the yearly rate as shown.

NPER	The number of total periods on an annuity.
PMT	The payment made each period and must remain constant. Typically, it includes principal and interest.
FV	The future value or cash balance you want to attain upon the last payment. For a loan it would be zero.
TYPE	The payment timing. When the payments are due.
GUESS	What you assume the rate will be. If omitted, Excel assumes 10%.

Figure 6.33
RATE returns the per period interest of an annuity.

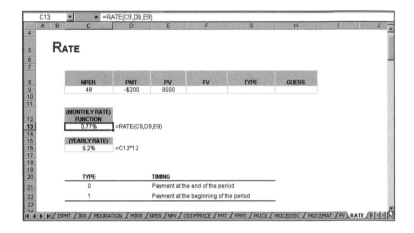

RECEIVED

Based on a fully invested security, RECEIVED returns the amount received at maturity.

`=RECEIVED(settlement,maturity,investment,discount,basis)`

The RECEIVED function returns the maturity amount based on the fully invested security. The RECEIVED function is found only if the Analysis Toolpak is installed. It must be turned on using the <u>A</u>dd-Ins command from the <u>T</u>ools menu. Figure 6.34 shows the function with the dates in the formula and as a cell reference. The settlement date is 11/15/1999 and the maturity date is 2/15/2000. You also see that the total amount of the security investment is $500,000 and the discount rate is 5.75% with a day count basis of 2 or Actual/360. The amount received at maturity results in $507,457.

SETTLEMENT	The security's settlement date. This is the date after the issue date when the security is traded to the buyer.
MATURITY	The security's maturity date—the date when the security expires.
INVESTMENT	The total amount invested in the security.
DISCOUNT	The discount rate of the security.
BASIS	The day count basis to use.

RECEIVED can be calculated as follows:

$$RECEIVED = \frac{investment}{1 - (discount \times \frac{DIM}{B})}$$

Figure 6.34
Based on a fully
invested security,
RECEIVED returns
the amount received
at maturity.

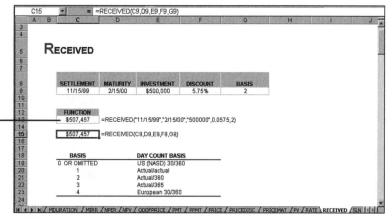

❶ Build the
RECEIVED results
with cell referencing

SLN

Based on one period, SLN returns the straight-line depreciation on an asset.

=SLN(cost,salvage,life)

The SLN function returns the straight-line depreciation on an asset. In the example in Figure 6.35, the cost of the asset is $700,000 and the salvage value of the asset is $350,000. The useful life of the asset is 8 years. The result returns the straight-line depreciation for one period of $43,750.

COSTE   The asset's initial cost.

SALVAGE   The value at the end of the useful life of the asset.

LIFE   The number of periods over which the asset will be depreciated.

Figure 6.35
Based on one
period, *SLN* returns
the straight-line
depreciation on
an asset.

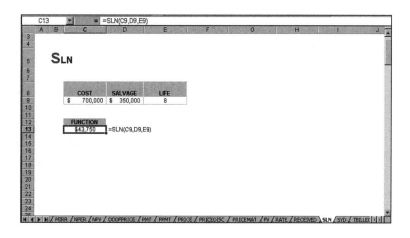

SYD

Based on a specified period, SYD returns the sum-of-years' digits depreciation of an asset.

`=SYD(cost,salvage,life,per)`

The SYD function returns the sum-of-years' digits depreciation of an asset. In the example in Figure 6.36, if you bought an asset for $700,000 and the salvage value is $350,000, the useful life of the asset is 8 years. The sum-of-years' digits depreciation is for the fifth period, resulting in $38,889.

COST	The asset's initial cost.
SALVAGE	The value at the end of the useful life of the asset.
LIFE	The number of periods over which the asset will be depreciated.
PER	The period for which you're looking for the sum-of-year's digits depreciation.

Figure 6.36
Based on a specified period, *SYD* returns the sum-of-years' digits depreciation of an asset.

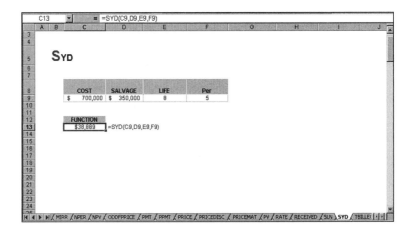

TBILLEQ

For a treasury bill, TBILLEQ returns the bond equivalent yield.

`=TBILLEQ(settlement,maturity,discount)`

The TBILLEQ function returns the bonds equivalent yield for a treasury bill. The TBILLEQ function is found only if the Analysis Toolpak is installed. It must be turned on using the Add-Ins command from the Tools menu. As you see in Figure 6.37, the treasury bill's settlement date is 11/15/1999 and the maturity date is 2/25/2000. The treasury bill's discount rate is 8.9% and the result is 9.26%.

SETTLEMENT	The treasury bill's settlement date. This is the date after the issue date when the security is traded to the buyer.
MATURITY	The treasury bill's maturity date—when the security expires.
DISCOUNT	The discount rate of the treasury bill.

Figure 6.37
For a treasury bill,
TBILLEQ returns the
bond equivalent yield.

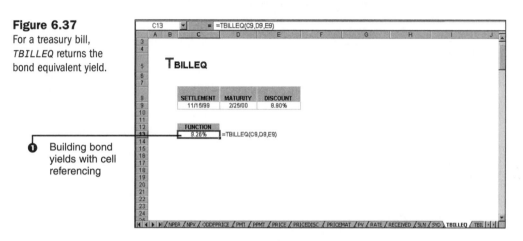

❶ Building bond
yields with cell
referencing

TBILLPRICE

For a treasury bill, TBILLPRICE returns the price per $100 face value.

=TBILLPRICE(settlement,maturity,discount)

The TBILLPRICE function returns the price per $100 face value of a treasury bill. The TBILLPRICE function is found only if the Analysis Toolpak is installed. It must be turned on using the Add-Ins command from the Tools menu. In Figure 6.38, for example, the treasury bill's settlement date is 11/15/1999 and the maturity date is 2/25/2000. The treasury bill's discount rate is 8.9% and the result is $97.48 price per $100 face value.

SETTLEMENT	The treasury bill's settlement date. This is the date after the issue date when the security is traded to the buyer.
MATURITY	The treasury bill's maturity date—when the security expires.
DISCOUNT	The discount rate of the treasury bill.

TBILLPRICE is calculated as follows:

$$TBILLPRICE = 100 \times (1 - \frac{discount \times DSM}{360})$$

Figure 6.38
For a treasury bill,
TBILLPRICE returns
the price per $100
face value.

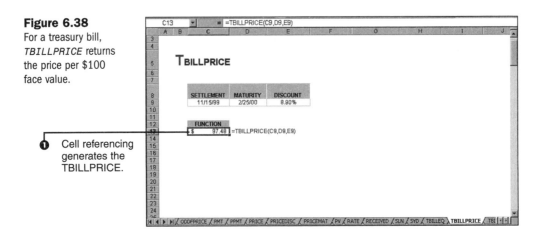

❶ Cell referencing
generates the
TBILLPRICE.

TBILLYIELD

For a treasury bill, TBILLYIELD returns the yield.

=TBILLYIELD(settlement,maturity,pr)

The TBILLYIELD function returns the yield for the treasury bill. The TBILLYIELD function is found only if the Analysis Toolpak is installed. It must be turned on using the Add-Ins command from the Tools menu. As you see in Figure 6.39, the treasury bill's settlement date is 11/15/1999 and the maturity date is 2/25/2000. The treasury bill's discount rate is $97.64 and the yield result is 8.53%.

SETTLEMENT   The treasury bill's settlement date. This is the date after the issue date when the security is traded to the buyer.

MATURITY   The treasury bill's maturity date—when the security expires.

PR   The price per $100 for the treasury bill.

TBILLYIELD is calculated as:

$$TBILLYIELD = \frac{100 - par}{par} \times \frac{360}{DSM}$$

Figure 6.39
For a treasury bill,
TBILLYIELD
returns the yield.

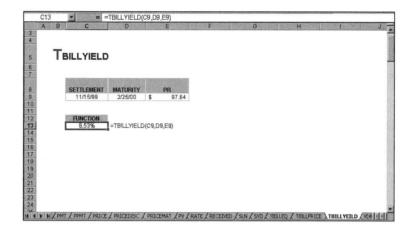

VDB

For a period you specify, VDB returns the depreciation of an asset.

```
=VDB(cost,salvage,life,start_period,end_period,factor,no_switch)
```

The VDB function is the variable declining balance method of depreciation and returns the depreciation of an asset for a full or partial period that you specify. Notice Figure 6.40 where the cost of the asset is $50,000, the salvage value of the asset is $14,000, and the life is for 10 years or 120 periods. The start period is for period 1 through the end period of 12 (the first year) and the factor assumes 2 because it's omitted. The no switch is omitted and assumes the staight-line method. This produces a first year result of $3,300.

COST	The asset's initial cost.
SALVAGE	The value at the end of the useful life of the asset.
LIFE	The number of periods over which the asset will be depreciated.
START_PERIOD	The start period for which you want the depreciation calculated.
END_PERIOD	The end period for which you want the depreciation calculated.
FACTOR	The rate the balance declines. If omitted, it is assumed to be 2 (double-declining balance method).
NO_SWITCH	When True, the formula uses the double-declining balance. When False or omitted, it switches to straight-line depreciation.

Figure 6.40
For a period you specify, *VDB* returns the depreciation of an asset.

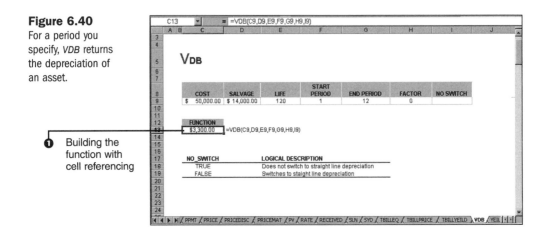

① Building the function with cell referencing

XIRR

For a schedule of cash flows that are not necessarily periodic, XIRR returns the internal rate of return.

`=XIRR(values,dates,guess)`

The XIRR function returns the internal rate of return for a schedule of cash flows. The XIRR function is found only if the Analysis Toolpak is installed. It must be turned on using the Add-Ins command from the Tools menu.

VALUES   A series of cash flows that corresponds to a series of dates.

DATES   A series of payment dates that corresponds to a series of payments.

GUESS   A guess number of the result.

XIRR is calculated as follows:

$$0 = \sum_{i=1}^{N} \frac{P_i}{(1+rate)^{\frac{(d_i - d_1)}{365}}}$$

XNPV

For a schedule of cash flows that are not necessarily periodic, XNPV returns the present value.

`=XNPV(rate,values,dates)`

The XNPV function returns the present value for a series of cash flows. This function is found only if the Analysis Toolpak is installed. It must be turned on using the Add-Ins command from the Tools menu.

RATE   The discount rate applied to the cash flows.

VALUES   A series of cash flows that corresponds to a series of dates.

DATES   A series of payment dates that corresponds to a series of payments.

XNPV is calculated as follows:

$$XNPV = \sum_{i=1}^{N} \frac{P_i}{(1+rate)^{\frac{(d_i - d_1)}{365}}}$$

YIELD

Based on a yield that pays periodic interest, YIELD returns the yield of the security.

=YIELD(settlement,maturity,rate,pr,redemption,frequency,basis)

The YIELD function returns the yield on a security that pays on period interest. This is a function found only if the Analysis Toolpak is installed. It must be turned on using the Add-Ins command from the Tools menu. In Figure 6.41, for example, the settlement date of the security is 11/15/1999 and the maturity date is 2/9/2009. The rate is 5.8% and the security's price per $100 face value is $98. The frequency is semiannually, and the basis is 30/360(4), resulting with 6.08%.

SETTLEMENT   The security's settlement date. This is the date after the issue date when the security is traded to the buyer.

MATURITY   The security's maturity date—when the security expires.

RATE   The interest rate of the security.

PR   The price of the security.

REDEMPTION   The redemption value of the security per $100 face value.

FREQUENCY   The number of the payments per year—Annual = 1; Semiannual = 2; Quarterly = 4.

BASIS   The day count basis to use.

YIELD can be calculated as:

$$YIELD = \frac{(\frac{redemption}{100} + \frac{rate}{frequency}) - (\frac{par}{100} + (\frac{A}{E} \times \frac{rate}{frequency}))}{\frac{par}{100} + (\frac{A}{E} \times \frac{rate}{frequency})} \times \frac{frequency \times E}{DSR}$$

Figure 6.41
Based on a yield that pays periodic interest, this function returns the yield of the security.

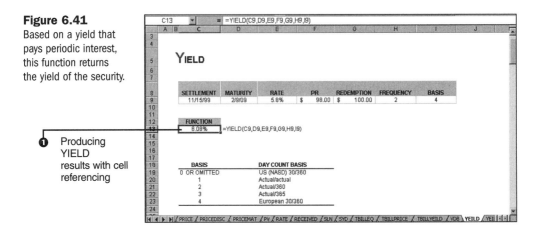

❶ Producing YIELD results with cell referencing

YIELDDISC

For a discounted security, YIELDDISC returns the annual yield.

=YIELDDISC(settlement,maturity,pr,redemption,basis)

The YIELDDISC function returns the annual yield of a discounted security. The YIELDDISC function is found only if the Analysis Toolpak is installed. It must be turned on using the Add-Ins command from the Tools menu. As you'll see in Figure 6.42, the settlement date of the security is 11/15/1999 and the maturity date is 2/9/2000. The security's price per $100 face value is $98 and the basis is 30/360(4). This produces an annual yield of 8.75%.

SETTLEMENT	The security's settlement date. This is the date after the issue date when the security is traded to the buyer.
MATURITY	The security's maturity date—when the security expires.
PR	The price of the security.
REDEMPTION	The redemption value of the security per $100 face value.
BASIS	The day count basis to use.

Figure 6.42
For a discounted security, *YIELDDISC* returns the annual yield.

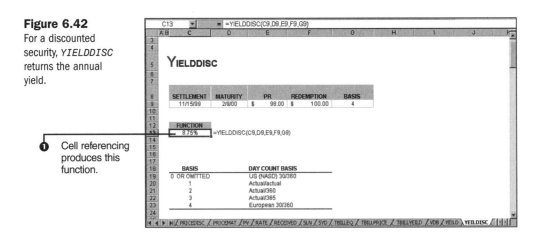

❶ Cell referencing produces this function.

YIELDMAT

Based on a security that pays interest at maturity, YIELDMAT returns the annual yield.

`=YIELDMAT(settlement,maturity,issue,rate,pr,basis)`

The YIELDMAT function returns the yield annually for a security that pays interest at maturity. It can be found only if the Analysis Toolpak is installed. It must be turned on using the Add-Ins command from the Tools menu. The example in Figure 6.43 shows the settlement date of the security is 11/15/1999 and the maturity date is 6/9/2009. The issue date of the security is 6/18/1999. The rate is 5.8% and the securities price per $100 face value is $98 and the basis is 30/360(4). This means that the annual interest for the security result is 9.30%.

SETTLEMENT	The security's settlement date. This is the date after the issue date when the security is traded to the buyer.
MATURITY	The security's maturity date—when the security expires.
ISSUE	The issue date of the security.
RATE	The interest rate of the security.
PR	The price of the security.
BASIS	The day count basis to use.

Figure 6.43

YIELDMAT returns the annual yield based on a security that pays interest at maturity.

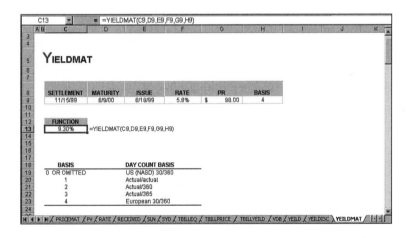

Information Functions

Information Functions Overview

Information functions generally are made up of logical results and can be used in many business situations. Combined with other functions, the information functions can manage lists of data and provide feedback based on a logical result. An example of this is: if you were tracking dates where certain items were received and then delivered, you could use the ISBLANK function combined with the IF function to return the result. For a more in-depth explanation of this, see the example for ISBLANK.

The following information functions are discussed in this chapter.

▶ CELL

▶ COUNTBLANK

▶ ERROR.TYPE

▶ INFO

▶ IS

▶ ISBLANK

▶ ISERR

▶ ISERROR

▶ ISEVEN

▶ ISLOGICAL

▶ ISNA

▶ ISNONTEXT

▶ ISNUMBER

▶ ISODD

▶ ISREF

▶ ISTEXT

▶ N

▶ NA

▶ TYPE

CELL

CELL returns information about a cell's location, formatting, or contents in the upper-left cell in a reference.

`=CELL(info_type,reference)`

The CELL function returns information about the cell such as the format, or whether it's general or some type of number format. The CELL function is primarily for compatability with other spreadsheet programs. Notice the following Table 7.1 with its descriptions, and then the function results as shown in Figure 7.1. If the INFO_TYPE is "Format", and the format of the cell in the reference argument changes, the cell function will not update the value until the worksheet is recalculated.

Here's an example of the CELL function used to determine whether a cell is protected: `Y5:Y100` contains cell functions that determine the protection of `D5:D100.Ex:` `Y5=CELL("protect",D5)`, `Y6=CELL("protect",D6)`, and so on.

To add up unprotected cells in a range in the form of an array the example could be: `{=SUM((Y5:Y100=0)*D5:D100)}`, where the array entered formula will only add up the unprotected cells in the range `D5:D100`.

INFO_TYPE   This is the text that tells Excel what kind of value your looking for. See Table 7.1 for examples and descriptions.

REFERENCE   This is the cell in which you want information about. See Table 7.2 for examples and descriptions.

Table 7.1 INFO_TYPE Examples and Descriptions

Info Type	Return
Address	Reference of the first cell in reference as text
Col	The column number of the cell referenced
Color	Returns zero unless formatted in color for negative values, then it returns 1
Contents	Contents of the upper-left cell in reference
Filename	Full path and filename as text
Format	The text value of the number format in a cell
Parentheses	If the cell is formatted with parentheses, Excel returns 1; otherwise it returns zero
Prefix	Text value of the label prefix
	Returns (') for left-aligned text
	Returns (") for right-aligned text

Table 7.1 INFO_TYPE **Examples and Descriptions**

Info Type	Return
	Returns (^) for centered text
	Returns (\) for fill-aligned text and empty text
	Returns (" ") for anything else
Protect	Zero for unlocked cells and 1 for locked
Row	Row number of the cell referenced
Type	The text value of the type of data in a cell
	Returns (b) for blank cells
	Returns (l) for text
	Returns (v) for anything else
Width	The column width of the cell referenced, rounded off to an integer

Figure 7.1
The *CELL* function
returns formatting,
location, and content
information about the
cell referenced or
selected.

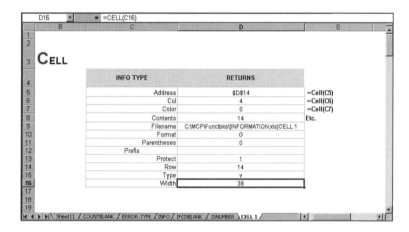

Additional cell formatting return types are shown in Table 7.2.

Table 7.2 REFERENCE **Examples and Descriptions**

If Format Is...	Cell Returns...
General	G
0	F0
#,##0	,0

continues

Table 7.2   Continued

If Format Is...	Cell Returns...
0.00	,F2
#,##0.00	,2
$#,##0_);($#,##0)	C0
$#,##0_);[Red]($#,##0)	C0 -
$#,##0.00_);($#,##0.00)	C2
$#,##0.00_);[Red]($#,##0.00)	C2 -
0%	P0
0.00%	P2
0.00E+00	S2
#?/?or#??/??	G
m/d/yy or m/d/yyh:mm or mm/dd/yy	D4
d-mmm-yy or dd-mmm-yy	D1
d-mmm or dd-mmm	D2
mmm-yy	D3
mm/dd	D5
h:mm AM/PM	D7
h:mm:ss AM/PM	D6
h:mm	D9
h:mm:ss	D8

COUNTBLANK

COUNTBLANK counts the number of empty cells in a specified range.

=COUNTBLANK(range)

The COUNTBLANK function returns the number of blank cells. If you have a formula that returns a blank text result, that cell is also counted. Notice the example in Figure 7.2, the COUNTBLANK function can be used to track percent complete in tables where you have steps in process.

RANGE   This is the range your looking for blank cells in.

The formula:

=COUNTBLANK(H8:H13) returns the result of 4, because 4 of the six cells within the step 5 range are blank. When a date is entered the number of blank cells decreases.

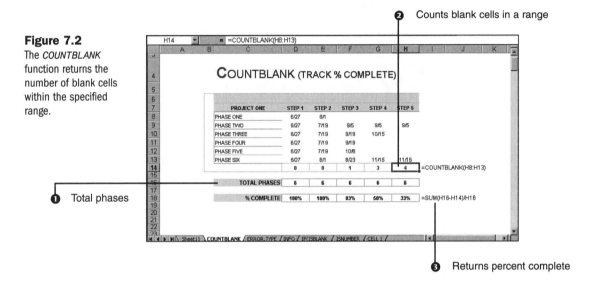

Figure 7.2
The *COUNTBLANK* function returns the number of blank cells within the specified range.

ERROR.TYPE

Returns the corresponding number value associated with an error type in Microsoft Excel.

=ERROR.TYPE(error_val).

The ERROR.TYPE function returns a number associated with an Excel error type. The table example in Figure 7.3 shows the Excel number result and the error type. You can use the ERROR.TYPE function with the IF function to display custom text messages instead of errors as shown in cell C22 of Figure 7.3.

ERROR_VAL   This is the error value of the number you're looking for. This is usually used in the form of a reference to another cell. So, for example, it would be a cell.

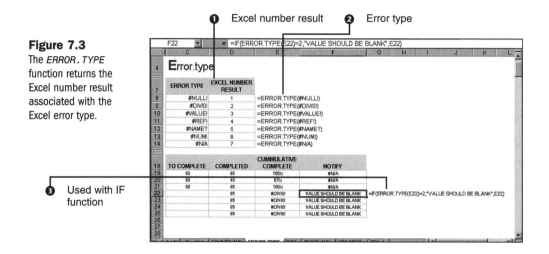

Figure 7.3
The *ERROR.TYPE* function returns the Excel number result associated with the Excel error type.

INFO

INFO returns operating environment information.

=INFO(type_text)

The INFO function can be used to retrieve vital information about your current operating environment. For example, if you are working within a workbook created by another person, and, for some reason the calculations weren't working, you could type the formula =INFO("recalc") and Excel would return either manual or automatic. The INFO text types and descriptions are in Table 7.3 and the formulas in practice with the return results are shown in Figure 7.4.

TYPE_TEXT   This can be any value such as number, text, logical value, and so on.

Table 7.3   INFO Text Types and Descriptions

Text Type	Return
Directory	Path of the current directory or folder
Memavail	Amount of memory available in bytes
Memused	Amount of memory being used for current data
Numfile	Number of active worksheets currently open
Origin	Absolute A1 style reference as text
Osversion	Current operating system version as text
Recalc	Current recalculation mode Automatic/Manual
Release	Version of Microsoft Excel
System	Name of operating environment (PC or Mac)
Totmem	Total memory available including in-use

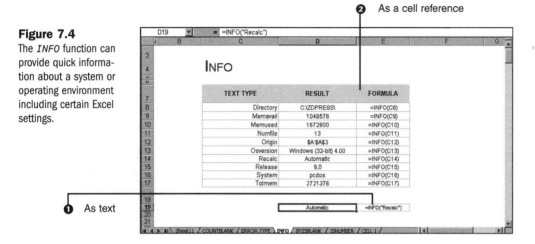

Figure 7.4
The *INFO* function can provide quick information about a system or operating environment including certain Excel settings.

IS Functions

`=ISFUNCTION(NUMBER)`

Keep in mind that the function portion is replaced by one of the IS functions options in the syntax.

The IS functions return logical results after a test on a cell or a range of cells. These functions alone provide the logical test. However, when combined with other functions like the IF function, they become a powerful decision making tool for analyzing data and returning a logical test with a numeric result. The following IS functions in Table 7.4 are available in Excel.

Table 7.4   IS Function Returns

IS Function	Returns True If...
ISBLANK	The value refers to blank cells
ISERR	The value refers to an error type, except #NA
ISERROR	The value refers to any error value
ISEVEN	The value returns True if the number is even, False if not
ISLOGICAL	The value refers to a logical value
ISNA	The value refers to the #NA error value (value not available)
ISNONTEXT	The value refers to any item that is nontext (returns True on blank cells)
ISNUMBER	The value refers to a number
ISODD	The value returns True if the number is odd, False if not
ISREF	The value refers to a reference
ISTEXT	The value refers to text

Again, the IS functions alone provide only a TRUE/FALSE result. However, when used in conjunction with other functions, they can be powerful management tools. Note some of the following IS functions in use with others.

Using the **ISBLANK** Function

ISBLANK returns the value associated with the number of empty cells.

=ISBLANK(value)

The ISBLANK function can be used in accordance with the SUM and IF functions to track information based on the input of dates within a cell. Note the formula as shown in Figure 7.5 in cell I19:

> VALUE   This is the cell or range you want tested.

{=SUM(IF(ISBLANK(I8:I18),0,$D$8:$D$18))}   Ctrl+Shft+Enter to activate the array.

The formula looks up the cells with dates in them within the range and returns the actual page count from the column D range. For example, let's say you are tracking steps in a process. In this case, the chapters in a book have to go through four steps before being complete. When you place a date completed in the intersecting cell for the chapter and step completed, the formula takes into account the actual page count from column D and adds up the column. The percent complete shows the total chapters complete through the steps.

Figure 7.5
Combine the
ISBLANK function
with *SUM* and *IF* to
lookup entered dates
in a range and return
a numeric result from
another range.

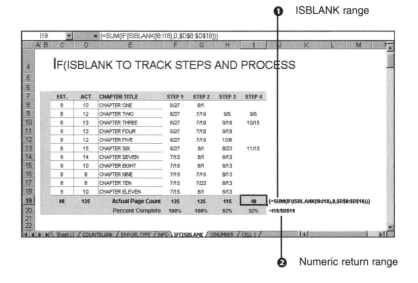

❶ ISBLANK range

❷ Numeric return range

ISNUMBER

ISNUMBER returns a value if the cell has a number.

=ISNUMBER(value)

The ISNUMBER function can be combined with cell references to return a text result based on whether a number meets the criteria of the number specified in the formula. Notice the example in Figure 7.6.

VALUE   This is the cell or range you want tested.

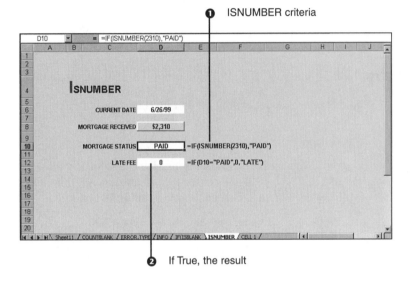

Figure 7.6
Combine the *ISNUMBER* function with the *IF* function to return results based on whether the criteria is met.

❶ ISNUMBER criteria

❷ If True, the result

N

N returns the value converted to a number.

=N(value)

The N function converts values listed in Table 7.5. This function is generally not needed by Excel and is provided primarily for compatibility with other spreadsheet programs.

VALUE   This is the value you want converted.

The values in the following table show the values and the return results based on the VALUE reference.

Table 7.5   N Conversion Values

The Value Refers to...	Returns the Result
A number	The number
A date from built-in date formats	The serial number of that date
True	1
Anything Else	0

NA

NA returns the error value associated with #NA.

`=NA()`

As with the N function, the NA function is generally not needed by Excel and is provided for compatibility with other spreadsheet programs. You could use the NA function to return #N/A (no value is available) or you could simply type #N/A into the cell.

TYPE

Use TYPE when the behavior of another function depends on the type of value a particular cell has.

`=TYPE(value)`

The TYPE function is primarily used when using functions that can accept several different types of data. Use type to find out the type of data that is returned by the particular function or cell. Notice the return result as shown in Table 7.6.

VALUE   This is the value you want converted.

The values in the following table show the values and the return results based on the VALUE reference.

Table 7.6 Return Results of TYPE

If the Value Is...	Returns the Result
Number	1
Text	2
Logical Value	4
Formula	8
Error Value	16
Array	64

CHAPTER 8

Logical Functions

Logical Functions Overview

Logical functions test cells and ranges and return a logical result in the form of text and numbers. A logical function operates under a logical test. For example, if you want to apply a simple addition based on whether a cell has a number in it, you could use an IF function to test the cell then apply the simple addition if the logical result is true.

The following functions are discussed in this chapter.

▶ AND

▶ FALSE

▶ IF

▶ NOT

▶ OR

▶ TRUE

AND

AND returns TRUE if all the arguments are true in the formula, and FALSE if any one argument is false.

```
=AND(logical1,logical2,...)
```

The AND function can operate on text, numbers, or cell references. The AND function alone serves as a simple logical test function. However, when it is combined with other formulas, the AND function gives you the ability to combine several tests into one, then apply the results depending on whether the test result is true or false. Notice the example in Figure 8.1. The AND function operates on the text applying False if the range appears with a false category. However, in the range C5:D5, all tests are True, thus applying the True Result. Notice the second and third examples in Figure 8.1. The AND function is combined with IF to perform a logical test on multiple combinations. The example in cell F12—=IF(AND(C12>10,C12<30), "QUALIFY")—states, if the value in C12 is greater than 10 and the value in C12 is less than 30, apply the text QUALIFY. Conditions/tests/arguments in the AND function must be met for the person to QUALIFY. If the next test applies the same logic, except the result as false.

> LOGICAL VALUE 1, 2, ...   This is the value of 1 to 30 conditions you wish to test. The test results in a logical True or False return.

TIP When using text results within formulas, it's important to note that the text must be enclosed with quote symbols. Also, talk through the formula as expressed in the previous sentence.

The last example applies the same logic, however, it uses cell referencing.

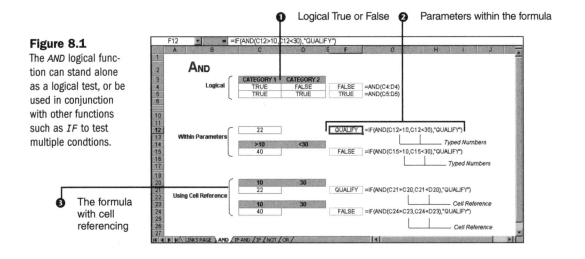

Figure 8.1
The *AND* logical function can stand alone as a logical test, or be used in conjunction with other functions such as *IF* to test multiple condtions.

❸ The formula with cell referencing

Another example of using the AND function with the IF function is in conjunction with time-lines. If you want to plot names, numbers, symbols, text, or colors over time you can create dynamic time lines by moving giant charts. Notice the example in Figure 8.2. The formula in cell G8—=IF(AND(G$7>=$D8,H$7<$E8),$F8," ")—states, if the date in G7 is greater than or equal to the start date in cell D8, and the date in cell H7 is less than the stop date in cell E8, then plot the result in cell F8 for $50. Otherwise, leave the cell blank.

TIP Apply relative referencing with dollar signs to anchor the formula reference. This means, when you drag the formula to the right, it holds either the row number or the column letter depending on which one you have the dollar sign in front of.

Figure 8.2
Use the *AND* function in conjunction with the *IF* formula when building dynamic time lines to automatically move money, names, colors, and symbols.

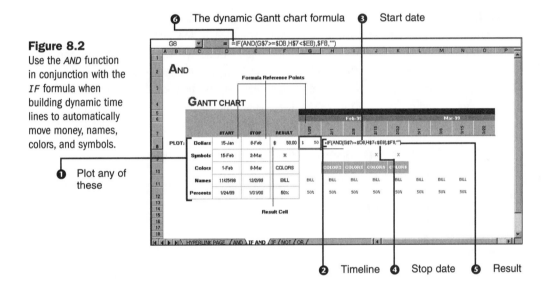

FALSE

FALSE returns the value FALSE. There are no arguments associated with this function.

=FALSE()

The FALSE function can be typed directly into a cell as false and Excel will interpret the text as the false function. The FALSE and TRUE functions are primarily for compatibility with other spreadsheet programs (Lotus 1-2-3 in particular). If you know you will be sharing/exporting a workbook to another spreadsheet program, it would be to your advantage to use the functions to express TRUE or FALSE so that those other programs interpret them as real true/false expressions. Failure to do so might yield unexpected results (in those other programs) because a TRUE or FALSE entered directly into a cell may be interpreted as text rather than as a logical expression.

IF

IF returns a value if one condition is TRUE, and returns another value if the condition is FALSE.

=IF(logical_test,value_if_true,value_if_false)

The IF function is one of the most commonly used logical functions in Excel. This function can be used in conjuction with other formulas, embedded within itself to perform up to seven logical tests per cell, or used with cell referencing to apply text results. We've already seen the IF function in action in the AND function example. Notice the example in Figure 8.3. There are three different logics used in conjuction with IF. The first example applies the logic of whether a student has passed or failed. The result is applied to cell E4. The formula in E4—=IF(D4="PASS","GRADE 7","GRADE 6")—states, if the text result is in cell D4 = "PASS" then apply the result GRADE 7 else GRADE 6. The first value applied is the true value, and the second value applied is the false value based on whether the logical test is met.

LOGICAL_TEST   This is a value that can be evaluated in a True or False condition.

VALUE IF TRUE   This is the True result if the condition is met. If omitted, assumes True. The value if True can also be another formula.

VALUE IF FALSE   This is the False result if the condition is not met. If omitted, assumes False. The value if False can also be another formula.

❶ Applied text result   **❷** Applied formula result

Figure 8.3
The *IF* formula performs the logical test and applies the true result value first after the logical test is met and the false value following the true value.

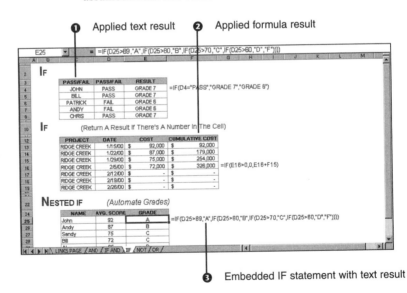

❸ Embedded IF statement with text result

Notice the second example in Figure 8.3. The formula in cell F16 asks the logical question—if cell E16 equals zero, then apply zero, else apply the formula E16 + F16. The last example in Figure 8.3 shows an automated grading formula with an embedded IF statement. The formula applies the text results of the grades A–F based on the whether the logical test is met. The formula is structured in a way that there is only one false value and that value is F and only occurs if all other true values are not met. The formula—=IF(D25>89,"A",IF(D25>80,"B", IF(D25>70,"C",IF(D25>60,"D","F"))))—states the following conditions:

If the value in cell D25 is greater than 89, apply the result of A else
If the value in cell D25 is greater than 80, apply the result of B else
If the value in cell D25 is greater than 70, apply the result of C else
If the value in cell D25 is greater than 60, apply the result of D else
F

The formula embeds an IF function with only the True values being met and the last value after all other logical tests are applied is F or the False value.

NOT

NOT returns the reverse value of its arguments.

`=NOT(logical)`

NOT returns the opposite of the logical value. If the logical value is False, NOT returns True. If two cells are equal, NOT returns False. NOT can be used when evaluating two cells in lists of information. For example, if two cells can never equal each other, NOT will return a False logical value if the cells match. Notice the example in Figure 8.4. The first condition in cell D4 is the logical value False and the formula returns True. The second example shows two cells not equaling each other in cells C8 and D8 and the logical value again returns True. If cell C9 is less than D9 in the third example the logical value is False even when the condition appears True. The last example could be used if you were planning holidays for workers within a plant. If one employee always has to be on call, the NOT function would call out a False logical value to notify that two employees were taking off the same week.

LOGICAL — This is the value that can be evaluated with a True or False condition. If True, NOT returns False, if False, NOT returns True.

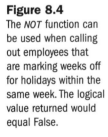

Figure 8.4
The *NOT* function can be used when calling out employees that are marking weeks off for holidays within the same week. The logical value returned would equal False.

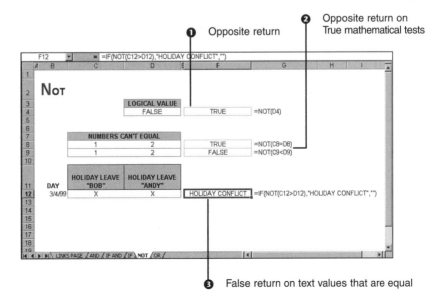

❶ Opposite return

❷ Opposite return on True mathematical tests

❸ False return on text values that are equal

OR

OR returns FALSE if all arguments are False, and TRUE if one argument is True.

`=OR(logical1,logical2,...)`

The OR function can be used as a stand-alone function when looking for one true statement or can be used in conjuction with other functions to return logical information. The first example in Figure 8.5 shows one true test being met in the range D7:F7. The second example displays no true values in the range D8:F8 and returns the logical value of False. The last example displays the OR function used in conjunction with the exact function in the form of an Array. The Array range is D17:D23. If you have a list of ISBN numbers, SKU's, and so on, that span 1,000 rows long and you want to know if there is a match with a number, this formula will tell you if the number exists in the list with a True result. After the formula is entered, remember to press Ctrl+Shft+Enter to activate the Array.

LOGICAL1, LOGICAL2, ... These are the conditions to be met from 1 to 30 for OR to test a logical true or false result.

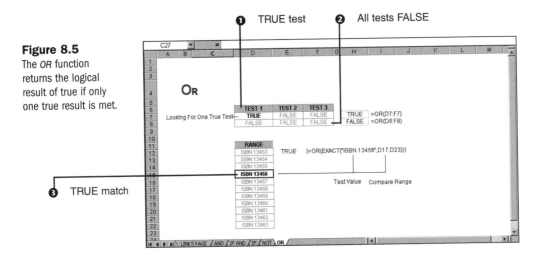

Figure 8.5
The *OR* function returns the logical result of true if only one true result is met.

TRUE

TRUE returns the value TRUE. There are no arguments associated with this function.

`=TRUE()`

The TRUE value can be entered directly into cells and formulas without using the function. The function was included for compatability with other spreadsheet programs.

Lookup and Reference Functions

Lookup and Reference Functions Overview

Lookup and reference functions are probably some of the most frequently asked, "How do I?" questions of all functions. Because so many people use Excel to manage data stored in lists in some form or fashion, at times you'll need to look up information associated with an item. For example, what if you have several product names in a database and want to look up the associated ISBN number for the product? You could do this several ways using Excel's lookup functions. You could, for example, use the VLOOKUP function or combine the INDEX and MATCH functions to pinpoint the ISBN number.

The following functions will be discussed in this chapter.

- ADDRESS
- AREAS
- CHOOSE
- COLUMN
- HLOOKUP
- HYPERLINK
- INDEX (Array Form)
- INDEX (Reference Form)
- INDIRECT
- LOOKUP (Array Form)
- LOOKUP (Vector Form)
- MATCH
- OFFSET
- ROW
- ROWS
- TRANSPOSE
- VLOOKUP

ADDRESS

Given specified row and column numbers, ADDRESS creates a cell address as text.

`=ADDRESS(row_num,column_num,abs_num,A1,sheet_text)`

The ADDRESS function returns the address of the cell in relative and in absolute form. This function is mostly used in combination with other functions to produce an address where the row or column (or both) are not known or may change. For example:

`=ADDRESS(MATCH(MAX(D2:D100),D2:D100,0),4)`

ROW_NUM is the row number to use in the cell reference.

COLUMN_NUM is the column number to use in the cell reference.

ABS_NUM specifies the reference type to return.

Abs_Num	Return Type
1 or omitted	Absolute
2	Absolute: Relative Column
3	Relative Row: Absolute Column
4	Relative

`=ADDRESS(2,2)` returns the result =$B$2 Absolute Reference.

`=ADDRESS(2,2,2)` returns the result =B$2 Absolute Row, Relative Column.

`=ADDRESS(2,2,3)` returns the result =$B2 Absolute Column, Relative Row.

`=ADDRESS(2,2,4)` returns the result =B2 Relative Column, Relative Row.

AREAS

Based on a reference, AREAS returns the number of areas.

`=AREAS(reference)`

The AREAS function returns the number of areas in a reference. For example, the formula `=Areas(B3:B10)` results in 1, because there is just one range selected. The formula `=Areas((B3:B10,C3:C10))` would result in two because there are two ranges referenced. When inheriting a workbook with range names, you can audit the range names with the AREAS function to specify the number of references the named range is referencing. For example, if you have a range name called Costs that referred to 1998 costs in A3:A100 and 1999 costs in B3:B100, `=AREAS(Costs)` would equal 2.

REFERENCE   This is the reference to a cell or range of cells the formula refers to. It can also refer to multiple areas.

CHOOSE

Based on a list of arguments, CHOOSE returns the index number from the list.

=CHOOSE(index_num,value1,value2,...)

The CHOOSE function can be used as a standalone function or in conjunction with other functions. The CHOOSE function can also be automated with form controls where the index number is the cell link and value 1, value 2 are automatic results from the form controls cell link. Because of the number of examples in Figure 9.1, the examples are numbered down the left side. The CHOOSE premise is quite simple, the index number indexes the value within the formula, the value can be text, cells, and ranges. The index number can also be a cell reference.

INDEX_NUM
Specifies which value argument is selected and must be a number between 1 and 29.

VALUE 1, VALUE 2,...
The values are arguments from 1 to 29. These numbers can be cell references, formulas, functions text, and defined names.

Consider the following examples using the CHOOSE function:

1. =CHOOSE(1,1,2,3,4,5,6,7,8,9) results in 1 because the index number calls for the first choice in the value list (1–9).

2. =CHOOSE(9,1,2,3,4,5,6,7,8,9) results in 9 because the index number calls out for 9 index spaces to the right.

3. =SUM(CHOOSE(1,**D20:D33**,E20:E33)) results in the sum of D20:D33 because the index number calls out for the sum of the first range over.

4. =COUNT(CHOOSE(1,**D20:D36**,E20:E36)) results in the count of record in the range D20:D36 because the index number calls out for the count of the first range over.

5. =SUM(**E$20**:CHOOSE(1,**E$22**,E$26,E$30)) results in the sum of the range E20:E22.

6. =SUM(**E$20**:CHOOSE(2,E$22,**E$26**,E$30)) results in the sum of the range E20:E26.

7. =SUM(**E$20**:CHOOSE(3,E$22,E$26,**E$30**)) results in the sum of the range E20:E30.

A more powerful way to use the CHOOSE function is to automate its index number with a cell reference. For example, use the CHOOSE function with the Option button from the Form Control toolbar. Notice that in the example in Figure 9.2, the CHOOSE formula references the cell link cell D7, which prompts an automated response for the indexing result. In this example, Approve equals 1 and would produce the text result of APPROVE. If Decline equals 2, it would produce a text result of DECLINE. Where Send To Mgr. equals 3, the text result would be SEND TO MGR. To learn more about formulas and form controls, see Chapter 2, "Managing Your Business with Functions." A simple nested IF statement returns a result based on the CHOOSE result; and a final IF statement returns a result based on the previous nested IF result. This simple example of using one formula response generated from another formula's result demonstrates how forms are created using form controls.

Figure 9.1
The *CHOOSE* function indexes values within the formula to return an exact result within a list.

❶ Examples 1 through 7

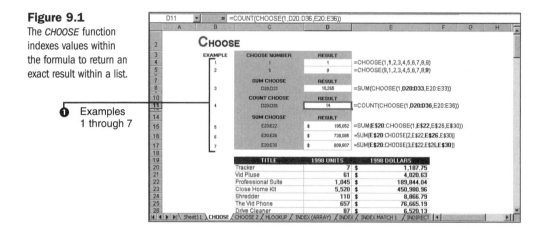

❶ Cell link **❷** CHOOSE function index

Figure 9.2
The *CHOOSE* function with form controls creates an automated indexing result based on the cell link.

❺ How forms are built

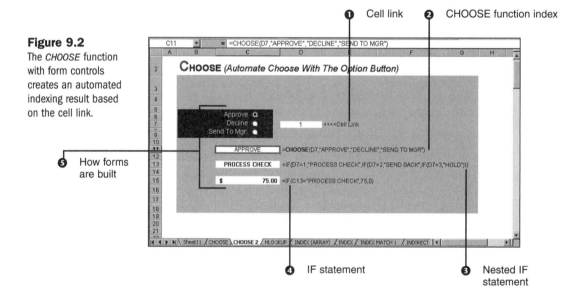

❹ IF statement **❸** Nested IF statement

COLUMN

Based on a given reference, COLUMN returns the column number.

=COLUMN(reference)

The COLUMN function returns the column number of a reference. For example, Column A = 1, so cell A5 would equal 1.

REFERENCE   This is the cell or range of cell for which you want the column number.
=COLUMN(A5) results in 1.
=COLUMN(B5) results in 2, and so on.

COLUMNS

Based on an array or reference, COLUMNS returns the number of columns.

=COLUMNS(array)

Similar to the COLUMN function, however, it returns the number of columns in an array or reference. If you have several columns and you want a quick reference as to how many columns are being used, you can use the COLUMNS function. For example:

ARRAY   This is the array formula or reference to a range of cells that will return the number of columns within the array.

=COLUMNS(B5) results in 1.

=COLUMNS(B5:D5) results in 3, and so on. It simply adds up the number of columns referenced.

HLOOKUP

HLOOKUP searches for a specified value in an array or a table's top row.

=HLOOKUP(lookup_value,table_array,row_index_number,range_lookup)

The HLOOKUP function searches for a column heading that is defined in the table array and then it returns a number associated with the row index.

You can use text reference for the lookup value as shown in the first example in Figure 9.3. Using text for the lookup value produces the following formula and result: =HLOOKUP("Q2",D5:G9,2) results in $65,087. The quarter specifies the column heading, the table array includes the entire data table and the headings, and 2 is the number of rows indexed down. The range lookup argument is not necessary in this example.

The second example is a more efficient way to use the HLOOKUP function. The reason for this is that the formula acts upon the values input in the cells to the left. With cell referencing your formula becomes a live working model. Now you can apply different region numbers for index values as well as column headings, and the function will return the index and column heading result.

If you look at the second example in Figure 9.3, you'll see that =HLOOKUP(B8,D5:G9,C18) results in $33,929. The quarter reference for the lookup value is Q3, the table array includes the column heading, and the index value is referenced to the number of rows down the left side.

LOOKUP_VALUE   This is the value to be looked up in the first row of the table. This can be values, references, and text strings.

TABLE_ARRAY   The table or range in which you are looking up information. You can also use references to names or range names for the table array.

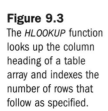

Figure 9.3
The *HLOOKUP* function looks up the column heading of a table array and indexes the number of rows that follow as specified.

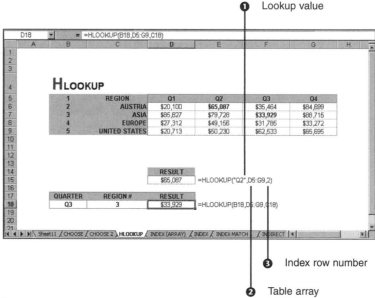

HYPERLINK

HYPERLINK creates a shortcut to jump to a document stored on a network server.

`=HYPERLINK(link_location,friendly_name)`

The HYPERLINK function can be used for several applications. For example, if you have a workbook that contains 50 or 60 worksheets, you might want to create a main page and call out all the pages on one page with hyperlinks to their respective pages. Take a look at the workbooks on the CD accompanying this book for examples. They are all set up with a main page and hyperlinks to the respective pages. You can create a hyperlink to specific cells or ranges on a specific sheet in the current workbook, to another external file, or even to a Web address. There are a couple of ways to do this. One is from the Insert menu, choose Hyperlink. The second way is with the HYPERLINK formula. Notice the formula shown in Figure 9.4. For example, =HYPERLINK(CHOOSE!B2) results in a jump to the CHOOSE page. Another way to use the HYPERLINK function is with a Web address or another office document.

LINK_LOCATION   This is the file location or path to the document that will be displayed as text. This can be UNC (the path on a server called the universal naming convention) or URL (the path on a intranet site or the Internet called the Uniform Resource Locator).

FRIENDLY_NAME   This is the text or numeric value that is displayed in a cell, previously called cell contents. The Friendly_Name is displayed in blue and is underlined. If it is omitted, the cell displays the Link_Location as the jump text.

Page reference (text location of link)

Figure 9.4

The *HYPERLINK* function can be used to create main pages in your workbooks that enable you to navigate through large workbooks— similar to a portal site on the Web.

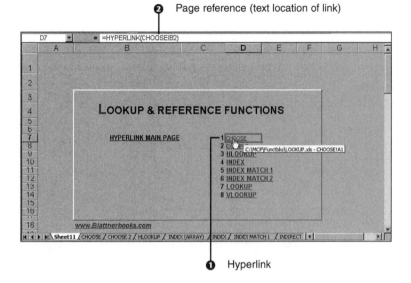

Hyperlink

INDEX (Array Form)

Based on a table or array, INDEX (Array Form) returns the value of an element selected by the row number and column letter indexes.

```
=INDEX(array,row_num,column_num)
```

The INDEX function in the form of an array allows you to expand the flexibility of the array function by specifying a row number and column number over several rows and columns, as you should notice in the examples in Figure 9.5.

ARRAY This is the range of cells or the array constant in the formula.

ROW_NUM Specifies the row within the array in which to return the value from.

The first example:

=INDEX(C10:E20,2,3) results in $4,021 because it is the second row and the third column over in the table array.

The second example:

=INDEX(C10:E20,5,1) results in 5 because it is the fifth row down in the first column of the range or table array.

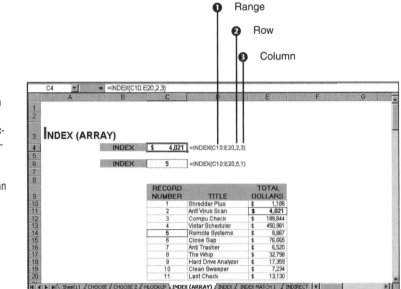

Figure 9.5
The *INDEX* function in the form of an array creates database function flexibility by allowing you to specify a range of columns and rows and looking up an intersecting point.

INDEX (Reference Form)

Based on the intersection of a particular row and column, INDEX (Reference Form) returns the reference of the cell.

```
=INDEX(reference,row_num,column_num,area_num)
```

The INDEX function in the form of a reference is one of the more useful lookup functions in that it can be used with other functions or form controls, as a cell reference, or with text reference. To illustrate, Figure 9.6 shows three examples using the index function on a list. The first example: =INDEX(D7:D17,6) results in 6, because it is the sixth row down on the single-column range.

The second example is used with the MATCH function to match text from another column shown as: =INDEX(E6:F17,MATCH(E21,E6:F17,),MATCH("PRODUCT",E6:F6,)).

The result is the product name, where E6 through F17 specifies the range of the ISBN number and the product names, the first nested match function specifies the ISBN input number cell reference. The MATCH range includes the same range as the index, and the second nested MATCH function calls out the column title heading in quotes and specifies the column heading range. Notice the last example, it takes into account a form control. The form control cell reference link is in cell D27, and indexes down to the fifth record and returns the index range of the fifth record in the range from G7:G17. When formatting the form control, use the F7:F17 product range. To learn more about form controls and functions see Chapter 2, "Managing Your Business with Functions."

REFERENCE	The reference to cell ranges. You can use one or more.
ROW_NUM	The number of the row within the reference for which to return the reference.
COLUMN_NUM	The number of the column within the reference from which to return the reference.
AREA_NUM	This is the range within the reference for which to return a result from a specified range. For example, 1 may refer to the first range and 2 would refer to the second, and so on.

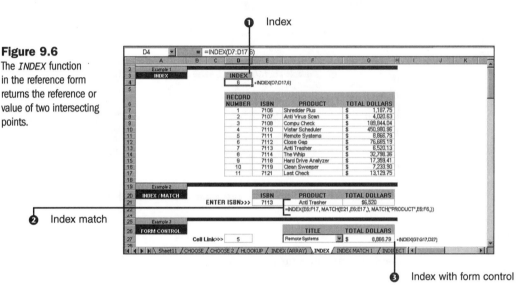

Figure 9.6

The *INDEX* function in the reference form returns the reference or value of two intersecting points.

Because the INDEX and MATCH functions are so critical and useful, Figure 9.7 shows the importance of these functions. As you see in the figure, the INDEX function is combined with the nested MATCH function performed over another list. Based on a lookup value such as an ISBN number or any number that identifies a product in a list over a range, you can look up numbers or text. Notice how the ISBN identifier returns the text value of the product title highlighted in the list. Take a look at what this formula might look like:

`=Index(D10:E25,Match(D8,D10:D25,),Match(Title,D10:E10,))`

Where `D10:E25` is the table range.

Where `D8,D10:D25` references the first match of 7407 in the ISBN range.

Where `Title,D10:E10` references the word title from the range of title range.

The formula returns the text result of the title.

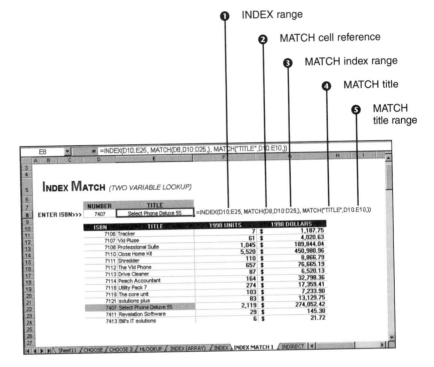

Figure 9.7
The *INDEX* function with the *MATCH* function can include the return of a value or of text.

INDIRECT

Based on a text string, INDIRECT returns the reference.

```
=INDIRECT(ref_text,A1)
```

The INDIRECT function points to one cell containing a reference to another cell. For example, you should notice in Figure 9.8 that cell D11 contains an INDIRECT function that uses a text reference in cell D8 that points to cell E8, so the result is the value found in E8, 5000. On the other hand, if the Ref_Text argument points to a cell containing a range name, the same result occurs. For example, if D15 contains text that refers to the range name for cell E15, then the indirect result is still E15 or the value of 5000.

REF_TEXT   The reference to a cell that contains an A1 style of reference. This is a name defined as a cell refence.

A1   The logical value that explains which kind of reference is displayed in the cell.

Figure 9.8
The *INDIRECT* function returns the value from an independent text reference pointing to another reference.

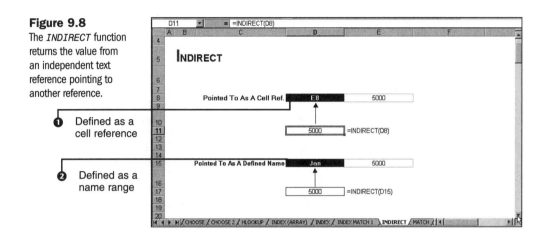

❶ Defined as a cell reference

❷ Defined as a name range

LOOKUP (Array Form)

LOOKUP (Array Form) looks in the first row or column of an array, and returns the specified value from the same position in the last row or column of the array.

=LOOKUP(lookup_value,array)

The LOOKUP function Array Form differs from the Vector Form in that the Vector Form looks up the value in the first row or column, and the Array Form allows you to specify the location of the lookup value. Notice that in Figure 9.9, the LOOKUP value is outside the array in the formula and can be referenced as text shown in the first example, or as a cell reference as shown in the second, third, and fourth examples.

LOOKUP_VALUE	This is the value LOOKUP searches for in the first vector.
LOOKUP_VECTOR	The range that contains only one row or column.

❶ LOOKUP value as text

Figure 9.9
The *LOOKUP* function as an array can be used as a text reference or cell reference.

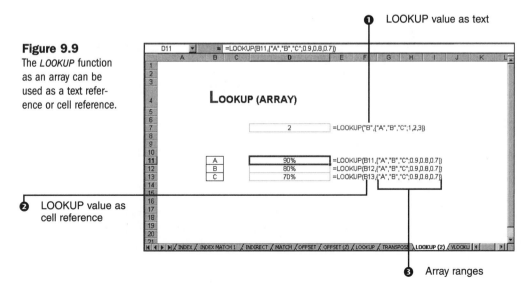

❷ LOOKUP value as cell reference

❸ Array ranges

LOOKUP (Vector Form)

Based on a range of one row or one column, LOOKUP (Vector Form) returns the value from the same position in a second row or column.

=LOOKUP(lookup_value,lookup_vector,result_vector)

The LOOKUP function Vector Form looks for the value in the first vector and returns the result from the second vector. More simply put, it looks up the value from the first range and returns the result of the cell in the same position in the second range as shown in Figure 9.10. Notice in the timeline example, the LOOKUP function searches for the greatest value in the range. Use this form when the value you want to look up is in the first row or column.

LOOKUP_VALUE   This is the value LOOKUP searches for in the first vector.

LOOKUP_VECTOR   The range that contains only one row or column.

RESULT_VECTOR   The range that contains only one row or column and must be the same as the Lookup_Vector.

❶ Looks up the greatest value in the range

Figure 9.10
The *LOOKUP* function looks up values in one vector (range) and returns the result of another vector (range).

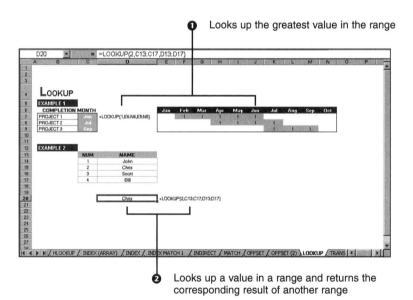

❷ Looks up a value in a range and returns the corresponding result of another range

MATCH

MATCH returns the relative position of an item in an array that matches a specified value in a specified order, or the position of an item.

=MATCH(lookup_value,lookup_array,match_type)

Use the MATCH function instead of the LOOKUP function when you specifically want to retrieve the position of the item and not its value. The position of the item means if there are five digits—1, 2 , 3, 4, 5—the position of the number 3 is three because it's the third item in the list.

LOOKUP_VALUE	The value used to find the specific value you want in the table.
LOOKUP_ARRAY	The contiguous range of cells containing lookup values.
MATCH_TYPE	Specifies whether to find an exact match (0), to find the largest value that is less than or equal to the lookup value (1), or to find the smallest value that is greater than or equal to the lookup value (-1).

Notice the example in Figure 9.11, the two formulas:

- =MATCH(5,C7:C17,0) where 5 is lookup value, and C7:C17 is the lookup array or range, and the MATCH type is zero. The MATCH type is simply a mechanism Excel uses to provide a type return in a formula. With the MATCH type zero, the return results in the record position.

- =MATCH(5,C7:C17,1) where 5 is the lookup value, and C7:C17 is the lookup array or range, and the MATCH type is 1, the return result is order of the number.

Figure 9.11
The *MATCH* function can include the return of a value or of text.

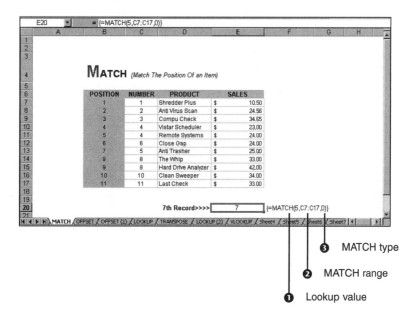

① Lookup value
② MATCH range
③ MATCH type

OFFSET

OFFSET returns a reference to a range that is a specific number of rows and columns from a cell or range of cells.

=OFFSET(reference,rows,columns,height,width)

The OFFSET function offsets a current location or position with another. For example, if you were giving a presentation and wanted the presentation to be interactive, you could use the OFFSET function to return different locations for a chart reference as shown in Figure 9.12. The first example in the figure shows the OFFSET function being used to look up or offset the Year 1 unit sales for Asia to Year 2. The formula: =OFFSET(C5,0,2) where C5 is the current location, or ground zero. The number of rows down is 0, and 2 is the number of columns over. The height of the return is the first row and the first column from the new position. If the row reference was 2, the return would have been 9,878. However, the result returns the value in cell E5 of 8,696.

It's important for you to note that the examples don't need the last two arguments (height and width). They are assumed to be 1 and 1 if they are omitted. When used within another function, the last two arguments help create a new range height and width starting at the new offset position. Using height and width numbers other than 1 in a cell containing just an offset formula will result in an error. If OFFSET is used inside of another function that is expecting to see a reference, then OFFSET returns the address and not the value.

REFERENCE	The range or cell of adjacent cells on which you want to base the offset.
ROWS	The number of rows up or down you want the base to refer or offset to.
COLUMNS	The number of columns left or right you want the base to refer or offset to. For example, using three would mean the upper-left cell is three columns to the right of the reference.
HEIGHT	(Optional) The height in the number of rows that you want the reference to return. This must be a positive number.
WIDTH	(Optional) The width in the number of columns that you want the reference to return. This must be a positive number.

Figure 9.12
The *OFFSET* function returns a location offset from the current location on the worksheet.

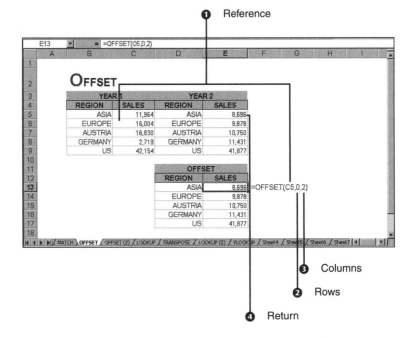

As you can see in Figure 9.13, you can use the OFFSET function in conjunction with other functions. In this particular example, the OFFSET function is used with the IF function to trigger a response based on a cell reference. The cell reference in C13 results in an offset of Year 2, and if the logical value of the cell reference of Year 2 is not Year 2 it defaults to the Year 1 cell of C5 as shown in Figure 9.14. See also, Chapter 2, "Managing Your Business with Functions."

Figure 9.13
The *OFFSET* function in conjunction with the *IF* function can be used to create a table that corresponds with the logical result in cell C14. The chart is based on the offset table.

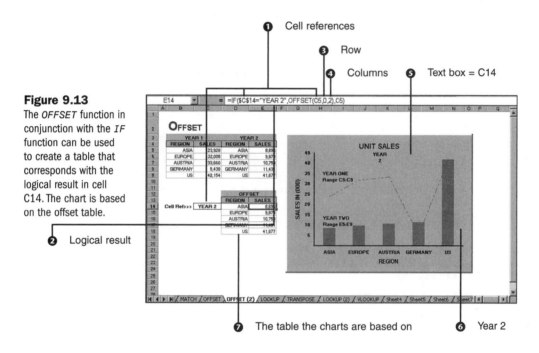

Figure 9.14
With the *OFFSET* function, if the logical result is not met, the result defaults to Year 1.

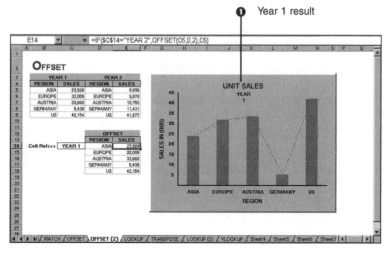

ROW

Based on a reference, ROW returns the row number.

`=ROW(reference)`

The ROW function returns the row of the cell of the reference. If the reference is ommitted, the ROW function assumes the row in which the function is entered. For example, =Row(C4) would result in 4. If the refernce is omitted, such as =Row(), then the result is the row of the cell the formula is entered into.

      REFERENCE   This is the range or cell you want the row number to refer to.

ROWS

Based on a reference or array, ROWS returns the number of rows.

`=ROWS(array)`

The ROWS function returns the number of rows in the form of an array. For example, the formula {=ROWS(C20:C25)} generates the number of rows in the array reference, which is 6. The same formula not entered as an array produces the same result of 6.

TRANSPOSE

TRANSPOSE returns a horizontal range of cells as vertical or vice versa.

`=TRANSPOSE(array)`

The TRANSPOSE function operates similar to the TRANSPOSE in the Paste Special command. The trick to making this function work better is by selecting your destination range first before typing the TRANSPOSE function. Use Ctrl+Shft+Enter instead of Enter to fill the entire high-lighted range with the new transposed data. Notice how Figure 9.15 shows building the TRANSPOSE function in progress and Figure 9.16 shows the final result. This function must be entered in the form of an array for the function to work. Select Ctrl+Shft+Enter to activate the array. Should your initial range not contain the same number of columns and rows, you will need to select the destination range in the opposite configuration. For example, if the initial range is B5:E7 (3 rows by 4 columns), you will need to select B9:D12 (4 rows by 3 columns) as a destination range.

      ARRAY   This is the range of cells you want to transpose on the worksheet. This starts with the first row of the range and then transposes starting with the first column of the new array.

Figure 9.15
Be sure to select the
region of the destination
of the transposed table.

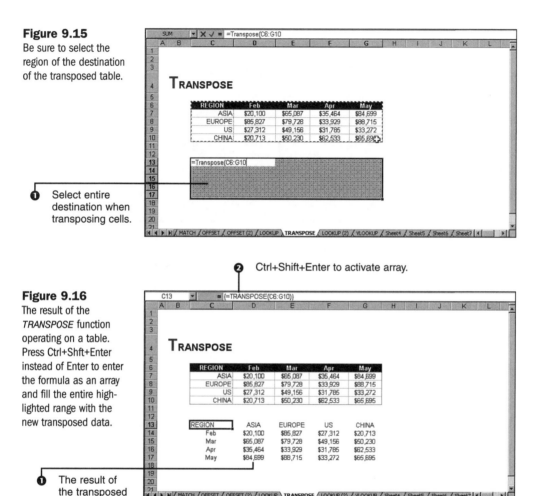

❶ Select entire
destination when
transposing cells.

❷ Ctrl+Shift+Enter to activate array.

Figure 9.16
The result of the
TRANSPOSE function
operating on a table.
Press Ctrl+Shft+Enter
instead of Enter to enter
the formula as an array
and fill the entire high-
lighted range with the
new transposed data.

❶ The result of
the transposed
table.

VLOOKUP

VLOOKUP looks for a value in the leftmost column of a table and returns a value from the
column number that you specify.

=VLOOKUP(lookup_value,table_array,column_index_num,range_lookup)

The VLOOKUP is one of those functions that has multiple purposes, and is useful in just about every
walk of business life. If you have employee time sheets on a weekly or daily basis, this is a good
formula to use when looking up the rate for the employee and matching it to the name of the
employee in the list. Notice the example in Figure 9.17: =VLOOKUP(F6,$C$6:$D$8,2,false)
produces the rate of the employee from the rate table. In this example, F6 is the lookup value of
the employee's name, C6:D8 is the rate table referenced, and 2 is the column index number from
the rate table in which you want a value return. The range lookup is what Excel uses as a result.

Figure 9.17
The *VLOOKUP* function can be used to combine employee rates with the names in a list.

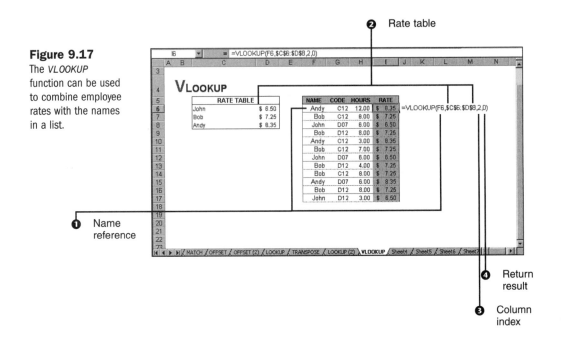

❷ Rate table

❶ Name reference

❹ Return result

❸ Column index

CHAPTER 10

Math and Trigonometry Functions

Math and Trigonometry Functions Overview

Math and Trigonometry functions in Excel can be used to perform calculations as standalone functions or combined together to create complex formulas.

ABS

The ABS function returns the absolute value of a number—the number without its sign.

=ABS(number)

The ABS function always returns a positive number. The NUMBER argument can be a value, a single-cell range, such as ABS(A1), or a multiple-cell range, which returns an array of values. An example of using ABS in a multiple-cell range is shown below.

This is the function you would use for looking at the absolute differences of a set of data from a given value. As you see in Figure 10.1, ABS can be used to find the value from a data range that is closest to the average of that data. This formula creates an array of absolute differences, as calculated by the ABS function, between the data and the average of the data. This is matched to the minimum difference, and the INDEX function returns the desired value based on that match. The formula as shown in the figure is an array formula. To enter an array formula, hold down Ctrl+Shift+Enter. Also notice less complex uses of the ABS function that return the absolute value of a real number.

NUMBER   Is the real number you want to convert to an absolute.

Figure 10.1
The *ABS* function can be used to create arrays of absolute differences to be used in complex formulas.

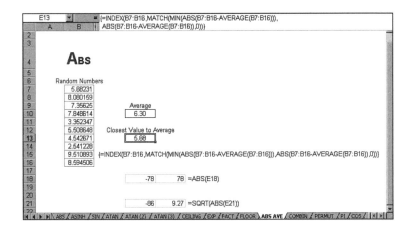

ACOS

The ACOS function returns the arccosine of a number, in radians in the range 0 (zero) to pi. The arccosine is the angle of which the cosine is number.

=ACOS(number)

The number is the cosine of the angle you want and it is restricted to the range of –1 to 1. As with all normal trigonometric functions in Excel, you can convert the result from radians to degrees by multiplying it by 180/PI().

Notice the example of the ACOS function shown in Figure 10.2.

NUMBER   This is the cosine of the angle you want. It must be from –1 to 1. To convert the result from radians to degrees multiply the number by 180/PI().

Figure 10.2
The *ACOS* function returns an angle of which cosine is the given number.

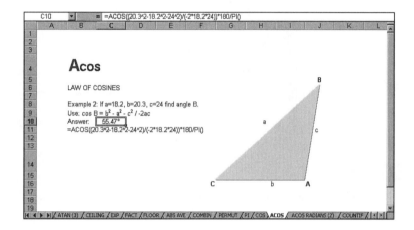

ACOSH

ACOSH returns the inverse hyperbolic cosine of a NUMBER. The number must be greater than or equal to one.

=ACOSH(number)

An inverse hyperbolic cosine is the value in which the hyperbolic cosine is the number. For example, ACOSH(COSH(number)) equals the number.

NUMBER   The real number greater than or equal to one.

ASIN

The ASIN function returns the arcsine of a number. The arcsine is the angle of which sine is number. The returned angle is given in radians in the range –pi/2 to pi/2.

=ASIN(number)

The number is the sine of the angle you want and it is bounded by the range of –1 to 1.

As with all normal trigonometric functions in Excel, you can convert the result from radians to degrees by multiplying it by 180/PI().

Notice the example of the ASIN function shown in Figure 10.3. The destination of the plane flying at 450 miles per hour is at 16 degrees south of west. If the wind velocity is 30 miles per hour from the east, what course should the pilot set?

NUMBER   The sine of the desired angle. It must be from –1 to 1.

Figure 10.3
The *ASIN* function returns an angle in which sine is the given number.

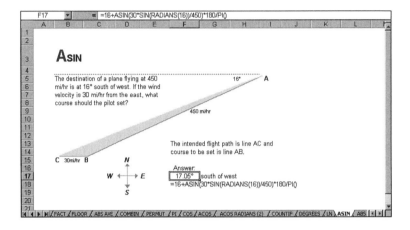

ASINH

The ASINH function returns the inverse hyperbolic sine of a number. The inverse hyperbolic sine is the value in which the hyperbolic sine is number, so ASINH(SINH(number)) equals that number.

=ASINH(number)

NUMBER   The NUMBER argument can be any real number.

Notice the example in Figure 10.4 where ASINH(5) equals 2.3124.

Figure 10.4
The *ASINH* function returns an angle in which sine is the given number.

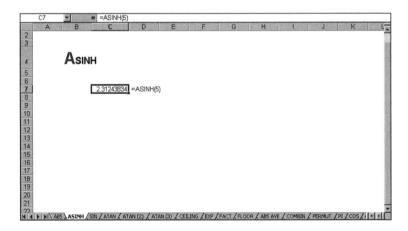

ATAN

The ATAN function returns the arctangent of a number. The arctangent is the angle in which tangent is number. The returned angle is given in radians in the range –pi/2 to pi/2.

=ATAN(number)

The NUMBER argument is the tangent of the angle you want.

As with all normal trigonometric functions in Excel, you can convert the result from radians to degrees by multiplying it by 180/PI().

Notice the example in Figure 10.5 where ATAN(0.5) equals 0.4636.

NUMBER   Where the number is the desired tangent angle.

Figure 10.5
The *ATAN* function generates the arctangent of a number.

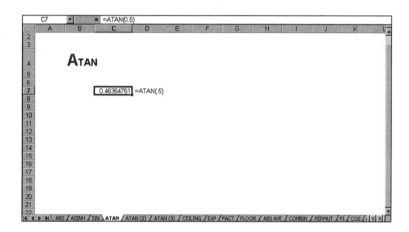

ATAN2

The ATAN2 function returns the four-quadrant arctangent of the specified x- and y-coordinates. The arctangent is the angle from the x-axis to a line containing the origin (0, 0) and a point with coordinates (x, y). The angle is given in radians between –pi and pi, excluding –pi.

=ATAN2(x,y)

The argument x is the x-coordinate of the point and the argument y is the y-coordinate of the point. Notice the example in Figure 10.6.

X_NUM   This is the x-coordinate of the point.
Y_NUM   This is the y-coordinate of the point.

Figure 10.6
The *ATAN2* function
returns the arctangent
of the specified x and y
coordinates.

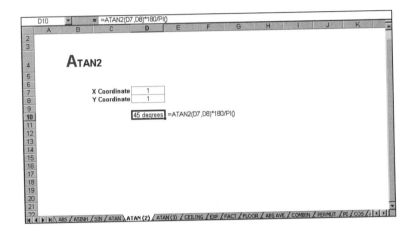

ATANH

The ATANH function returns the inverse hyperbolic tangent of a number. Number must be between –1 and 1 (excluding –1 and 1). The inverse hyperbolic tangent is the value in which the hyperbolic tangent is number, so ATANH(TANH(number)) equals number.

=ATANH(number)

Notice the example in Figure 10.7 where the number equals .1 and the inverse hyperbolic of the number from the ATANH function equals 0.1003.

NUMBER   Any real number between –1 and 1.

Figure 10.7
The *ATANH* function
returns the inverse
hyperbolic tangent of a
number between –1
and 1.

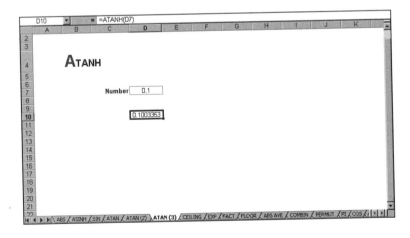

CEILING

The CEILING function returns a number rounded up, away from zero, to the nearest multiple of significance.

=CEILING(number,significance)

The NUMBER argument is the value you want to round, and the significance argument is the multiple to which you want to round. For NUMBER arguments that are negative, use a negative significance argument. Otherwise, CEILING returns an error value. If a nonnumeric entry is made for either argument, CEILING returns an error value.

An interesting use for the CEILING function is in the adjustment of time periods. The following formula uses the NOW function as the number argument and a fraction as the significance argument as shown in Figure 10.8. =CEILING(NOW(),1/96) is the formula that returns the date serial number corresponding to the time, rounded up to the next 15-minute period. So, if the current time is 9:02 (and the cell containing this formula has a time number format), this formula returns 9:15.

| NUMBER | The number you want to round. |
| SIGNIFICANCE | The multiple in which you want to round. |

Figure 10.8
The *CEILING* function with the *NOW* function can be used to return 15-minute increments when formatted to a time.

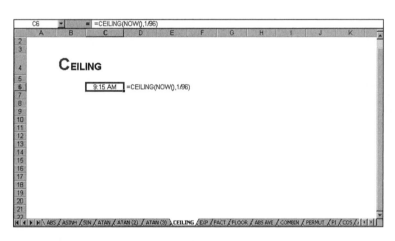

COMBIN

The COMBIN function returns the number of combinations for a given number of items. Use COMBIN to determine the total possible number of groups for a given number of items.

=COMBIN(number,items)

The number argument is the number of items.

The ITEMS argument is the number of items in each combination and it must be between zero and the value of the number argument for the function to work correctly. Although non-integer values can be used in the COMBIN function, they have no mathematical significance, and they are automatically rounded to integers.

Combinations are similar to permutations in that groupings of objects are made from a larger set of objects. However, with permutations, the internal order is significant, while it is not with combinations.

Notice the example in Figure 10.9. An example of the similar PERMUT function (see Chapter 11, "Statistical Functions") is also shown. In the example, there are 8 linemen, 6 receivers, 4 running backs, and 2 quarterbacks on a given football team. How many different ways can a team of 11 offensive players be chosen if 5 linemen, 3 receivers, 4 running backs, and 1 quarterback are used? The answer: 13,440.

NUMBER	The number of items.
ITEMS	The number of items in each combination.

$$\binom{n}{k} = \frac{P_{k,n}}{k!} = \frac{n!}{k!(n-k)!}$$

Figure 10.9
Use the *COMBIN* function to return the number of combinations that can be used with different sets of data.

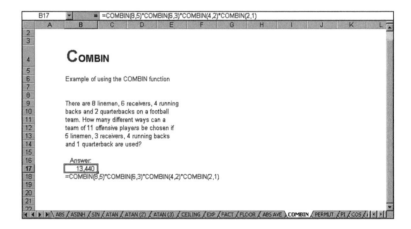

COS

The COS function returns the cosine of the given angle.

`=COS(number)`

The NUMBER argument is the angle in radians for which you want the cosine.

As with all normal trigonometric functions in Excel, you can convert the result from radians to degrees by multiplying it by 180/PI().

The COS function is useful for determining the lengths of sides and central angles of geometric shapes, as shown in Figure 10.10. The degrees symbol was created with a custom number format and can be accessed from the CD included with this book.

NUMBER   The number is the angle in radians that you are looking for. If the angle is in degrees, you can multiply it by 180/PI() to convert it to radians.

Figure 10.10
The *COS* function returns the cosine of a given angle.

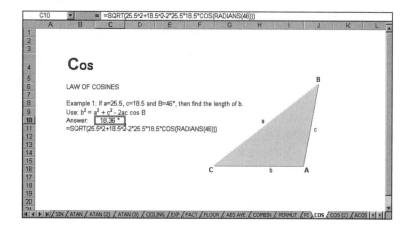

COSH

The COSH function returns the hyperbolic cosine of a number.

=COSH(number)

NUMBER   Is the NUMBER argument of any real number for which you want to find the hyperbolic cosine.

COSH(n) is equivalent to (EXP(n)+EXP(-n))/2.

$$\mathrm{COSH}(z) = \frac{e^z + e^{-z}}{2}$$

Example: COSH(0.5) equals 1.128.

COUNTIF

The COUNTIF function counts the number of cells within a range that meet the given criteria.

=COUNTIF(range,criteria)

The RANGE argument is the range of cells from which you want to count cells. It is important to note that this argument cannot be a calculated array, unlike many functions that do not differentiate between a worksheet range and an array.

The CRITERIA argument is the criteria in the form of a number, expression, or text that defines which cells will be counted. Whatever you decide to use in this argument, Excel must be able to convert it into a Boolean (TRUE/FALSE) expression that defines the criteria.

The second argument of the COUNTIF function also can accept a range of data. An outstanding example of using this range argument is in the formula that returns the count of unique items in a rectangular range. The COUNTIF function can be used to count those items individually, as indicated by the formulas in B5:B14 (formula shown for B1) in Figure 10.11. However, the array formula in E9 is able to perform this calculation in a collective manner. The formula as shown in the figure is an array formula. To enter an array formula, press Ctrl+Shift+Enter.

The key part of this formula is 1/COUNTIF(B5:B14, B5:B14), which affords an array of ratios, which evaluates as shown below.

{1/2;1/2;1/3;1/2;1/3;1/2;1/1;1/1;1/1;1/3}

So, if an item appears three times in the range A1:A10, as indicated by the use of the COUNTIF function in column B, the array will contain three occurrences of the value.

RANGE   The range of cells to count.

CRITERIA   The criteria in the form of an expression. Such as ">10".

Figure 10.11
The *COUNTIF* function can be used in an array formula to calculate the number of unique items in a range.

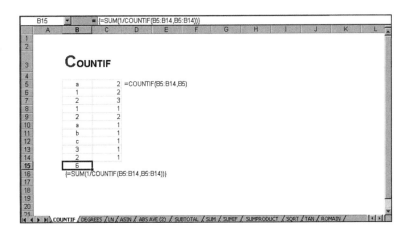

DEGREES

The DEGREES function converts radians into degrees.

=DEGREES(angle)

The ANGLE argument is the angle in radians that you want to convert. Using this function is equivalent to multiplying a value in radians by 180/PI(). The formula DEGREES(PI()) equals 180 because pi radians describes an arc of a hemisphere.

Notice the example of the DEGREES function shown in Figure 10.12.

ANGLE   The angle in the form of radians you want to convert.

Figure 10.12
The *DEGREES* function converts radian measure to central angle measure.

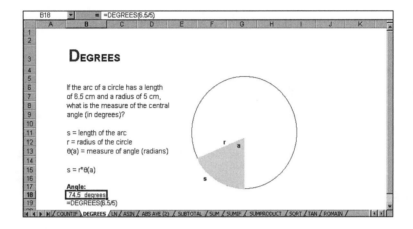

EVEN

The EVEN function returns a number rounded up away from zero to the nearest even integer.

=EVEN(number)

The NUMBER argument is the value to round.

For example, If number is an even integer, no rounding occurs. If the number in A1 is 1.1, then =EVEN(A1) returns 2. If the number in A1 is 2.1, then =EVEN(A1) returns 4.

NUMBER   The value in which to round.

EXP

The EXP function returns e raised to the power of number. The constant e equals approximately 2.71828182845904, the base of the natural logarithm.

=EXP(number)

NUMBER   The NUMBER argument is the exponent applied to the base e. This can be any real number. The returned value, if the NUMBER argument is less than zero, will be between 0 and 1.

Notice the example of using EXP in Figure 10.13. You will also notice that LN is also the inverse of EXP as shown in cell C9.

Figure 10.13
The *EXP* function returns the e raised to the power of the number.

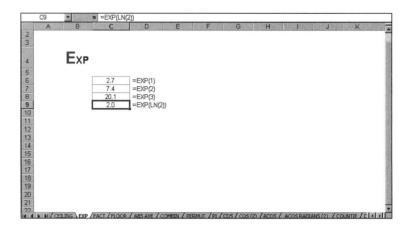

FACT

The FACT function returns the factorial of a number. The factorial of a number is equal to the product of integers from 1 to number.

=FACT(number)

The NUMBER argument is the non-negative number you want the factorial of. If number is not an integer, it is truncated (see the TRUNC function later in this chapter).

Example: FACT(4) equals 24, which is equivalent to =1*2*3*4.

You also might want to calculate the sum of a series of factorials from n to m, where n and m are positive integers. You can do this with a formula such as =FACT(n)+FACT(n+1)..+FACT(m) but the formula might get a little long. Instead, you can use an array formula to perform this task. This formula is of the form =SUM(FACT(ROW(n:m))). As an example, the formula =SUM(FACT(ROW(2:5))) returns 152, which is the sum of FACT(2), FACT(3), FACT(4), and FACT(5). Notice the example in Figure 10.14.

 T I P The use of the ROW function with a RANGE argument allows you to create an array of numbers. The array created by the formula ROW(1:10) is an array of numbers from 1 to 10.

To use this formula you must remember that it must be entered as an array formula (by holding down the Ctrl and Shift keys when pressing Enter).

NUMBER   Returns the factorial of a number. For example 1*2*3....

Figure 10.14
Calculate the sum of a
series of factorials with
this array.

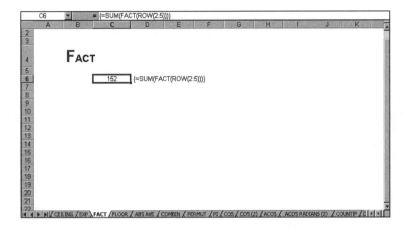

FACTDOUBLE

The FACTDOUBLE function returns the double factorial of a number.

=FACTDOUBLE(number)

This function is available from the Analysis ToolPak add-in and can be accessed using the Tools, Add-Ins command. Check the box for that add-in. If it is not on the add-in list, run Setup to install it. The NUMBER argument is the value for which to return the double factorial. If number is not an integer, it is truncated. If the number is even, this function returns the product of values from 1 to number that are even. If the number is odd, this function returns the product of values from 1 to number that are odd. The FACTDOUBLE function returns an error value if the NUMBER argument is not a positive number.

NUMBER   The value you want the double factorial for. The number is
                       truncated if not an integer.

For example: FACTDOUBLE(11) equals 10395.

FLOOR

The FLOOR function returns a number rounded down, toward zero, to the nearest multiple of significance.

=FLOOR(number,significance)

The NUMBER argument is the value you want to round, and the SIGNIFICANCE argument is the multiple to which you want to round. For NUMBER arguments that are negative, use a NEGATIVE SIGNIFICANCE argument. Otherwise, FLOOR returns an error value. If a nonnumeric entry is made for either argument, FLOOR returns an error value. The FLOOR function can be used to round a monetary amount down to the nearest cent. Notice the example in Figure 10.15. If A1 contains $46.234 then =FLOOR(A1,.01) returns $46.23.

NUMBER   The value you want to round.

SIGNIFICANCE   The multiple to which to round the value to.

Figure 10.15
Use the *FLOOR* function to round values to the nearest multiple.

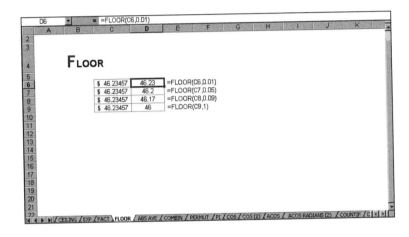

GCD

The GCD function returns the greatest common divisor of two or more integers. The greatest common divisor is the largest integer that divides both number1 and number2 without a remainder.

=GCD(number1,number2, ...)

This function is available from the Analysis ToolPak under Tools, Add-Ins in the menu if the box for that add-in is checked. If it is not in the add-in list, run Setup to install it. For example, GCD(16,28) equals 4.

NUMBER   The NUMBER arguments are 1 to 29 values. If any value is not an integer, it is truncated. If any argument is 0, it is ignored. If any argument is nonnumeric or less than 0, an error value is returned. You also can use ranges of values in place of single-number values in this function.

INT

The INT function rounds a number down to the nearest integer.

=INT(number)

For example: INT(2.6) equals 2 and INT(-2.6) equals –3.

You also can use the TRUNC function. INT and TRUNC operate the same for positive numbers. With negative numbers INT rounds away from zero and TRUNC rounds toward zero.

NUMBER	The NUMBER argument is the real number you want to round down to an integer.

LCM

The LCM function returns the least common multiple of integers. The least common multiple is the smallest positive integer that is a multiple of all integer arguments number1, number2, and so on. Use LCM to add fractions with different denominators.

```
=LCM(number1,number2, ...)
```

This function is available from the Analysis ToolPak under Tools, Add-Ins in the menu if the box for that add-in is checked. If it is not in the add-in list, run Setup to install it. For example, LCM(16,28) equals 112.

NUMBER	The NUMBER arguments are 1 to 29 values. If any value is not an integer, it is truncated. If any argument is 0, it is ignored. If any argument is nonnumeric or less than 0, an error value is returned. You also can use ranges of values in place of single number values in this function.

LN

The LN function returns the natural logarithm of a number. Natural logarithms are based on the constant (2.71828182845904).

```
=LN(number)
```

The LN function can be used in problems that calculate exponential growth, such as the population growth in Figure 10.16. In this example, the cells are named cells. You can access the CD and plug numbers into the cells in the live workbook instead of recreating this example.

NUMBER	The NUMBER argument is the positive real number for which you want the natural logarithm.

LN is the inverse of the EXP function, so the formula LN(EXP(22.3)) equals 22.3. You also can use LOG if a more flexible approach is needed.

Figure 10.16
Use the *LN* function to estimate population growth over time.

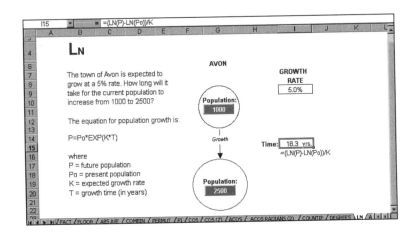

LOG

The LOG function returns the logarithm of a number to the base you specify.

=LOG(number,base)

For example, LOG(10,3) equals 2.0959.

NUMBER   The NUMBER argument is the positive real number for which you want the logarithm.

BASE   The BASE argument is the base of the logarithm. If base is omitted, it is assumed to be 10. The LOG function performs the inverse operation of the POWER function.

LOG10

The LOG10 function returns the base-10 logarithm of a number.

=LOG10(number)

For example, LOG10(50) equals 1.6990.

NUMBER   The NUMBER argument is the positive real number for which you want the base-10 logarithm. You also can use the LOG if a more flexible approach is needed.

MDETERM

The MDETERM function returns the matrix determinant of an array.

=MDETERM(array)

The argument can be an actual array, such as {1,2;3,4}, or a square worksheet range, such as A1:B2. Matrix determinants are generally used for solving systems of linear equations where the number of equations is the same as the number of variables. For example,

`MDETERM({1,2;3,4})` equals –2. Thus, each element of the array argument must be a numeric value or an error value is returned.

ARRAY   The ARRAY argument is a numeric array that must have an equal number of rows and columns or an error value is returned.

MINVERSE

The MINVERSE function returns the inverse matrix for the matrix stored in an array.

`=MINVERSE(array)`

Inverse matrices, like determinants, are generally used for solving systems of mathematical equations involving several variables. The product of a matrix and its inverse is the identity matrix—the square array in which the diagonal values equal 1, and all other values equal 0. The determinant for a noninvertible matrix is 0. For example, `MINVERSE({1,2,1;4,1,2;3,3,1})` equals `{-0.625,0.125,0.375;0.25,-0.25,0.25;1.125,0.375,-0.875}`.

ARRAY   The ARRAY argument is a numeric array that must have an equal number of rows and columns, which can be given as a cell range— for example, A1:C3; as an array constant, such as {1,2,3;4,5,6;7,8,9}; or as a name to either of these. Functions that return arrays must be entered as array formulas (by pressing Ctrl+Shift+Enter).

 TIP You can use the INDEX function to return individual items from a matrix created by functions such as MINVERSE. For example, INDEX(matrix,1,1) will return the value from the upper-left corner of an array named "matrix".

MMULT

The MMULT function returns the matrix product of two arrays. The result is an array with the same number of rows as array1 and the same number of columns as array2.

`=MMULT(array1,array2)`

array1 and array2 can be given as cell ranges, array constants, or references. If any cells are empty or contain text, or if the number of columns in array1 is different from the number of rows in array2, MMULT returns an error value. Functions that return arrays must be entered as array formulas (by pressing Ctrl+Shift+Enter). For example: `MMULT({1,2;3,1},{2,2;3,-1})` equals `{8,0;9,5}`.

ARRAY   The array1 and array2 arguments are the arrays you want to multiply. The number of columns in array1 must be the same as the number of rows in array2, and both arrays must contain only numbers.

The matrix product array a of two arrays b and c is

$$a_{ij} = \sum_{k=1}^{n} b_{ik} c_{kj}$$

MOD

The MOD function returns the remainder after number is divided by divisor. The result has the same sign as divisor.

```
=MOD(number,divisor)
```

For example: MOD(6,5) equals 1 and MOD(5,5) equals 0. Sometimes it may be desirable to use the following equivalent formula.

```
MOD(n,d) = n - d*INT(n/d)
```

NUMBER	The NUMBER argument is the number for which you want to find the remainder.
DIVISOR	The DIVISOR argument is the number by which you want to divide your number. If divisor is 0, MOD returns an error value.

MROUND

The MROUND function returns a number rounded to the desired multiple.

```
=MROUND(number,multiple)
```

This function is available from the Analysis ToolPak under Tools, Add-Ins in the menu if the box for that add-in is checked. If it is not in the add-in list, run Setup to install it. For example: =MROUND(5000, 75) returns 5025.

NUMBER	The NUMBER argument is the value to round.
MULTIPLE	The MULTIPLE argument is the multiple to which you want to round the number.

MULTINOMIAL

The MULTINOMIAL function returns the ratio of the factorial of a sum of values to the product of factorials.

```
=MULTINOMIAL(number1,number2, ...)
```

This function is available from the Analysis ToolPak under Tools, Add-Ins in the menu if the box for that add-in is checked. If it is not in the add-in list, run Setup to install it. For example: MULTINOMIAL(5,7) equals 792.

NUMBER 1, NUMBER 2, ...	The NUMBER arguments are 1 to 29 values. If any value is not an integer, it is truncated. If any argument is 0, it is ignored. If any argument is nonnumeric or less than 1, an error value is returned. You also can use ranges of values in place of single number values in this function.

The MULITNOMINAL is

$$\text{MULTINOMIAL}(a,b,c) = \frac{(a+b+c)!}{a!b!c!}$$

ODD

The ODD function returns number rounded up away from zero to the nearest odd integer.

`=ODD(number)`

If number is an odd integer, no rounding occurs. If the number in A1 is 0.1, then `=ODD(A1)` returns 1. If the number in A1 is 3.1, then `=ODD(A1)` returns 5.

NUMBER   The NUMBER argument is the value to round.

PERMUT

The PERMUT function returns the number of permutations for a certain number of objects that can be selected from number objects.

`=PERMUT(Number,Number_chosen)`

The PERMUT function operates on the subset of the whole, where the order of the subset is of importance. Notice the example in Figure 10.17. There are 9 players on a baseball team. If the pitcher is excluded, what is the number of ways to arrange the first 5 positions in the batter order? The result is 6,720.

NUMBER   The integer that describes the number of the total set.
NUMBER CHOSEN   The number of objects in the permutation.

Figure 10.17
Use the *PERMUT* function to find the number in order of a subset of the whole.

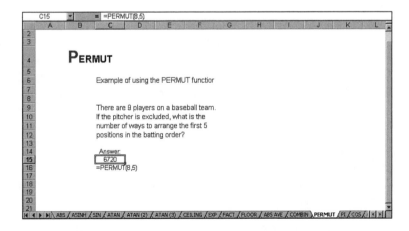

PI

The PI function returns the approximate number 3.14159265358979, the mathematical constant pi, accurate to 15 digits.

`=PI()`

Where the radius of the circle is 6.75, the calculation to find the area from the radius is `=PI()*(D11^2)` and the result is 143.14 (as shown in Figure 10.18).

Figure 10.18
To find the area of a circle with the known radius, use the *PI* function.

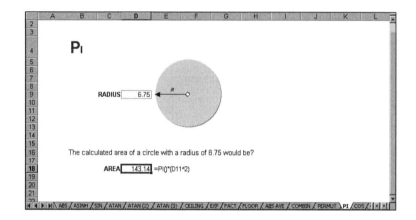

POWER

The POWER function returns the result of a number raised to a power.

`=POWER(number,power)`

For example: POWER(5,3) equals 125.

NUMBER	The NUMBER argument is the base number, and it can be any real number.
POWER	The POWER argument is the exponent to which the base number is raised. The POWER function performs the inverse operation of the LOG function. An equivalent formula to the POWER function is =x^y versus POWER(x,y).

PRODUCT

The PRODUCT function multiplies all the numbers given as arguments and returns the product.

`=PRODUCT(number1,number2, ...)`

For example: PRODUCT(2,5,10) equals 100. Acceptable arguments are numbers, logical values, and numbers entered as text. Error values or text that cannot be translated into numbers return errors. If an argument is an array or reference, only numbers in the array or reference are counted. Empty cells, logical values, text, or error values in the array or reference are ignored.

> NUMBER 1, NUMBER 2, ...   The arguments can be from 1 to 30 numbers that you want to multiply.

QUOTIENT

The QUOTIENT function returns the integer portion of a division.

=QUOTIENT(numerator,denominator)

This function is available from the Analysis ToolPak under Tools, Add-Ins in the menu if the box for that add-in is checked. If it is not in the add-in list, run Setup to install it. For example: QUOTIENT(5,2) equals 2.

> NUMERATOR   The NUMERATOR argument is the dividend.
>
> DENOMINATOR   The DENOMINATOR argument is the divisor.

RADIANS

The RADIANS function converts degrees to radians.

=RADIANS(angle)

Notice the example in Figure 10.19. The ACOS function returns the angle in degrees and the RADIANS function converts the degrees to radians.

Figure 10.19
Use the *RADIANS* function to convert degrees to radians.

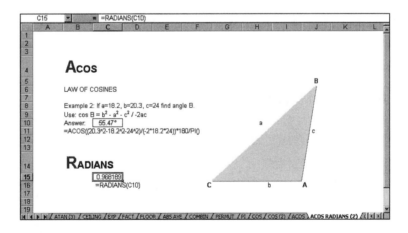

The angle argument is an angle in degrees that you want to convert.

RAND

The RAND function returns an evenly distributed random number greater than or equal to 0 and less than 1. A new random number is returned every time the worksheet is calculated.

=RAND()

The RAND function is a volatile function. This means that the value returned by that function is changed each time the worksheet is recalculated. If the result of the RAND is to be stored, the formula must be converted to its value. This can be accomplished by using Edit, Copy, then Edit Paste Special and choosing the Values option from the dialog box, or by highlighting the formula in the formula bar and pressing F9 and Enter.

Example: You can return a value between 0 and 2 with RAND()*2. Notice the example in Figure 10.20, the RAND function returns random numbers between point A and B: =RAND()*(b-a)+a. (See also RANDBETWEEN in this chapter.)

Figure 10.20
The *RAND* function can be used to create random numbers between two points as shown.

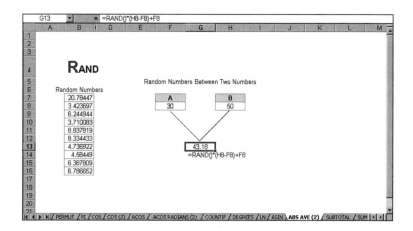

RANDBETWEEN

The RANDBETWEEN function returns a random integer between the integers you specify. A new random number is returned every time the worksheet is calculated.

=RANDBETWEEN(bottom,top)

This function is available from the Analysis ToolPak under Tools, Add-Ins in the menu if the box for that add-in is checked. If it is not in the add-in list, run Setup to install it. An example is RANDBETWEEN(5,10) and can return 5, 6, 7, 8, 9, or 10.

BOTTOM	The BOTTOM argument is the smallest integer RANDBETWEEN will return.
TOP	The TOP argument is the largest integer RANDBETWEEN will return.

ROMAN

The ROMAN function converts an Arabic numeral to Roman, as text.

```
=ROMAN(number,form)
```

The NUMBER argument is the Arabic numeral you want converted and the FORM argument is a number specifying the type of Roman numeral you want. If number is negative or greater than 3,999, an error value is returned. The Roman numeral style ranges from Classic to Simplified (0 to 4), becoming more concise as the value of form increases. You can see an example of the result of the formula =ROMAN(999,n) in the table shown in Figure 10.21.

Figure 10.21
Use the *ROMAN* function to convert Arabic numerals to Roman.

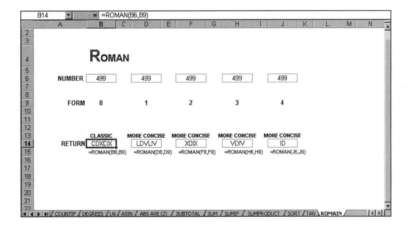

ROUND

The ROUND function rounds a number to a specified number of digits.

```
=ROUND(number,digits)
```

If digits is greater than 0 (zero), then number is rounded to the specified number of decimal places. If digits is 0, then number is rounded to the nearest integer. If digits is less than 0, then number is rounded to the left of the decimal point. For example: ROUND(9.95, 1) equals 10.0 and ROUND(5025,-2) results in 5000.

NUMBER	The NUMBER argument is the number you want to round.
DIGITS	The DIGITS argument specifies the number of digits to which you want to round the number.

ROUNDDOWN

The ROUNDDOWN function rounds a number down, toward zero.

=ROUNDDOWN(number, digits)

ROUNDDOWN behaves like ROUND, except that it always rounds a number down.

If digits is greater than 0 (zero), then number is rounded down to the specified number of decimal places. If digits is 0 or omitted, then number is rounded down to the nearest integer. If digits is less than 0, then number is rounded down to the left of the decimal point. For example: ROUNDDOWN(10.3, 0) equals 10.

NUMBER	The NUMBER argument is any real number that you want rounded down.
DIGITS	The DIGITS argument is the number of digits to which you want to round number.

ROUNDUP

The ROUNDUP function rounds a number up, away from 0 (zero).

=ROUNDUP(number, digits)

ROUNDUP behaves like ROUND, except that it always rounds a number up.

If digits is greater than 0 (zero), then number is rounded up to the specified number of decimal places. If digits is 0 or omitted, then number is rounded up to the nearest integer. If digits is less than 0, then number is rounded up to the left of the decimal point. For example: ROUNDUP(9.4,0) equals 10.

NUMBER	The NUMBER argument is any real number that you want rounded up.
DIGITS	The DIGITS argument is the number of digits to which you want to round number.

SERIESSUM

The SERIESSUM function returns the sum of a power series that uses the following formula:

$$SERIES(x,n,m,a) = a_1x^n + a_2x^{(n+m)} + a_3x^{(n+2m)} +\ldots+ a_ix^{(n+(i-1)m)}$$

This function is available from the Analysis ToolPak under Tools, Add-Ins in the menu if the box for that add-in is checked. If it is not in the add-in list, run Setup to install it.

X	The X argument is the input value to the power series.
N	The N argument is the initial power to which you want to raise X.
M	The M argument is the step by which to increase N for each term in the series.

The COEFFICIENT (or A) argument is a set of coefficients by which each successive power of X is multiplied. The number of values in coefficients determines the number of terms in the power series. For example, if there are three values in coefficients, then there will be three terms in the power series. For example: =SERIESSUM(2,1,1,{1,2,3}) equals 34.

If any argument is nonnumeric, SERIESSUM returns an error value.

SIGN

The SIGN function determines the sign of a number.

=SIGN(number)

For example: SIGN(100) equals 1 and SIGN(-100) equals –1.

NUMBER — The NUMBER argument is any real number. The SIGN function returns 1 if the number is positive, zero (0) if the number is 0, and 1 if the number is negative.

SIN

The SIN function returns the sine of the given angle.

=SIN(number)

The SIN function is useful for determining the lengths and direction of vectors, as illustrated in Figure 10.22. In this problem, a course correction is needed due to a tailwind. The SIN function returns a value from the angle converted to radians that is used in a formula with the ASIN function to return the desired result.

NUMBER — The NUMBER argument is the angle in radians for which you want the sine. If your argument is in degrees, multiply it by PI()/180 to convert it to radians.

Figure 10.22
The SIN function is important in calculating vectors.

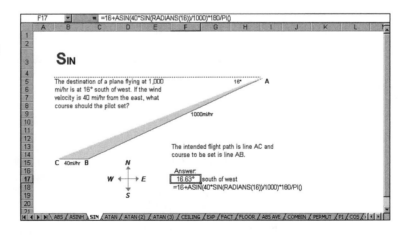

SINH

The SINH function returns the hyperbolic sine of a number.

=SINH(number)

SINH(n) is equivalent to (EXP(n)-EXP(-n))/2.

For example: SINH(3) equals 10.0179.

NUMBER   The NUMBER argument is any real number.

SQRT

The SQRT function returns a positive square root.

=SQRT(number)

Notice the example in Figure 10.23. The SQRT function can be used to return the positive square root of a number or in conjunction with the cosine and radians to return the length of an unknown where the square root of 64 is 8, as shown.

NUMBER   The NUMBER argument is the number for which you want the square root. If number is negative, SQRT returns an error value.

Figure 10.23
The *SQRT* function can be used to return the positive square root of a number or in con-junction with the cosine and radians to return the length of an unknown.

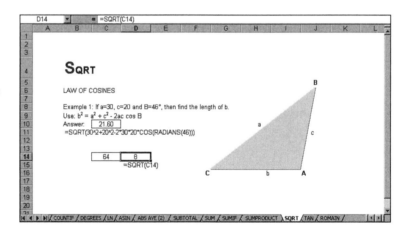

SQRTPI

The SQRTPI function returns the square root of (number * pi).

=SQRTPI(number)

This function is available from the Analysis ToolPak under Tools, Add-Ins in the menu if the box for that add-in is checked. If it is not in the add-in list, run Setup to install it. For example: SQRTPI(10) equals 5.6050.

NUMBER   The NUMBER argument is the number by which pi is multiplied. If the num-ber argument is < 0, SQRTPI returns an error value.

SUBTOTAL

The SUBTOTAL function returns a subtotal in a list or database. You can apply this function to a data table automatically by using the Subtotals command (Data menu). After the subtotal list is created, you can modify it by editing the SUBTOTAL function.

```
=SUBTOTAL(fnum,ref1,ref2,...)
```

The capability of the SUBTOTAL function to return information from a filtered list makes it one of the most powerful of Excel's functions.... If there are other subtotals within ref1, ref2,... (or nested subtotals), these nested subtotals are automatically ignored. SUBTOTAL will ignore any hidden rows that result from a list being filtered. This is important when you want to subtotal only the visible data that results from a list that you have filtered. If any of the references are 3D references, SUBTOTAL returns an error value.

The SUBTOTAL function can be used either with the normal filter (available by selecting Data, Filter from the menu) or by using the advanced filter (Data, Filter, Advanced Filter). The example shown in Figure 10.24 uses the advanced filter. In this case the data table has been filtered to show only unique records. If the status bar is visible during this operation, the number of unique records will be displayed there. However, to return that number to the worksheet, the SUBTOTAL function with a first argument of 3 gives the number of unique items in cell B28.

FNUM	The FNUM argument is a number from 1 to 11 that specifies which function to use in calculating subtotals within a list. There can be up to 29 ref arguments.
CELL REFERENCE or RANGE	The cell or range in which to reference.

Where the FNUM arguments are as follows:

1. AVERAGE
2. COUNT
3. COUNTA
4. MAX
5. MIN
6. PRODUCT
7. STDEV
8. STDEVP
9. SUM
10. VAR
11. VARP

Figure 10.24

Use the *SUBTOTAL* function with *FNUM* arguments to reference information quickly in lists.

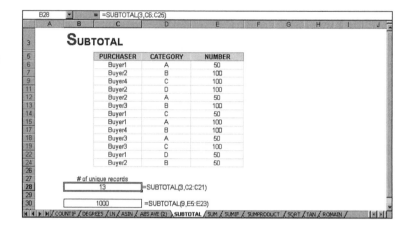

SUM

The SUM function adds all the numbers in a range of cells.

```
=SUM(number1,number2, ...)
```

If an argument is an array or reference, only numbers in that array or reference are counted. Empty cells, logical values, text, or error values in the array or reference are ignored. (See the third example following.) Arguments that are error values or text that cannot be translated into numbers cause errors.

T I P   A quick way to create a SUM formula with multiple reference arguments is to type "=SUM(" then click the first cell or group of cells to be used in the formula. Then, press Shift+F8. Each range that you highlight from that point will be added to the formula with the necessary comma separator for that argument.

There are problems associated with the summing of numbers in Excel that you should be aware of. Certain arguments can be coerced into numbers when directly entered into a SUM function. SUM(4, "2", TRUE) equals 7 because the text value 2 is translated into the number 2, and the logical value TRUE is translated into the number 1. However, if these same entries are made in a range (B6:B8 as shown in Figure 10.25), the SUM function returns a value of 4 as calculated by the formula in C1 because Excel does not translate the entries in this case. To further confuse the issue, Excel translates the entries if they are summed using the + operator, as calculated by the formula in C2. These two forms of summing are useful and complementary, as long as you know the strengths and limitations of each form.

NUMBER
The NUMBER arguments are 1 to 30 arguments for which you want the total value or sum.

It is true that the SUM function can accept only 30 arguments, but there is a simple workaround to this limitation. Each argument can contain up to 30 arguments of its own as long as they are enclosed by parentheses. The following example illustrates how this is done.

```
=SUM((A1,B2,C3),(A2,B3,C4))
```

The SUM function is one of the functions in Excel that can operate on a 3D range. The following formula is an example of the use of a 3D-range argument.

```
=SUM(Sheet1:Sheet4!A1)
```

In this case, the values in the sheets from Sheet1 to Sheet4 inclusive are summed. However, sheet names do not necessarily reflect sheet positions and only those sheets that are "between" Sheet1 and Sheet4 will be included in the result.

Figure 10.25
Use the *SUM* function to sum information in lists or across worksheets.

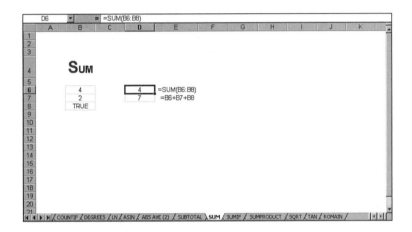

SUMIF

The SUMIF function adds the cells specified by a given criteria.

```
=SUMIF(range,criteria,sumrange)
```

It is important to note that the RANGE and SUMRANGE arguments do not have to reside on the same worksheet (example shown later in this section).

```
=SUMIF(Sheet1!A1:A10,">5",Sheet2!A1:A10)
```

In this case, the values in the range Sheet2!A1:A10 are summed if the corresponding values in the range Sheet1!A1:A10 are greater than 5.

An example of the utility of the SUMIF function is shown in Figure 10.26. The table represents sales data from a variety of regions. The formulas shown in C17 and C20 summarize this information according to region names that fit given criteria. The formula in B12 looks at the descriptive text in A12 and uses it in the criteria argument to return the sum of the data in C7:C14 that matches any word in B7:B14 that starts with "north". So, the result is 73.9 because the SUMIF function sums the values in cells A2, A3, and A9. The formula in B13 works in a similar manner, summing the cells in C7:C14 that matches any word in B7:B14 that ends with "east". In both cases, the wildcard character "*" is concatenated with the cell text to allow matches based on strings contained in text. You might also notice that the CRITERIA and SUMRANGE arguments in these formulas are partially relative references. This allows the formulas to be filled across for each region column and then filled down for the "south" and "west" summary rows.

| RANGE | The RANGE argument is the range of cells you want evaluated. |
| CRITERIA | The CRITERIA argument is the criteria in the form of a number, expression, or text that defines which cells will be added. |

It is important to note that the RANGE argument cannot be a calculated array, unlike many functions that do not differentiate between a worksheet range and an array. Whatever you decide to use in this argument, Excel must be able to convert it into a Boolean expression that defines the criteria.

| SUMRANGE | The SUMRANGE argument is the actual cells to sum. The cells in SUMRANGE are summed only if their corresponding cells in range match the criteria. If SUMRANGE is omitted, the cells in range are summed. |

Figure 10.26
The *SUMIF* function can use wildcard characters.

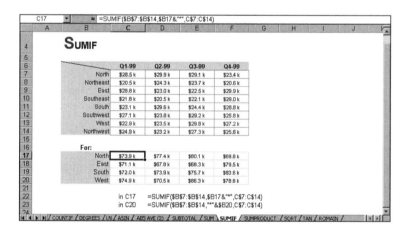

SUMPRODUCT

The SUMPRODUCT function multiplies corresponding components in the given arrays, and returns the sum of those products.

```
=SUMPRODUCT(array1,array2,array3, ...)
```

The ARRAY arguments must have the same dimensions. If they do not, SUMPRODUCT returns an error value. If there are entries in an array that are nonnumeric, SUMPRODUCT treats them as if they were zeros.

In the example shown in Figure 10.27, the SUMPRODUCT function is used to construct a rating system for employees. The table in the range C6:H10 provides a set of weightings for employee qualities based on their job type. To allow comparison across job types, the sum of the weightings must be equal to 1. Each row range of weightings has been given a name by highlighting C6:H10 and selecting Insert, Name, Create from the menu and checking the box for Create names in the left column and then pressing Enter. The employees are then given a ranking for each quality in the table B13:H22. The formula shown in cell I22 uses the SUMPRODUCT function to apply the correct weighting for the person in cell B22 by using the INDIRECT function with the job type name in C11 as the second array argument, which returns the named range SectionHead (D6:H6). This formula was filled down to I19 to return the weighted rating for each person, based on their job type.

ARRAY — The ARRAY arguments are 2 to 30 arrays, the components of which you want to multiply and then add.

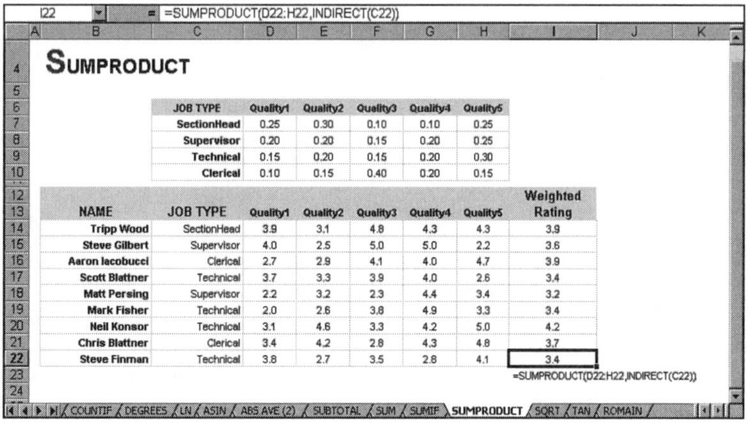

JOB TYPE	Quality1	Quality2	Quality3	Quality4	Quality5
SectionHead	0.25	0.30	0.10	0.10	0.25
Supervisor	0.20	0.20	0.15	0.20	0.25
Technical	0.15	0.20	0.15	0.20	0.30
Clerical	0.10	0.15	0.40	0.20	0.15

NAME	JOB TYPE	Quality1	Quality2	Quality3	Quality4	Quality5	Weighted Rating
Tripp Wood	SectionHead	3.9	3.1	4.8	4.3	4.3	3.9
Steve Gilbert	Supervisor	4.0	2.5	5.0	5.0	2.2	3.6
Aaron Iacobucci	Clerical	2.7	2.9	4.1	4.0	4.7	3.9
Scott Blattner	Technical	3.7	3.3	3.9	4.0	2.6	3.4
Matt Persing	Supervisor	2.2	3.2	2.3	4.4	3.4	3.2
Mark Fisher	Technical	2.0	2.6	3.8	4.9	3.3	3.4
Neil Konsor	Technical	3.1	4.6	3.3	4.2	5.0	4.2
Chris Blattner	Clerical	3.4	4.2	2.8	4.3	4.8	3.7
Steve Finman	Technical	3.8	2.7	3.5	2.8	4.1	3.4

Figure 10.27
The *SUMPRODUCT* function can produce weighted employee ratings.

SUMSQ

The SUMSQ function returns the sum of the squares of the arguments.

```
=SUMSQ(number1,number2, ...)
```

For example: SUMSQ(2,3) equals 13.

An array formula of the form =SUM(A1:C3^n) provides a general method of sum of a series of numbers raised to a power n. You can enter an array formula by holding down the Ctrl+Shift while pressing Enter.

NUMBER 1, NUMBER 2,... — The NUMBER arguments are 1 to 30 arguments for which you want the sum of the squares. You also can use a single array or a reference to an array instead of arguments separated by commas.

SUMX2MY2

The SUMX2MY2 function returns the sum of the difference of squares of corresponding values in two arrays. Therefore, the order that you enter the arguments into this function is important.

=SUMX2MY2(x, y)

If an ARRAY or REFERENCE argument contains text, logical values, or empty cells, those values are ignored; however, cells with the value zero are included. If the x and y arrays are different sizes, SUMX2PY2 returns an error value.

For example: =SUMX2MY2(3, 2) equals 5, whereas =SUMX2MY2(2, 3) equals –5.

X	The X argument is the first array or range of values.
Y	The Y argument is the second array or range of values. The arguments can be numbers or names, arrays, or references that contain numbers.

SUMX2PY2

The SUMX2PY2 function returns the sum of the sum of squares of corresponding values in two arrays.

=SUMX2PY2(x, y)

If an ARRAY or REFERENCE argument contains text, logical values, or empty cells, those values are ignored; however, cells with the value zero are included. If the x and y arrays are different sizes, SUMX2PY2 returns an error value. For example: SUMX2PY2(2, 3) equals 13.

X	The X argument is the first array or range of values.
Y	The Y argument is the second array or range of values. The arguments can be numbers or names, arrays, or references that contain numbers.

SUMXMY2

The SUMXMY2 function returns the sum of squares of differences of corresponding values in two arrays.

=SUMXMY2(x, y)

If an array or reference argument contains text, logical values, or empty cells, those values are ignored; however, cells with the value zero are included. If x and y have a different number of values, SUMXMY2 returns an error value. For example: SUMXMY2({2,3}, {3,4}) equals 2.

X	The X argument is the first array or range of values.
Y	The Y argument is the second array or range of values and the arguments can be numbers or names, arrays, or references that contain numbers.

TAN

The TAN function returns the tangent of the given angle.

```
=TAN(number)
```

As with all normal trigonometric functions in Excel, you can convert the result from radians to degrees by multiplying it by 180/PI().

Notice the example of TAN function shown in Figure 10.28 at the bottom of the figure. The angle of a is 56 degrees and the measurement from the survey point is 145 feet. What is the height of the tower? The result is 214.97 ft.

Figure 10.28
The *TAN* function can be used in survey measurements along with *RADIANS* to return results that are not directly measurable.

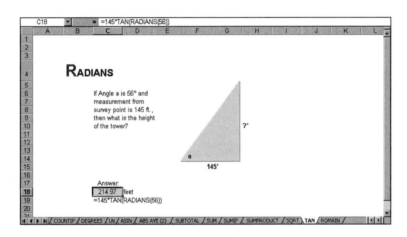

TANH

The TANH function returns the hyperbolic tangent of a number.

```
=TANH(number)
```

TANH(n) is equivalent to (EXP(n)-EXP(-n))/(EXP(n)+EXP(-n)).

For example: TANH(2) equals 0.9640.

NUMBER   The NUMBER argument is any real number.

TRUNC

The TRUNC function truncates a number to an integer by removing the fractional part of the number.

```
=TRUNC(number, digits)
```

You also can use the INT function. TRUNC and INT operate the same for positive numbers. With negative numbers INT rounds away from zero and TRUNC rounds toward zero.

For example: TRUNC(-3.3) equals –3.

NUMBER   The NUMBER argument is the number you want to truncate.

DIGITS   The digits is a number specifying the precision of the truncation. If not specified, the default value for digits is zero.

Statistical Functions

Statistical Functions Overview

Statistical functions are among the most widely used functions in Excel. You can calculate the average of a group of numbers and determine probabilities, distributions, and trends. Each of the 80 statistical functions in Excel are described in this chapter and most are accompanied by a figure to help illustrate the usage of the function.

The following functions are discussed in this chapter.

▶ AVEDEV	▶ FINV	▶ MAX	▶ SKEW
▶ AVERAGE	▶ FISHER	▶ MAXA	▶ SLOPE
▶ AVERAGEA	▶ FISHERINV	▶ MEDIAN	▶ SMALL
▶ BETADIST	▶ FORECAST	▶ MIN	▶ STANDARDIZE
▶ BETAINV	▶ FREQUENCY	▶ MINA	▶ STDEV
▶ BINOMDIST	▶ FTEST	▶ MODE	▶ STDEVA
▶ CHIDIST	▶ GAMMADIST	▶ NEGBINOMDIST	▶ STDEVP
▶ CHIINV	▶ GAMMAINV	▶ NORMDIST	▶ STDEVPA
▶ CHITEST	▶ GAMMALN	▶ NORMINV	▶ STEYX
▶ CONFIDENCE	▶ GEOMEAN	▶ NORMSDIST	▶ TDIST
▶ CORREL	▶ GROWTH	▶ NORMSINV	▶ TINV
▶ COUNT	▶ HARMEAN	▶ PEARSON	▶ TREND
▶ COUNTA	▶ HYPGEOMDIST	▶ PERCENTILE	▶ TRIMMEAN
▶ COUNTBLANK	▶ INTERCEPT	▶ PERCENTRANK	▶ TTEST
▶ COUNTIF	▶ KURT	▶ PERMUT	▶ VAR
▶ COVAR	▶ LARGE	▶ POISSON	▶ VARA
▶ CRITBINOM	▶ LINEST	▶ PROB	▶ VARP
▶ DEVSQ	▶ LOGEST	▶ QUARTILE	▶ VARPA
▶ EXPONDIST	▶ LOGINV	▶ RANK	▶ WEIBULL
▶ FDIST	▶ LOGNORMDIST	▶ RSQ	▶ ZTEST

AVEDEV

AVEDEV returns the average of the absolute deviations of data points from their mean.

`=AVEDEV(number1,number2,...)`

The AVEDEV function is one of several functions used to measure the dispersion, or spread, in a set of data. In Figure 11.1, the AVERAGE calculation shows that both departments have an average age of 40. But the AVEDEV calculation clearly highlights a wider spread in ages for Department B, the average deviation is 17 points from the mean (average).

> NUMBER N   Number N are the arguments, which can be cell references, arrays, or range names. You can have up to 30 arguments. Blank cells or cells containing text or logical values are ignored. Cells that contain a zero (0) are included in the AVEDEV calculation.

The equation for the AVEDEV function takes 1 divided by the number of values in a data set (n), then multiplies that by the result of the sum of the absolute value of each data point $(x_1, x_2,...,x_n)$ less the mean of the data set.

$$\frac{1}{n}\sum |x - \bar{x}|$$

Figure 11.1

AVEDEV is an indication of the dispersion or spread of the data points.

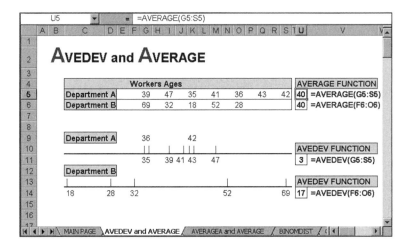

AVERAGE

AVERAGE returns the average (also known as *arithmetic mean*) of its arguments.

`=AVERAGE(number1,number2,...)`

AVERAGE is one of the most widely used functions by Excel users. It is calculated by taking the sum of the values in a data set and dividing by the number of values in the data set. Refer to Figures 11.1 and 11.2 for examples of the AVERAGE function.

NUMBER N You can specify up to 30 arguments for the AVERAGE function. The arguments can be cell references, arrays, or range names. Blank cells or cells containing text or logical values are ignored. Cells that contain a zero (0) are included in the Average calculation.

AVERAGEA

The AVERAGEA function calculates the average of the *values* in the list of arguments.

```
=AVERAGEA(value1,value2,...)
```

Similar to AVERAGE, the AVERAGEA function calculates the average of its arguments. The difference is that AVERAGEA does not ignore text or logical values (TRUE and FALSE). Text and FALSE are evaluated as zero (0) and TRUE is evaluated as one (1).

VALUE N Cells that contain a zero (0), text, or logical values are included in the AVERAGEA calculation. Arguments can be cell references, arrays, or range names. Blank cells are ignored. You can specify up to 30 arguments for the AVERAGEA function.

Figure 11.2
Text arguments like "new account" evaluate to zero and are factored into the *AVERAGEA* function.

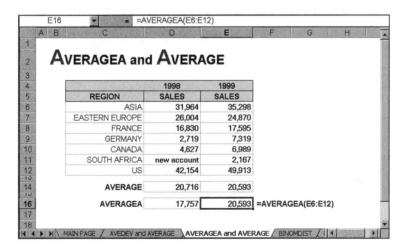

BETADIST

BETADIST returns the cumulative beta probability density function.

```
=BETADIST(x,alpha,beta,A,B)
```

X Is the value between A and B at which to evaluate the function, so that A<=X<=B.

ALPHA	Is a parameter to the distribution and must be a positive number.
BETA	Is a parameter to the distribution and must be a positive number.
A	Is an optional lower bound to the interval of x; is omitted, assumed to be zero (0).
B	Is an optional upper bound to the interval of x; if omitted, assumed to be one (1).

For example, =BETADIST(2,6,12,1,3) equals 0.9282684.

BETAINV

BETAINV returns the inverse of the cumulative beta probability density function.

=BETAINV(probability,alpha,beta,A,B)

The BETAINV function takes the probability you predict and returns the X value in the BETADIST function. So, if the probability is 0.9282684, then the BETAINV function returns 2.

PROBABILITY	Is the probability you predict or expect.
ALPHA	Is a parameter to the distribution and must be a positive number.
BETA	Is a parameter to the distribution and must be a positive number.
A	Is an optional lower bound to the interval of X; is omitted, assumed to be zero (0).
B	Is an optional upper bound to the interval of X; if omitted, assumed to be one (1).

For example, =BETAINV(0.9282684,6,12,1,3) equals 2.

BINOMDIST

BINOMDIST returns the individual term binomial distribution probability.

=BINOMDIST(number_s,trials,probability_s,cumulative)

The BINOMDIST function is used to find the probability that an outcome will occur x times in n performances of an experiment or trial. The trials are known as *Bernoulli trials*. The BINOMDIST function is used when:

- The number of trials (or tests) is fixed.
- Each repetition of the trial results in one of two possible outcomes—success or failure.
- The trials are independent and performed under identical conditions.
- Probability of success (denoted by p) is constant throughout the experiment.

NUMBER_S	Represents the number of successes in trials; must be a positive number but smaller than the number of trials.
TRIALS	Is the number of trials.
PROBABILITY_S	Is the probability of success on each trial; must be a positive number less than 1.

CUMULATIVE

Is a logical value that determines the form of the function. If TRUE, then BINDOMIST returns the cumulative distribution function (the probability that there are no more than number_s successes). If FALSE, then BINOMDIST returns the probability mass function (the probability that there are exactly the number_s successes).

The cumulative binomial distribution (when the cumulative argument is TRUE) is:

$$B(x;n,p) = \sum_{y=0}^{x} b(y;n,p)$$

The binomial probability mass function (when the cumulative argument is FALSE) is:

$$b(x;n,p) = \binom{n}{x} p^{x} (1-p)^{n-x}$$

where

$$\binom{n}{x}$$

is the COMBIN(n,x) mathematical function, described in Chapter 10, "Math and Trigonometry Functions." (1-p) is the probability of failure and is sometimes denoted by q.

Figure 11.3 shows an example of the BINOMDIST function used to calculate the probabilities that a manufactured piece of equipment will pass a safety test. When the cumulative argument is FALSE, the probability is about 1% that the safety test will be passed *exactly* 9 out of 10 trials. Using the TRUE cumulative argument, the probability is almost 100% that the safety test will be passed in 1 to 9 of the 10 trials.

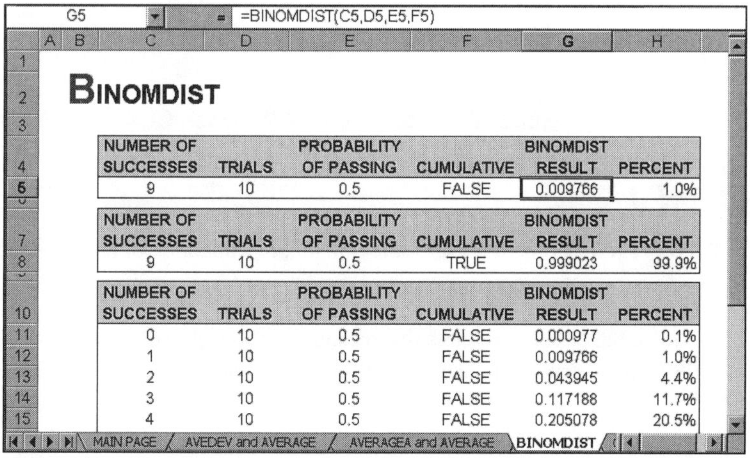

Figure 11.3
The Percent column displays the *BINOMDIST* results formatted as a percentage and rounded to one decimal place.

G5		=BINOMDIST(C5,D5,E5,F5)				
A B	C	D	E	F	G	H

BINOMDIST

NUMBER OF SUCCESSES	TRIALS	PROBABILITY OF PASSING	CUMULATIVE	BINOMDIST RESULT	PERCENT
9	10	0.5	FALSE	0.009766	1.0%

NUMBER OF SUCCESSES	TRIALS	PROBABILITY OF PASSING	CUMULATIVE	BINOMDIST RESULT	PERCENT
9	10	0.5	TRUE	0.999023	99.9%

NUMBER OF SUCCESSES	TRIALS	PROBABILITY OF PASSING	CUMULATIVE	BINOMDIST RESULT	PERCENT
0	10	0.5	FALSE	0.000977	0.1%
1	10	0.5	FALSE	0.009766	1.0%
2	10	0.5	FALSE	0.043945	4.4%
3	10	0.5	FALSE	0.117188	11.7%
4	10	0.5	FALSE	0.205078	20.5%

MAIN PAGE / AVEDEV and AVERAGE / AVERAGEA and AVERAGE \ BINOMDIST /

CHIDIST

CHIDIST returns the one-tailed probability of the chi-squared (X^2) distribution; the area in the right tail under the chi-squared distribution curve.

=CHIDIST(x,degrees_freedom)

The CHIDIST function is used in conjunction with the CHITEST function to perform hypothesis tests, including: experiments with more than two categories (goodness-of-fit tests or *multinomial experiments*); contingency tables (independence and homogeneity tests); and variance and standard deviation of a single population.

For example, an experiment might hypothesize that farmers who do not till the soil before planting a crop, will yield a larger harvest. By comparing the observed results with the expected ones, you can decide whether the hypothesis is valid.

X	Is the value at which you want to evaluate the distribution.
DEGREES FREEDOM	The degrees of freedom are typically the number of observations that can be chosen freely and is usually denoted by *df*.

Small degrees of freedom skew the distribution curve to the right. Large degrees of freedom skew the distribution curve to the left, making it more symmetrical like a normal distribution (bell-shaped curve). Figure 11.4 shows the results of several CHIDIST calculations using different values of X and degrees of freedom.

Figure 11.4
If the *CHITEST* result is more than the *CHIDIST* result, the hypothesis is typically rejected.

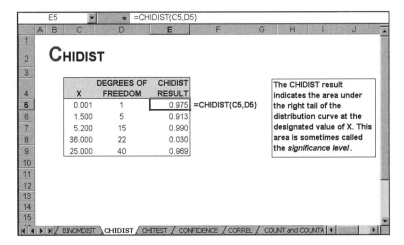

CHIINV

CHIINV returns the inverse of the one-tailed probability of the chi-squared (x^2) distribution.

=CHIINV(probability,degrees_freedom)

Where the CHIDIST returns the area under the right tail of the distribution curve, the CHIINV returns the remaining area under the distribution curve. The total area is 1.

PROBABILITY	Is the probability associated with the chi-squared (x^2) distribution.
DEGREES FREEDOM	The degrees of freedom are typically the number of observations that can be chosen freely and is usually denoted by *df*.

CHITEST

CHITEST returns the test for independence.

`=CHITEST(actual_range,expected_range)`

The CHITEST function is used with tables such as those shown in Figure 11.5. These tables are referred to as *contingency tables* or *cross-tabulation tables*. The tables show two characteristics—gender and opinion. The CHITEST function checks the independence of the characteristics, in other words that the option is or is not related to gender.

ACTUAL RANGE	Is the observed data.
EXPECTED RANGE	Is the ratio of the row and column totals to the grand total for the observed data.

Figure 11.5 shows the actual values and expected ratios. You need to calculate the expected ratios before you can perform the CHITEST. The actual range and expected range must have the same number of values. The expected ratios are calculated by multiplying the corresponding actual row and column totals and dividing by the actual grand total.

Figure 11.5
You need to calculate the expected ratios before you can perform the *CHITEST*.

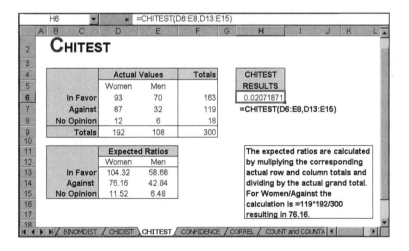

CONFIDENCE

CONFIDENCE returns the confidence interval for a population mean.

`=CONFIDENCE(alpha,standard_dev,size)`

The confidence interval is a range on either side of a sample mean, indicating the lowest (or earliest) and highest (or latest) values. Figure 11.6 shows the prices for efficiency apartments in various cities. After you calculate CONFIDENCE you subtract the result from the mean to get the low interval and add the result to the mean to get the high interval.

ALPHA Is the significance level used to determine the confidence level. The confidence level equals 1-alpha (shown as a percentage). If alpha (the significance level) is .1, then the confidence level is 90%. Typical confidence levels are 90%, 95%, and 99%.

STANDARD_DEV Is the standard deviation for the data set.

SIZE Is the the sample size.

Figure 11.6
Though not part of the
CONFIDENCE function,
you need to calculate
the mean, using the
AVERAGE function.

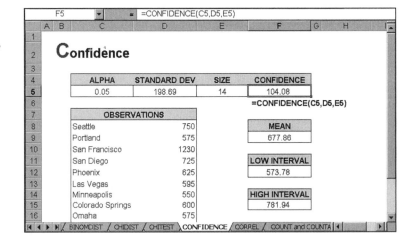

CORREL

CORREL returns the correlation coefficient between two data sets.

=CORREL(array1,array2)

The CORREL function is used to determine the relationship between two variables. For example, in Figure 11.7, the correlation between the monthly average temperature and the monthly average water usage (in gallons) is 0.954163749.

The value of the correlation coefficient always lies between –1 and +1. A correlation coefficient close to +1 indicates a positive correlation, as one variable increases, the other variable increases. A correlation coefficient close to –1 indicates a negative correlation, as one variable increases, the other variable decreases. A correlation coefficient close to zero (0) indicates there is little or no correlation between the variables.

ARRAY1 Is the first set of values; can be a cell range, range name, or array.

ARRAY2 Is the second set of values; can be a cell range, range name, or array.

N O T E The number of data points in each array must be the same. If array1 has 12 data points, array2 must also have 12 data points. ▪

The equation for the correlation coefficient is

$$\rho_{x,y} = \frac{Cov(X,Y)}{\sigma_x \cdot \sigma_y}$$

where

$$-1 \le \rho_{xy} \le 1$$

and

$$Cov(X,Y) = \frac{1}{n}\sum_{i=1}^{n}(x_i - \mu_x)(y_i - \mu_y)$$

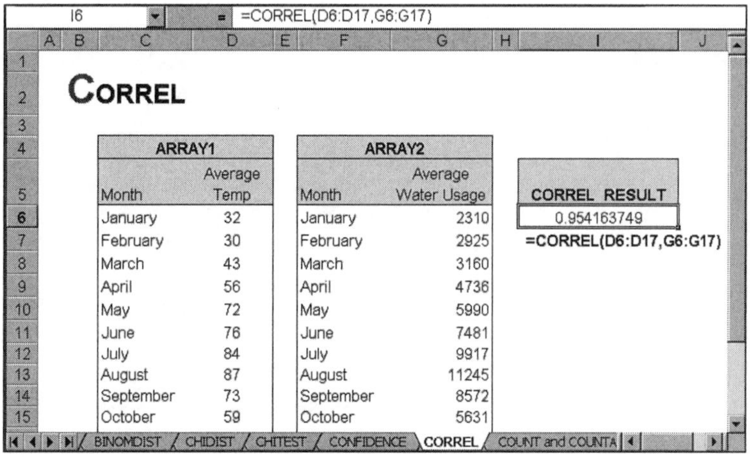

Figure 11.7
If the cells contain text, logical values, or are empty, they are ignored. Cells containing zero (0) are included in the *CORREL* calculation.

	I6			=CORREL(D6:D17,G6:G17)					
	A B	C	D	E F	G	H	I	J	

CORREL

	ARRAY1			ARRAY2			
		Average			Average		
Month		Temp	Month		Water Usage		CORREL RESULT
January		32	January		2310		0.954163749
February		30	February		2925		=CORREL(D6:D17,G6:G17)
March		43	March		3160		
April		56	April		4736		
May		72	May		5990		
June		76	June		7481		
July		84	July		9917		
August		87	August		11245		
September		73	September		8572		
October		59	October		5631		

BINOMDIST / CHIDIST / CHITEST / CONFIDENCE \ CORREL / COUNT and COUNTA

COUNT

COUNT counts the number of cells that contain *numbers* within the list of arguments.

=COUNT(value1,value2,...)

The COUNT function is used only to count the numerical entries in a range. Figure 11.8 shows a comparison between the COUNT and the COUNTA functions.

VALUE N   You can specify up to 30 arguments for the COUNT function. The arguments can be cell references, arrays, or range names. Blank cells or cells containing text are ignored. Cells that contain a zero (0) or dates are included in the COUNT calculation.

Figure 11.8
Numbers with symbols are treated as text by Excel and are therefore not included in the *COUNT* function calculation.

❶ Treated as text by Excel

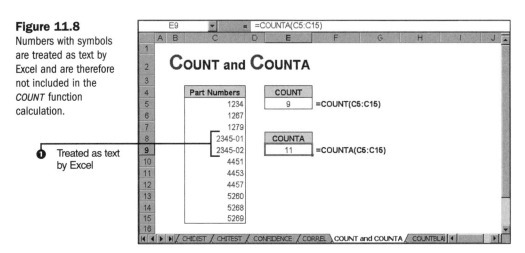

COUNTA

COUNTA counts the number of cells that are not empty.

`=COUNTA(value1,value2,...)`

Use the COUNTA function to count the number of cells in a range that contain text, numbers, or a combination of text and numbers. Although you can use COUNTA to generate the number of clients or employees in a list, it counts each entry, not unique entries.

TIP To count unique entries, combine the SUM and the COUNTIF functions. For example, if the range to be counted is C6:C46, the formula would be:

`=SUM(1/COUNTIF(C6:C46,C6:C46))`

You must array-enter the formula (using Ctrl+Shift+Enter) for this formula to count properly.

Refer to Figure 11.8 for a comparison between the COUNT and the COUNTA functions.

VALUE N   You can specify up to 30 arguments for the COUNTA function. The arguments can be cell references, arrays, or range names. Blank cells are ignored. All other cells are counted.

COUNTBLANK

COUNTBLANK counts the empty cells in a specified range.

`=COUNTBLANK(range)`

RANGE   Is the range to be counted.

In the COUNTBLANK function shown in Figure 11.9, any cells that are blank or formula that return "" (empty text) as the formula results are counted.

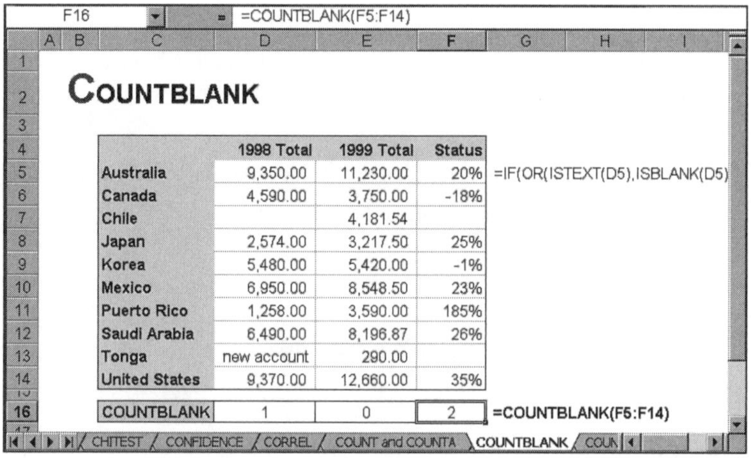

Figure 11.9

An *IF* function is used to avoid displaying an error message when a blank or text value is found in the 1998 column.

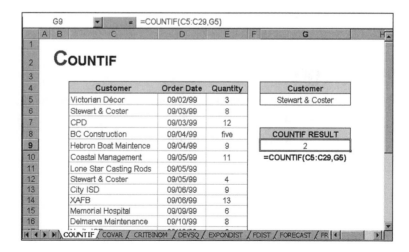

COUNTIF

COUNTIF counts the number of cells in a range that meet a given criteria.

=COUNTIF(range,criteria)

Use COUNTIF when you only want to count part of a range, as shown in Figure 11.10.

RANGE   Is the range to be counted.

CRITERIA   Is the criteria you want to evaluate; can be a number (14), a cell reference (G5), an expression (E5>10), or text ("Victorian Décor").

Figure 11.10

Use cells to store values (such as that shown in G5) to make your worksheets more flexible.

COVAR

COVAR returns covariance, the average of the products of deviations for each data point pair.

```
=COVAR(array1,array2)
```

The COVAR function is used to determine if a relationship exists between two data sets. The range of covariance is from –1 to +1. The data values must be integers. Figure 11.11 shows an example of the COVAR function.

ARRAY1 Is the first set of values; can be a cell range, range name, or array.

ARRAY2 Is the second set of values; can be a cell range, range name, or array.

The equation for the covariance is

$$Cov(X,Y) = \frac{1}{n}\sum_{i-1}^{n}(x_i - \mu_x)(y_i - \mu_y)$$

Figure 11.11
If the data set contains text, logical values, or blank cells, those cells are ignored. Cells that contain a zero (0) are included in the COVAR calculation.

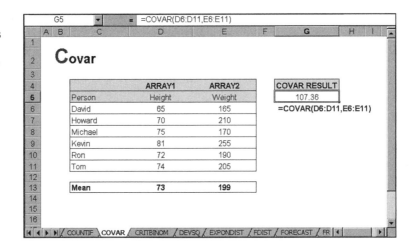

CRITBINOM

CRITBINOM returns the smallest value for which the cumulative binomial distribution is greater than or equal to a criterion value (*alpha*).

```
=CRITBINOM(trials,probability_s,alpha)
```

CRITBINOM is the probability that there are no more than a specified number of successes in the trial. This function is frequently used for quality assurance evaluations. For example, what is the largest number of defective products in a batch that is acceptable; more than that number and the batch is rejected. Figure 11.12 shows an example of this function.

TRIALS   Is the number of trials.

PROBABILITY_S   Is the probability of success on each trial; must be a positive number less than 1.

ALPHA   Is the criterion value that the cumulative binomial distribution must be below.

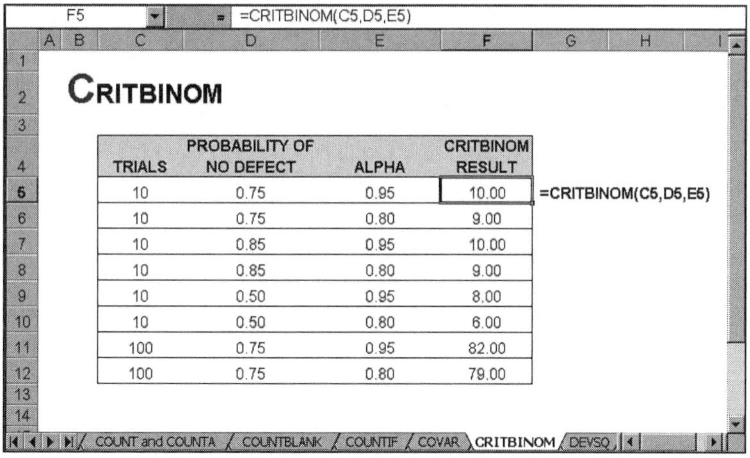

Figure 11.12
Increasing the probability while keeping the alpha unchanged has no impact on the *CRITBINOM* function result.

	TRIALS	PROBABILITY OF NO DEFECT	ALPHA	CRITBINOM RESULT	
5	10	0.75	0.95	10.00	=CRITBINOM(C5,D5,E5)
6	10	0.75	0.80	9.00	
7	10	0.85	0.95	10.00	
8	10	0.85	0.80	9.00	
9	10	0.50	0.95	8.00	
10	10	0.50	0.80	6.00	
11	100	0.75	0.95	82.00	
12	100	0.75	0.80	79.00	

DEVSQ

DEVSQ returns the sum of squares of deviations of a data set from their sample mean.

=DEVSQ(number1,number2,...)

The sum of the deviations is always equal to zero. Squaring the deviations, then summing them, enables you to calculate variance and standard deviation. The DEVSQ function calculates the deviations, the square of each deviation, and mean before returning the sum of the squares. These were included in Figure 11.13 only for illustration purposes.

NUMBER N   You can specify up to 30 arguments for the DEVSQ function. Arguments can be cell references, arrays, or range names. Blank cells or cells that contain a text, or logical values are ignored. Cells containing zero (0) are included in the calculation.

Figure 11.13
Manually calculating
the sum of the
squared deviations
yields the same result
as the *DEVSQ* function.

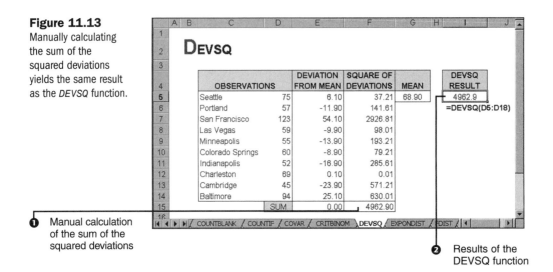

❶ Manual calculation
of the sum of the
squared deviations

❷ Results of the
DEVSQ function

EXPONDIST

EXPONDIST returns the exponential distribution.

=EXPONDIST(x,lambda,cumulative)

The exponential probability distribution deals with the lapse of time between two successive occurrences, when the average number of occurrences per unit of time is known. Figure 11.14 shows an example of this function.

X	Is the value of the function.
LAMBDA (λ)	Is the parameter value.
CUMULATIVE	Is a logical value that indicates which form of the exponential function to provide. If TRUE, then EXPONDIST returns the cumulative distribution function. If FALSE, then EXPONDIST returns the probability density function.

The formula for the probability density function is

$$f(x; \lambda) = \lambda e^{-\lambda x}$$

The formula for the cumulative distribution function is

$$F(x; \lambda) = 1 - e^{-\lambda x}$$

Figure 11.14
The cumulative argument dictates which formula is used to calculate *EXPONDIST*.

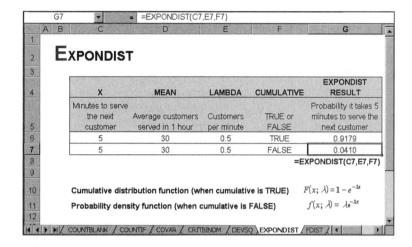

FDIST

FDIST returns the F probability distribution.

```
=FDIST(x,degrees_freedom1,degrees_freedom2)
```

The FDIST function is used for analysis of variance, that is to determine if two data sets have different degrees of diversity. This function returns the one-tailed probability of the FDIST distribution. Figure 11.15 shows an example where the FDIST is approximately .025, the area in the right tail under the FDIST distribution curve. This is the *significance level*. The significance level represents the probability of rejecting the statement you assume is true (the null hypothesis). In this case that probability is 2.5%.

X	Is the value at which to evaluate the function; must be a non-negative number.
DEGREES FREEDOM1	Is the numerator of freedom.
DEGREES FREEDOM2	Is the denominator of freedom.

Figure 11.15
FDIST returns the probability of rejecting the statement you assume is true.

H5 =FDIST(G5,D13,E13)

FDIST

College Entrance Scores	Juniors	Seniors
	1500	1350
	1290	1100
	920	1440
	1360	940
	1480	1270
		1210
		1050
Sample Size	5	7
Degrees of Freedom	4	6

X	FDIST
6.23	0.02497

=FDIST(G5,D13,E13)

Degrees of Freedom are typically calculated as the sample size minus one.

FINV

FINV returns the inverse of the F probability distribution.

`=FINV(probability,degrees_freedom1,degrees_freedom2)`

The FINV function is when you know the significance level you want to achieve and need to generate *x*. An example of an FINV function is `=FINV(.025,4,6)` which results in 6.23.

PROBABILITY	Is the probability associated with the F cumulative distribution—the significance level.
DEGREES FREEDOM1	Is the numerator of freedom.
DEGREES FREEDOM2	Is the denominator of freedom.

FINV uses an iterative technique for calculating the function. The default maximum number of iterations is 100. If a result is not reached within those iterations, the #N/A value is returned. You can change the number of iterations under Tools, Options, Calculation tab.

FISHER

FISHER returns the Fisher transformation at *x*.

`=FISHER(x)`

The FISHER function is used to perform hypothesis testing on the correlation coefficient. An example of a FISHER function is `=FISHER(.95)` which results in `1.831780823`.

X   Is the numeric value for which you want the transformation; must be between −1 and +1.

The equation for the Fisher transformation is

$$z' = \frac{1}{2}\ln\left(\frac{1+x}{1-x}\right)$$

FISHERINV

FISHERINV returns the inverse of the Fisher transformation.

`=FISHERINV(y)`

Use this transformation when analyzing correlations between ranges or arrays of data. If y=FISHER(x), then FISHERINV(y)=x. An example of a FISHERINV function is `=FISHERINV(1.5)`, which results in `0.905148254`.

Y   Is the value for which you want to perform the inverse of the transformation.

The equation for the FISHERINV transformation is

$$x = \frac{e^{2y} - 1}{e^{2y} + 1}$$

FORECAST

FORECAST calculates or predicts a future value by using existing values.

=FORECAST(x,known_y's,known_x's)

Use the FORECAST function when you want to predict a value based on the trend of the existing or known data. Figure 11.16 shows a forecast for the next year, based on sales from the past three years.

X	The data point of the value you want to predict.
KNOWN_Y'S	The known values for the known data points; the dependent variable.
KNOWN_X'S	The known data points—typically increments of time (years, quarters, months); the independent variable.

Figure 11.16

FORECAST can only predict one future value. See the TREND function to predict more than one value.

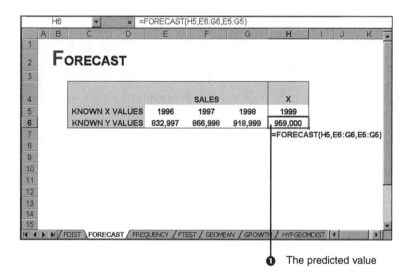

● The predicted value

FREQUENCY

FREQUENCY calculates how often values occur within a range of values, and then returns a vertical array of numbers.

=FREQUENCY(data_array,bins_array)

Figure 11.17 shows the FREQUENCY function used to count how the number of test scores that fall within ranges of scores. Because this function returns an array:

- The result range must be selected *before* you begin the function.
- The function must be *array entered* by using Ctrl+Shift+Enter, instead of just pressing Enter.

The data_array is the list of student scores. The bins_array is the list of max scores (G5:G9). Because this function always returns one more element than the number of elements in the bins_array, the range selected for the frequencies is H5:H10.

| DATA_ARRAY | Is the array of values for which you want to count frequencies (the test scores in Figure 11.17). |
| BINS_ARRAY | Is the array of intervals into which you want to group the values in the data_array. |

Figure 11.17
The range name Scores is used here to identify the *data_array*.

❷ bins_array

❶ data_array

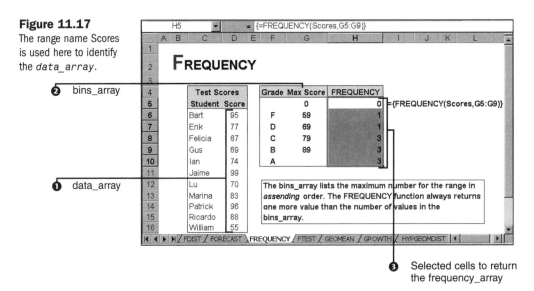

❸ Selected cells to return the frequency_array

FTEST

FTEST returns the result of an *F*-test.

```
=FTEST(array1,array2)
```

This function is used to compare the variances in two data sets. Specifically, it returns the one-tailed probability that the variances are not significantly different. Figure 11.18 shows an example of this function.

| ARRAY1 | Is the first data set. |
| ARRAY2 | Is the second data set. |

Data sets that contain text, logical values, or empty cells are ignored. However, if the data set contains a zero, that value is included in the calculation.

Figure 11.18
The *FTEST* function calculates the probability that the variances in the two data sets are not significantly different.

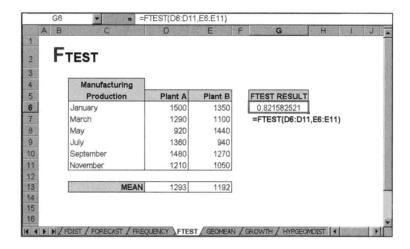

GAMMADIST

GAMMADIST returns the gamma distribution.

=GAMMADIST(x,alpha,beta,cumulative)

The GAMMADIST function is used to study variables that have a skewed distribution. For example, GAMMADIST(12,7,3,FALSE) results in 0.034731878 and GAMMADIST(12,7,3,TRUE) results in 0.110673977.

X	Is the value at which you want to evaluate the distribution; must be greater than zero (0).
ALPHA	A parameter to the distribution.
BETA	A parameter to the distribution. If beta equals one, the standard gamma distribution is returned.
CUMULATIVE	Is a logical value that determines the form of the function. If TRUE, the cumulative distribution function is returned. If FALSE, the probability mass function is returned.

The equation for the gamma distribution is

$$f(x; \alpha, \beta) = \frac{1}{\beta^\alpha \Gamma(\alpha)} x^{\alpha-1} e^{-\frac{x}{\beta}}$$

The equation for the standard gamma distribution is

$$f(x; \alpha) = \frac{x^{\alpha-1} e^{-x}}{\Gamma(\alpha)}$$

GAMMAINV

GAMMAINV returns the inverse of the gamma cumulative distribution.

=GAMMAINV(probability,alpha,beta)

The GAMMADIST function generates a probability p=GAMMADIST(x,...). The GAMMAINV function takes a probability as one of its arguments and generates x—GAMMAINV(p,...)=x. So that GAMMAINV(0. 110673977,7,3) results in 12 (when cumulative is TRUE in the GAMMADIST function).

PROBABILITY	Is the probability associated with the gamma distribution.
ALPHA	A parameter to the distribution.
BETA	A parameter to the distribution. If beta equals one, the standard gamma distribution is returned.

GAMMALN

GAMMALN returns the natural logarithm of the gamma function.

=GAMMALN(x)

For example if x=6, GAMMALN(6)=4.787491743.

X	Is the value for which you want to calculate the GAMMALN; must be a positive number.

GEOMEAN

GEOMEAN returns the geometric mean of an array or range of positive data.

=GEOMEAN(number1,number2,...)

Use the GEOMEAN when you want to calculate the average growth rate of compound interest, assuming variable interest rates. Figure 11.19 shows an example.

NUMBER N	Up to 30 arguments can be specified, including cell references or an array.

The equation for the geometric mean is

$$GM_{\bar{y}} = \sqrt[n]{y_1 y_2 y_3 \cdots y_n}$$

Figure 11.19
The *GEOMEAN* is not the same as the arithmetic mean *(AVERAGE)*.

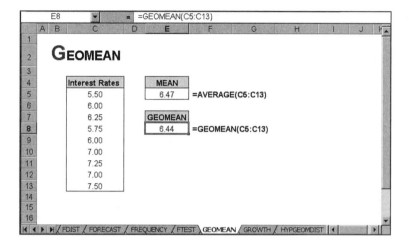

GROWTH

GROWTH calculates predicted exponential growth by using existing data.

=GROWTH(known_y's,known_x's,new_x's,const)

Using an existing data set of values and increments, and supplying a new set of increments, the GROWTH function generates the predicted set of corresponding values (the new y values). In Figure 11.20, the exponential growth values (the predicted y values) have been calculated. The known_y and known_x values are based on the formula y=b*m^x. A set of new y values is predicted for the entire time increment, not just for the additional time increments you specify. Because these new y values are based on the growth equation (and not on the known y values), the first three y values predicted do not match the known y values for the same increment.

KNOWN_Y'S	The known values for the known data points; the dependent variable. Each value must be a positive number.
KNOWN_X'S	The known data points—typically increments of time (years, quarters, months); the independent variable. An optional argument. If omitted assumed to be the array {1,2,3...}, the same size as the known_y's.
NEW_X'S	The data points of those values you want to predict. An optional argument. If omitted assumed to be the same as the known_x's.
CONST	TRUE or FALSE indicating whether the slope (b) is = 1 (FALSE) or not (TRUE).

Because this function returns an array:

- The result range must be selected *before* you begin the function.
- The formula must be *array entered* by using Ctrl+Shift+Enter, instead of just Enter.

Figure 11.20
You must select the range where the results are to appear before you begin the *GROWTH* function.

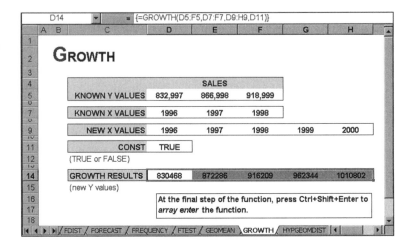

HARMEAN

HARMEAN returns the harmonic mean of a data set.

=HARMEAN(number1,number2,...)

The harmonic mean is the reciprocal of the arithmetic mean of reciprocals. The harmonic mean is always less than the geometric mean and arithmetic mean.

NUMBER N   Up to 30 arguments can be specified, including cell references or an array. Each number in the data set must be positive.

The equation for the harmonic mean is

$$\frac{1}{H_{y'}} = \frac{1}{n}\sum\frac{1}{Y_j}$$

If the data set is {5.50,6.00,6.25,5.75,6.00,7.00,7.25,7.00,7.5} the

arithmetic mean is 6.47.

geometric mean is 6.44.

harmonic mean is 6.40.

HYPGEOMDIST

HYPGEOMDIST returns the hypergeometric distribution.

=HYPERGEOMDIST(sample_s,number_sample,population_s,number_population)

The HYPGEOMDIST function returns the probability of a given number of sample successes, and is used when the population size is finite. Each observation is either a success or failure. Figure 11.21 shows an example of the HYPGEOMDIST function.

SAMPLE_S	Is the number of successes in the sample; s in the equation.
NUMBER_S	Is the size of the sample; n in the equation.
POPULATION_S	Is the number of successes in the population; M in the equation.
NUMBER_POPULATION	Is the population size; N in the equation.

The equation for the hypergeometric distribution function is

$$P(X = x) = h(x; n, M, N) = \frac{\binom{M}{x}\binom{N-M}{n-x}}{\binom{N}{n}}$$

Figure 11.21
The result in this *HYPGEOMDIST* example is a 30% probability that one of the cards is an Ace.

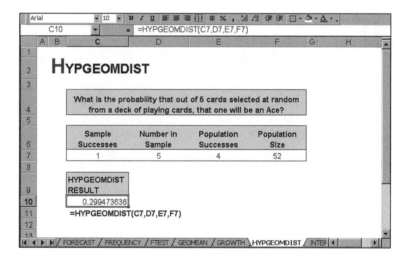

INTERCEPT

INTERCEPT calculates the point at which a line will intersect the y-axis by using existing x-values and y-values.

`=INTERCEPT(known_y's,known_x's)`

The INTERCEPT function will tell you the value of y when x is zero. Figure 11.22 shows an example.

KNOWN_Y'S	The known values for the known data points; the dependent variable.
KNOWN_X'S	The known data points. If increments of time (years, quarters, months), convert or substitute consecutive integers. The independent variable.

Figure 11.22
Use the Chart Wizard to plot the known values on a line chart.

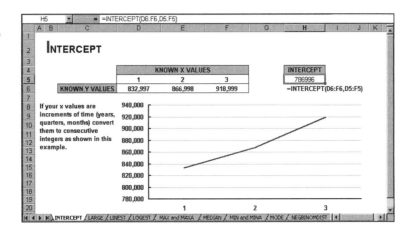

KURT

KURT returns the Kurtosis of a data set.

=KURT(number1,number2,...)

Kurtosis characterizes the relative peakedness or flatness of a distribution compared to the normal distribution. When the Kurtosis is positive, the distribution is relatively peaked. When the Kurtosis is negative, the distribution is relatively flat.

NUMBER N   The arguments (up to 30 argument), including cell references, range names, or arrays. More than four data points are required for the KURT function to calculate a result.

The calculation KURT(1,3,7,2,3,9,2,4) returns 0.384769378 and KURT (2,4,3,5,1,2,3,4) returns –0.7. The equation for KURT is

$$\left\{ \frac{n(n+1)}{(n-1)(n-2)(n-3)} \sum \left(\frac{x_j - \bar{x}}{s} \right)^4 \right\} - \frac{3(n-1)^2}{(n-2)(n-3)}$$

LARGE

LARGE returns the k-th largest value in a data set.

=LARGE(array,k)

The LARGE function is used to retrieve a value based on its standing or rank in the data set. Figure 11.23 shows an example of the LARGE function returning the third largest number from the list.

ARRAY   Is the range of data from which you want to return the k-th largest value.

K   Is the position (from the largest) of the data point you want to return.

Figure 11.23

LARGE returns the position of the specified largest value in the data set. To return the corresponding state, use the *VLOOKUP* function. To return the smallest value, use the *SMALL* function.

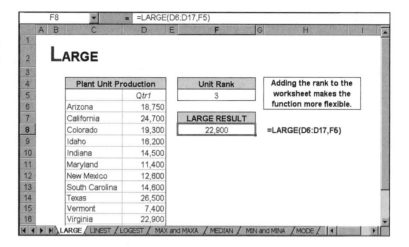

LINEST

LINEST calculates a straight line that best fits your data, using the "least squares" method.

`=LINEST(known_y's,known_x's,const,stats)`

The LINEST function uses the equation

`y = mx + b`

If there are multiple ranges of x values the equation is

`y = m1x1 + m2x2 + ... + b`

Because the result is an array, the formula must be *array entered* by using Ctrl+Shift+Enter, instead of just pressing Enter (see Figure 11.24).

KNOWN_Y'S	The known values for the known data points; the dependent variable.
KNOWN_X'S	The known data points. The independent variable. An optional argument. If omitted assumed to be the array {1,2,3...} the same size as the known_y's.
CONST	TRUE or FALSE indicating whether the y-intercept (b) is = 0 (FALSE) or not (TRUE).
STATS	If stats is TRUE, LINEST returns the additional regression statistics, so the returned array is {mn,mn-1,...,m1,b; sen,sen-1,...,se1,seb; r2,sey; F,df; ssreg,ssresid}. If stats is FALSE or omitted, LINEST returns only the m-coefficient and the constant b.(See Table 11.1.)

N O T E **Before you start the function** If stats will be FALSE, select a range of cells one cell high and two cells wide (as in this example). If stats will be TRUE, select a range of cells five cells high and two cells wide. ■

Figure 11.24

The *LINEST* results in both the slope (M) of the straight line and y-intercept (b) that fits the data.

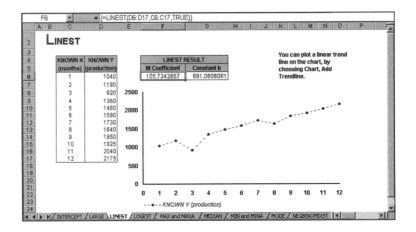

Table 11.1 Regression Statistics Returned When STATS Argument Is TRUE

Statistic	Description
$se_1, se_2, ..., se_n$	The standard error values for the coefficients $m_1, m_2, ..., m_n$.
se_b	The standard error value for the constant b (se_b = #N/A when const is FALSE).
r^2	The coefficient of determination. Compares estimated and actual y-values, and ranges in value from 0 to 1. The closer r^2 is to 1, the more correlation there is between the estimated y-value and the actual y-value. If r^2 is 0, the regression equation is not helpful in predicting a y-value.
se_y	The standard error for the y estimate.
F	The F statistic, or the F-observed value. Use the F statistic to determine whether the observed relationship between the dependent (y) and independent (x) variables occurs by chance.
df	The degrees of freedom. Use the degrees of freedom to help you find F-critical values in a statistical table. Compare the values you find in the table to the F statistic returned by LINEST to determine a confidence level for the model.
ss_{reg}	The regression sum of squares.
ss_{resid}	The residual sum of squares.

LOGEST

LOGEST calculates an exponential curve that fits your data and returns an array of values that describes the curve.

```
=LOGEST(known_y's,known_x's,const,stats)
```

The LOGEST function is used in regression analysis. The equation for the curve is y=b*m^x. Because the result is an array, the formula must be *array entered* by using Ctrl+Shift+Enter, instead of just Enter. Figure 11.25 shows an example of LOGEST.

KNOWN_Y'S   The known values for the known data points; the dependent variable.

KNOWN_X'S   The known data points. If omitted assumed to be the array {1,2,3...} the same size as the known_y's.

CONST   TRUE or FALSE indicating whether to force b to be = 1 (FALSE) or not (TRUE). When TRUE or omitted, b is calculated normally.

STATS   If stats is TRUE, LOGEST returns the additional regression statistics. If stats is FALSE or omitted, LOGEST returns only the M coefficient and the Constant b.

Figure 11.25
The *LOGEST* function returns values that describe the existing curve. Use the *GROWYH* function to predict future values on the curve.

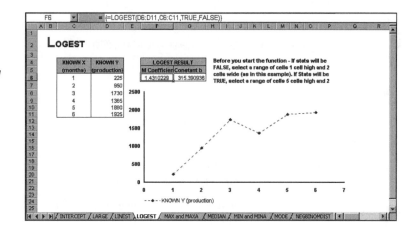

LOGINV

LOGINV returns the inverse of the LOGNORMDIST (lognormal cumulative distribution) function of x, where *ln(x)* is normally distributed with parameters mean and standard deviation.

=LOGINV(probability,mean,standard_dev)

The LOGNORMDIST function generates a probability p=LOGNORMDIST(x,...). The LOGINV function takes a probability as on of its arguments and generates x—LOGINV(p,...)=x. So that LOGINV(0.044534344,4.5,1.7) results in 5.

PROBABILITY   Is the probability associated with the lognormal distribution.

MEAN   Is the mean of the x.

STANDARD_DEV   Is the standard deviation of x.

The equation for LOGINV is

$$LOGINV(p,\mu,\sigma) = e^{[\mu+\sigma\times[NORMSINV(p)]]}$$

LOGNORMDIST

LOGNORMDIST returns the cumulative lognormal distribution of *x*, where *ln(x)* is normally distributed with parameters mean and standard deviation.

`=LOGNORMDIST(x,mean,standard_dev)`

The LOGNORMDIST function is used to analyze logarithmically transformed data. For example, LOGNORMDIST(5,4.5,1.7) equals 0.044534344.

X	Is the value at which to evaluate the function.
MEAN	Is the mean of the logarithm of *x*, *ln(x)*.
STANDARD_DEV	Is the standard deviation of the logarithm of *x*, *ln(x)*.

The equation for LOGNORMDIST is

$$\text{LOGNORMDIST}(x,\mu,\sigma) = \text{NORMSDIST}\left(\frac{\ln(x)-\mu}{\sigma}\right)$$

MAX

MAX returns the largest value in a set of values.

`=MAX(number1,number2,...)`

Use the MAX function to display the largest sales figure, production throughput, score, and so on, in a group of values. Figure 11.26 shows an example of the MAX function.

NUMBER N	Is the cell reference(s), range name, or array that makes up the data set. Up to 30 unique arguments (data sets) can be specified.

Figure 11.26

While the *MAX* function evaluates cells containing numerical data, you can use *MAXA* when you need to evaluate data containing text or logical values.

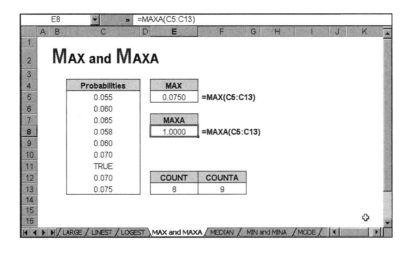

MAXA

MAXA returns the largest value in a list of arguments.

=MAXA(value1,value2,...)

The MAXA function differs from the MAX function in that it will also evaluate logical values such as TRUE and FALSE. TRUE evaluates to one (1); FALSE evaluates to zero (0). Arguments that contain text also evaluate to zero. Refer to Figure 11.26 for a comparison on MAX and MAXA.

VALUE N   Is the cell reference(s), range name, text representations of numbers, array, or logical values that makes up the data set. Up to 30 arguments (unique data sets) can be specified. Text values in an array argument are ignored.

MEDIAN

MEDIAN returns the median of the given numbers.

=MEDIAN(number1,number2,...)

The median is the number in the middle of the set of numbers, as opposed to the mean, which is the average of the set of numbers. When the data set contains an odd number of values, the value in the middle is returned (as shown in Figure 11.27). When the data set contains an even number of values, the middle two values are averaged to determine the median.

NUMBER N   Is the cell reference(s), range name, or array that makes up the data set. Up to 30 arguments (unique data sets) can be specified.

Figure 11.27

The *MEDIAN* function does not average the entire set of numbers, but simply returns the middle number in the set or the average of the two middle numbers (if the data set contains an even number of values).

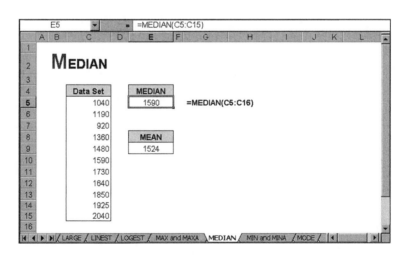

MIN

MIN returns the smallest number in a set of values.=MIN(number1,number2,...)

Use the MIN function to display the smallest sales figure, loss due to shrink, employee absentee rate, and so on, in a group of values. Figure 11.28 shows an example of the MIN function.

NUMBER N   Is the cell reference(s), range name, or array that makes up the data set. Up to 30 arguments (unique data sets) can be specified.

Figure 11.28
While the *MIN* function evaluates cells containing numerical data, use *MINA* when you need to evaluate data containing text or logical values.

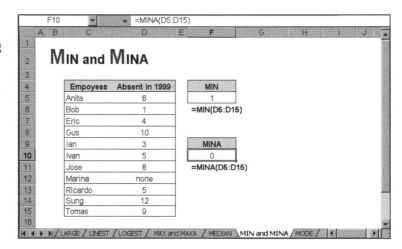

MINA

MINA returns the smallest value in a list of arguments.

=MINA(value1,value2,...)

The MINA function differs from the MIN function in that it will also evaluate logical values such as TRUE and FALSE. TRUE evaluates to one (1); FALSE evaluates to zero (0). Arguments that contain text also evaluate to zero. Refer to Figure 11.28 for a comparison of MIN and MINA.

VALUE N   Is the cell reference(s), range name, text representations of numbers, array, or logical values that makes up the data set. Up to 30 arguments (unique data sets) can be specified. Text values in an array argument are ignored.

MODE

MODE returns the most frequently occurring, or repetitive, value in an array or range of data.

=MODE(number1,number2,...)

Use MODE function when you need to know which value occurs most frequently in a data set. If each value is unique, there is no mode and the error #NA is returned. If two or more values occur with the same frequency, Excel returns the item with the smallest value regardless of the order in which it encounters the values in the data set. Figure 11.29 shows an example of MODE.

NUMBER N   Is the cell reference(s), range name, or array that makes up the data set. Up to 30 arguments (unique data sets) can be specified.

Figure 11.29

MODE does not return all values when more than one value occurs the same number of times.

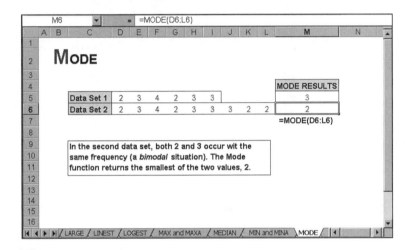

NEGBINOMDIST

NEGBINOMDIST returns the negative binomial distribution.

=NEGBINOMDIST(number_f,number_s,probability_s)

The NEGBINOMDIST returns the probability that there will be number_f failures before the number_s-th success, when the constant probability of a success is probability_s. With this function, the number of successes is fixed and the number of trials is variable (see Figure 11.30).

NUMBER_F   Is the number of failures.

NUMBER_S   Is the threshold number of successes.

PROBABILITY_S   Is the probability of success.

The equation for NEGBINOMDIST is

$$nb(x; r, p) = \binom{x + r - 1}{r - 1} p^r (1 - p)^x$$

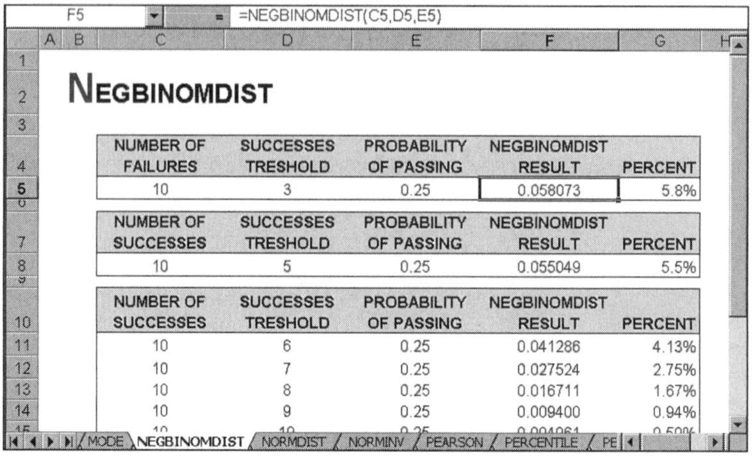

NUMBER OF FAILURES	SUCCESSES TRESHOLD	PROBABILITY OF PASSING	NEGBINOMDIST RESULT	PERCENT
10	3	0.25	0.058073	5.8%

NUMBER OF SUCCESSES	SUCCESSES TRESHOLD	PROBABILITY OF PASSING	NEGBINOMDIST RESULT	PERCENT
10	5	0.25	0.055049	5.5%

NUMBER OF SUCCESSES	SUCCESSES TRESHOLD	PROBABILITY OF PASSING	NEGBINOMDIST RESULT	PERCENT
10	6	0.25	0.041286	4.13%
10	7	0.25	0.027524	2.75%
10	8	0.25	0.016711	1.67%
10	9	0.25	0.009400	0.94%

Figure 11.30
While the *NEGBINOMDIST* returns failures, see the *BINOMDIST* function for testing successes.

NORMDIST

`NORMDIST` returns the normal cumulative distribution for the specified mean and standard deviation.

```
=NORMDIST(x,mean,standard_dev,cumulative)
```

The `NORMDIST` function is frequently used in statistics and hypothesis testing. There is also the *standard* normal distribution function (`NORMSDIST`) discussed later in this chapter. In Figure 11.31 the mean and standard deviation have been calculated for the data set, and are then fed into the `NORMDIST` function.

`X`	Is the value for which you want the distribution.
`MEAN`	Is the arithmetic mean of the distribution.
`STANDARD_DEV`	Is the standard deviation of the distribution.
`CUMULATIVE`	Is a logical value that determines the form of the function. If TRUE, the cumulative distribution is returned. If FALSE, the probability mass function is returned.

Figure 11.31
This figure shows the results (the cumulative distribution) when the cumulative argument is TRUE. Change the cumulative argument to FALSE to see the probability mass function.

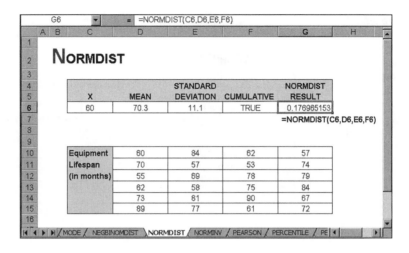

NORMINV

NORMINV returns the inverse of the normal cumulative distribution for the specified mean and standard deviation.

`=NORMINV(probability,mean,standard_dev)`

The NORMDIST function returns a probability, the NORMINV function returns x, the value that corresponds to the given probability, mean, and standard deviation. There is also an inverse for the *standard* normal distribution function (NORMSINV) discussed later in this chapter. NORMINV uses an iterative technique for calculating the function. The default maximum number of iterations is 100. If a result is not reached within those iterations, the #N/A value is returned. You can change the number of iterations under Tools, Options, Calculation tab.

Figure 11.32 shows an example of the NORMINV function.

PROBABILITY   Is the probability corresponding to the normal distribution.

MEAN   Is the arithmetic mean of the distribution.

STANDARD_DEV   Is the standard deviation of the distribution.

Figure 11.32
The *NORMINV* function returns the inverse of the normal cumulative distribution. You can see the inverse of the standard normal distribution function by using the *NORMSINV* function.

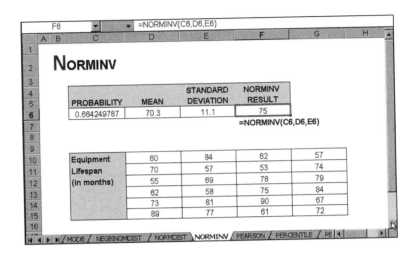

NORMSDIST

NORMSDIST returns the standard normal cumulative distribution function.

`=NORMSDIST(z)`

The standard distribution always has a mean of zero (0) and a standard deviation of one (1). This function is used in lieu of the statistical tables published for standard normal curves. If z (the value of the continuous random variable) is .6, then NORMSDIST(.6)= 0.725746935.

   z   Is the value for which you want the distribution.

NORMSINV

NORMSINV returns the inverse of the standard normal cumulative distribution.

`=NORMSINV(probability)`

Given the probability, the NORMSINV function returns the x value for that probability. If the probability is 0.815939908, then NORMSINV(0.815939908) returns 0.9.

   PROBABILITY   Is the probability corresponding to the normal distribution.

PEARSON

PEARSON returns the Pearson product moment correlation coefficient, *r*, a dimensionless index that ranges from –1.0 to 1.0 inclusive and reflects the extent of a linear relationship between two data sets.

`=PEARSON(array1,array2)`

The PEARSON function is illustrated in Figure 11.33.

ARRAY1   A set of independent values; can be cell references, range names, or arrays.

ARRAY2   A set of dependent values; can be cell references, range names, or arrays.

The equation for PEARSON is

$$r = \frac{n(\Sigma XY) - (\Sigma X)(\Sigma Y)}{\sqrt{\left[n\Sigma X^2 - (\Sigma X)^2\right]\left[n\Sigma Y^2 - (\Sigma Y)^2\right]}}$$

Figure 11.33
When using the *PEARSON* function, the arrays must have the same number of data points.

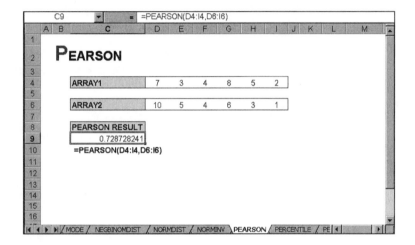

PERCENTILE

PERCENTILE returns the *k*-th percentile of values in a range.

=PERCENTILE(array,k)

The PERCENTILE function is used to a threshold of acceptance. In Figure 11.34, for example, the price earning ratios of 12 companies is given. To find the value of the seventieth percentile (the k value), the result is 28.3.

ARRAY   Is the data set that defines relative standing.

K   Is the percentile value between 0 and 1.

Figure 11.34

Use the *PERCENTILE* function to set a threshold of acceptance or rejection.

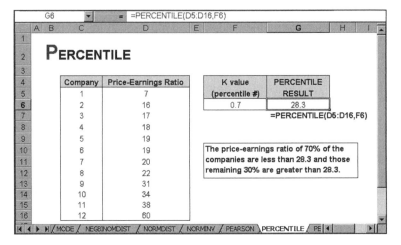

PERCENTRANK

PERCENTRANK returns the rank of a value in a data set as a percentage of the data set.

```
=PERCENTRANK(array,x,significance)
```

This function returns the percentage of values in the data set that are smaller than *x*—the relative standing of an observation in a data set. Figure 11.35 shows an example of this calculation.

ARRAY	Is the data set with numeric values that defines relative standing.
X	Is the value for which you want to know the rank.
SIGNIFICANCE	An optional value that identifies the number of significant digits for the percentage value that is returned. If omitted, three (3) digits are returned.

Figure 11.35

Use the *PERCENTRANK* function to determine the percentage for the value in which you are looking.

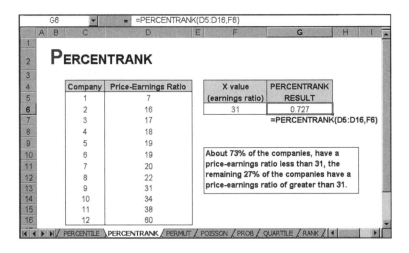

PERMUT

PERMUT returns the number of permutations for a given number of objects that can be selected from a range of numbers.

```
=PERMUT(number,number_chosen)
```

Permutations are not the same as combinations. With a combination, the numbers 1 2 3 is the same as 3 2 1, 1 3 2, 2 3 1, and so on; permutations sees each of these as distinct outcomes. For example, the PERMUT function will tell you how many different ways these numbers can appear if you select 3 numbers from 1 to 3. Figure 11.36 shows the result.

NUMBER   Is the number of objects in the range.

NUMBER_CHOSEN   Is the number of objects in each permutation.

Figure 11.36
With the *PERMUT* function, each number selected must be unique. It accounts for 1 2 3, but not 1 1 1 or 1 1 2.

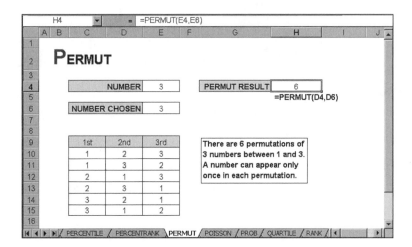

POISSON

POISSON returns the Poisson distribution.

```
=POISSON(x,mean,cumulative)
```

The Poisson probability distribution is applied to experiments with random and independent occurrences. The occurrences are always considered within an interval (time, space, or volume). Using a known average number of occurrences for the interval, the POISSON function computes the probability of a certain number of occurrences at the x interval. Figure 11.37 shows the Poisson probability distribution for the number of people arriving at a bank branch within a one hour time period.

X   Is the number of occurrences within the interval.

MEAN   Is the average and, therefore, expected number of occurrences.

CUMULATIVE   Is a TRUE/FALSE value that determines the form in which the Poisson probability distribution will be returned. If TRUE, the cumulative probability is returned (the probability that the number of occurrences will be *between* zero and *x*). If FALSE, the probability mass function is returned (the probability that exactly *x* events will occur).

X	MEAN	CUMULATIVE	POISSON
17	14	TRUE	0.797498995

Time	Monday	Tuesday	Wednesday	Thursday	Friday	Hourly Me
0900-1000	24	19	11	15	13	16
1000-1100	13	9	13	12	17	13
1100-1200	16	14	15	14	21	16
1200-1300	18	16	17	17	25	19
1300-1400	17	18	12	14	19	16
1400-1500	11	13	9	11	16	12
1500-1600	10	7	6	10	12	9
Daily Mean	16	14	12	13	18	14

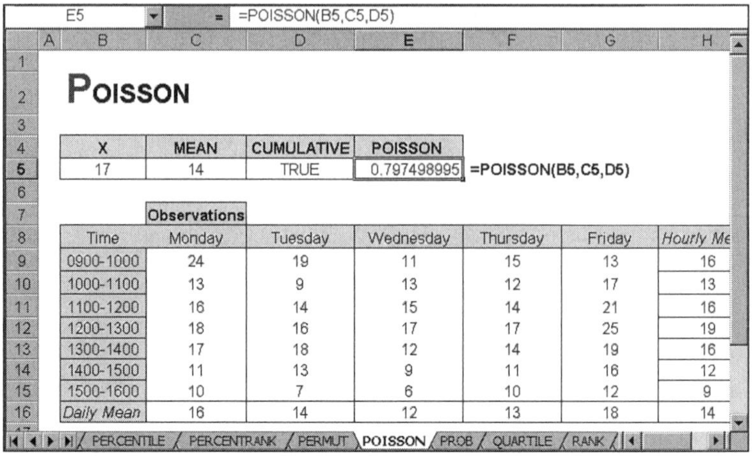

Figure 11.37
Cumulative can be TRUE or FALSE with regard to the *POISSON* function.

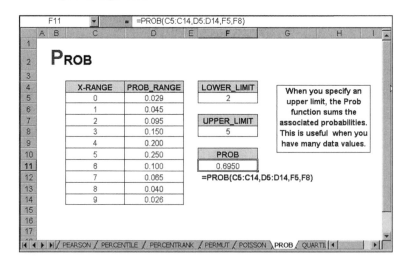

PROB

PROB returns the probability that values in a range are between two specified limits (as shown in Figure 11.38).

```
=PROB(x_range,prob_range,lower_limit,upper_limit)
```

X_RANGE	Is the range of values with which there are associated probabilities.
PROB_RANGE	Is a set of probabilities associated with the `x_values`. The sum of the probabilities in this range must equal one (1).
LOWER_LIMIT	Is the lower bound on the value for which you want a probability.
UPPER_LIMIT	Is the upper bound on the value for which you want a probability; an optional argument.

X-RANGE	PROB_RANGE
0	0.029
1	0.045
2	0.095
3	0.150
4	0.200
5	0.250
6	0.100
7	0.065
8	0.040
9	0.026

Figure 11.38
If *UPPER_LIMIT* is omitted, the function returns the probability that the values in *X_RANGE* are equal to *LOWER_LIMIT*.

QUARTILE

QUARTILE returns the quartile of a data set.

=QUARTILE(array,quart)

The QUARTILE function is used frequently to divide data into four equal parts and return the average of the quartile you specify. In Figure 11.39, the QUARTILE function is being used to locate the top twenty-fifth percentile of price-earnings ratios for 12 companies.

ARRAY   Is the data set of numeric values for which you want the quartile value.

QUART   Indicates the value you want to return. (See Table 11.2.)

Table 11.2   Quart Value Results

Quart Value	Result
0	Minimum value
1	First quartile (25th percentile)
2	Second quartile (50th percentile)
3	Third quartile (75th percentile)
4	Maximum value

Figure 11.39
The *MEDIAN* function returns the same result as *QUARTILE* when Quart is 2.

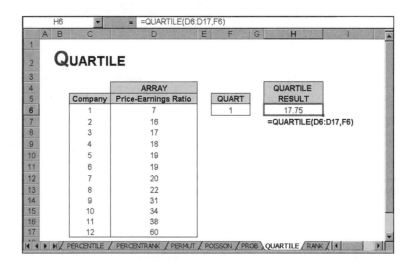

RANK

RANK returns the rank of a number in a list of numbers.

`=RANK(number,ref,order)`

As seen in Figure 11.40, the RANK function is used to provide the relative position of the number you specify in relation to the other numbers in the data set.

NUMBER — Is the number of the rank you want to determine.

REF — Is the data set of values being assessed.

ORDER — Is an indicator of how the numbers should be ranked. If zero (0) or omitted, the list is ranked as if it were in descending order. If any non-zero value, the list is ranked as if it were in ascending order.

Although duplicate numbers are treated as having the same rank, the numbering is effected when duplicates are present. In Figure 11.40, there are several duplicates; number 84 appears twice. 84 is ranked third, and 81 is ranked fifth; no number is ranked fourth.

Figure 11.40
Be sure the data set is sorted by the values, either ascending or descending.

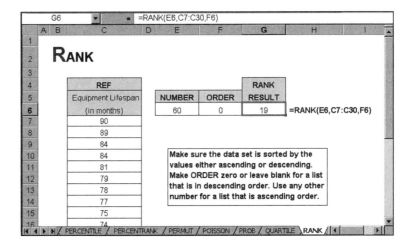

RSQ

RSQ returns the r^2 value of a linear regression line.

`=RSQ(known_y's,known_x's)`

The r^2 value is the proportion of the variance in y attributed to the variance in x. Also known as the Pearson product moment correlation coefficient (see the PEARSON function earlier in this chapter). The closer r^2 is to one (1), the better the regression line fits your data. Figure 11.41 shows an example of calculating this function. If you add a linear trendline to an Excel chart, you can have the r^2 value display on the chart.

KNOWN_Y'S   Is the set of data points or values.

KNOWN_X'S   Is the set of values that correspond to the known_y values. Intervals
of time are often the known_x value.

The equation for RSQ is

$$r = \frac{n(\Sigma XY) - (\Sigma X)(\Sigma Y)}{\sqrt{\left[n\Sigma X^2 - (\Sigma X)^2\right]\left[n\Sigma Y^2 - (\Sigma Y)^2\right]}}$$

Figure 11.41
The closer r^2 is to one, the better the regression line fits your data.

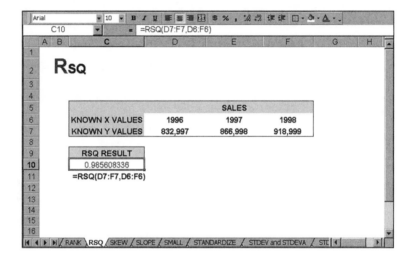

SKEW

SKEW returns the skewness of a distribution.

=SKEW(number1,number2,...)

Skewness refers to the asymmetry of a distribution around its mean. Positive skewness indicates a distribution with an asymmetric tail extending towards more positive values. Negative skewness indicates a distribution with an asymmetric tail extending towards more negative values. Figure 11.42 illustrates the SKEW function.

NUMBER N   You can specify up to 30 arguments for the SKEW function. Arguments
can be cell references, arrays, or range names. Blank cells or cells that
contain a text, or logical values are ignored. Cells containing zero (0)
are included in the calculation.

The equation for SKEW is

$$\frac{n}{(n-1)(n-2)}\sum\left(\frac{x_j - \overline{x}}{s}\right)^3$$

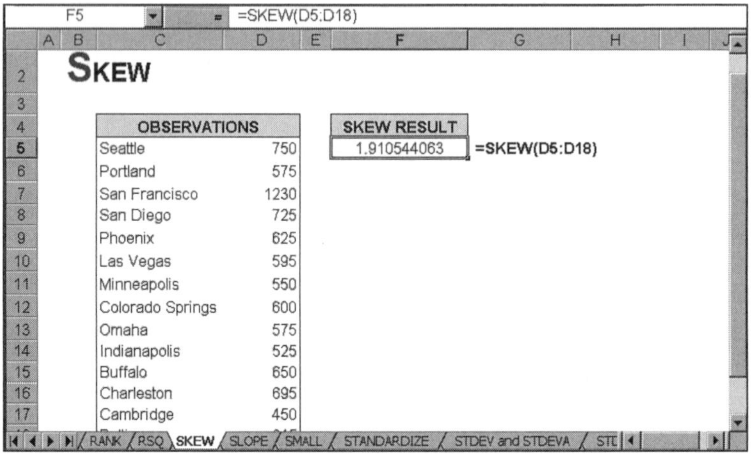

Figure 11.42
There must be at least three data points in the data set for the *SKEW* function.

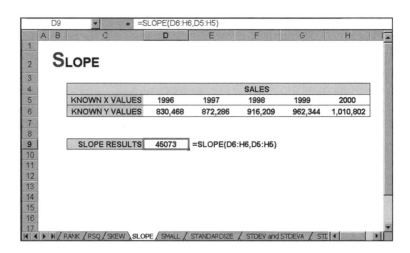

SLOPE

SLOPE returns the slope of the regression line through data points in known_y's and known_x's.

=SLOPE(known_y's,known_x's)

The slope of line is the vertical distance divided by the horizontal distance between any two points on the line. Figure 11.43 shows the result of calculating the slope for a set of sales data.

KNOWN_Y'S   Is the set of data points or values; the dependent variable.

KNOWN_X'S   Is the set of independent data points.

The equation for the slope of the regression line is

$$b = \frac{n \sum xy - \left(\sum x \right)\left(\sum y \right)}{n \sum x^2 - \left(\sum x \right)^2}$$

Figure 11.43
The slope of a line is the amount of change in y due to a change of one unit in x.

| | D9 | ▼ | = =SLOPE(D6:H6,D5:H5) | | | | |

SMALL

SMALL returns the *k*-th smallest value in a data set.

```
=SMALL(array,k)
```

The SMALL function is used to retrieve a value based on its standing or rank in the data set. Figure 11.44 shows an example of the SMALL function returning the third smallest number from the list.

ARRAY   Is the range of data from which you want to return the *k*-th smallest value.

K   Is the position (from the smallest) of the data point you want to return.

Figure 11.44

SMALL returns the position of the specified smallest value in the data set. To return the corresponding state, use the VLOOKUP function. To return the largest value, use the LARGE function.

❶ Shrink refers to loss due to spoilage, damage, and theft.

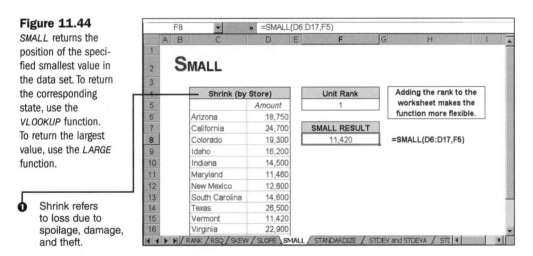

STANDARDIZE

STANDARDIZE returns a normalized value from a distribution characterized by mean and standard_dev.

```
=STANDARDIZE(x,mean,standard_dev)
```

The mean of a standard normal distribution is zero. However, in real-world situations, the mean is rarely zero. In order to make accurate comparisons, the x value must be *standardized*. The result, shown in Figure 11.45, is what the x value is equivalent to in a standard normal distribution (the z value in the equation).

X   Is the value you want to normalize.

MEAN   Is the arithmetic mean (average) of the data set.

STANDARD_DEV   Is the standard deviation of the data set.

The equation for STANDARDIZE is

$$Z = \frac{X - \mu}{\sigma}$$

Figure 11.45
In this example, the z value (the result of the *STANDARDIZE* function) is negative.

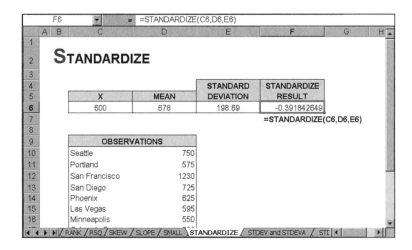

STDEV

STDEV estimates standard deviation based on a sample.

`=STDEV(number1,number2,...)`

The standard deviation is a measure of how widely dispersed values are from the arithmetic mean (the average) value. Figure 11.46 shows the STDEV calculated for a *random* sample of college entrance scores from a local high school. If your data set is the entire population, use the STDEVP function.

NUMBER N   Arguments can be cell references, arrays, or range names. Blank cells or cells that contain a text, or logical values are ignored. Cells containing zero (0) are included in the calculation. You can specify up to 30 arguments for the STDEV function.

The equation for STDEV is

$$\sqrt{\frac{n\sum x^2 - \left(\sum x\right)^2}{n(n-1)}}$$

Figure 11.46
The *STDEV* function is used with a sample data set. Use the *STDEVP* function if the data set represents the entire population and not a sample.

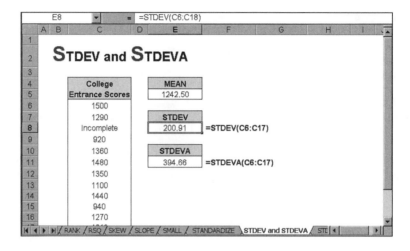

STDEVA

STDEVA estimates standard deviation based on a sample that may be comprised of numbers, text, or logical values.

=STDEVA(value1,value2,...)

Similar to STDEV, the STDEVA function calculates the average of its arguments. The difference is that STDEVA does not ignore text or logical values (TRUE and FALSE). Text and FALSE are evaluated as zero (0) and TRUE is evaluated as one (1). Refer to Figure 11.46 for a comparison of the STDEV and STDEVA functions.

VALUE N   Cells that contain a zero (0), text, or logical values are included in the STDEVA calculation. Arguments can be cell references, arrays, or range names. Blank cells are ignored. You can specify up to 30 arguments for the STDEVA function.

STDEVP

STDEVP calculates standard deviation based on the entire population.

=STDEVP(number1,number2,...)

Like the STDEV function, the STDEVP function is a measure of how widely dispersed values are from the arithmetic mean (the average) value. While the STDEV function is used with a sample of a population, the STDEVP function is used when you have the *entire* population. Figure 11.47 shows an example of the STDEVP function.

NUMBER N   Arguments can be cell references, arrays, or range names. Blank cells or cells that contain text or logical values are ignored. Cells containing zero (0) are included in the calculation. You can specify up to 30 arguments for the STDEVP function.

Figure 11.47
Use the *STDEVP* function when the data set is the entire population. If your data set is a sample of the population, use the *STDEV* function.

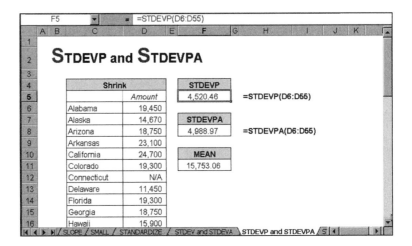

STDEVPA

STDEVPA calculates standard deviation based on the entire population given as arguments.

=STDEVPA(value1,value2,...)

The STDEVPA function differs from the STDEVP function in that it will also evaluate logical values such as TRUE and FALSE. TRUE evaluates to one (1); FALSE evaluates to zero (0). Arguments that contain text also evaluate to zero. Refer to Figure 11.47 for a comparison of STDEVP and STDEVPA.

  VALUE N   Is the cell reference(s), range name, text representations of numbers, array, or logical values that makes up the data set. Up to 30 arguments (unique data sets) can be specified.

STEYX

STEYX returns the standard error of the predicted y value for each x in the regression.

=STEYX(known_y's,known_x's)

The STEYX function is a measure of the amount of error in the prediction of y for an individual x. Figure 11.48 shows an example of the standard error that can be expected for the sales figures.

  KNOWN_Y'S   Is the set of data points or values; the dependent variable.
  KNOWN_X'S   Is the set of independent data points.

The equation for the STEYX is

$$S_{y \cdot x} = \sqrt{\left[\frac{1}{n(n-2)} \right] \left[n\Sigma y^2 - (\Sigma y)^2 - \frac{\left[n\Sigma xy - (\Sigma x)(\Sigma y) \right]^2}{n\Sigma x^2 - (\Sigma x)^2} \right]}$$

Figure 11.48
The *STEYX* function is used in regression analysis.

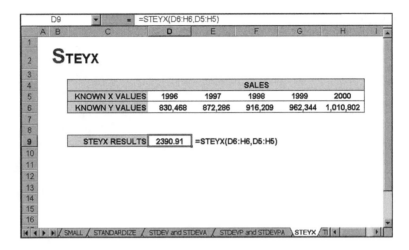

TDIST

TDIST returns the *t*-distribution.

```
TDIST(x,degrees_freedom,tails)
```

The TDIST function is similar to the normal distribution (bell-shaped) curve, except that it is typically used when the sample size is small (less than 30) and the standard deviation is not known. Like the standard normal distribution the mean of the t-distribution is zero (0). Figure 11.49 shows an example of a TDIST function. If you know the probability you want to achieve, use the TINV function instead.

X	Is the numeric value at which to evaluate the distribution.
DEGREES_FREEDOM	Is the integer number for the degrees of freedom.
TAILS	Is an indication whether to return a one-tailed distribution or two-tailed distribution.

Figure 11.49
The t-distribution
(TDIST) is sometimes called Student's t-distribution.

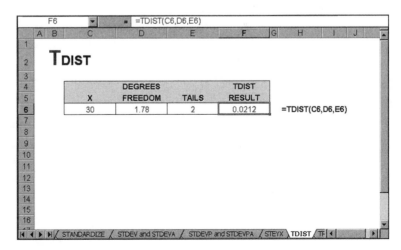

TINV

TINV returns the inverse of the t-distribution for the specified degrees of freedom.

`=TINV(probability,degrees_freedom)`

The TINV function is when you know the probability level you want to achieve and need to generate *x*. TINV uses an iterative technique for calculating the function. The default maximum number of iterations is 100. If a result is not reached within those iterations, the #N/A value is returned. You can change the number of iterations under Tools, Options, Calculation tab.

An example of a TINV function is `=TINV(.095,2)` which results in 0.071.

PROBABILITY	Is the probability associated with the two-tailed t-distribution.
DEGREES FREEDOM	The degrees of freedom to characterize the distribution.

TREND

TREND returns the y-values along a linear trendline that best fits the values in a data set.

`=TREND(known_y's,known_x's,new_x's,const)`

Using the least squares method, the TREND function determines the values that plot a straight line based on a data set. In Figure 11.50, the trend values have been calculated. The known_y and known_x values are based on the formula y=m*x+b. Because the new y values (the values that the function returns) are along the linear trendline that best fits your data (based on the trend equation), the new y values do not match the known y values.

Because this function returns an array:

- The result range must be selected *before* you begin the function.
- The formula must be *array entered* by using Ctrl+Shift+Enter, instead of just Enter.

KNOWN_Y'S	The known values for the known data points; the dependent variable.
KNOWN_X'S	The known data points. If omitted assumed to be the array {1,2,3...} the same size as the known_y's.
NEW_X'S	Are the new x-values for which you want TREND to return corresponding y-values. If omitted assumed to be the same as the known_x's.
CONST	TRUE or FALSE indicating whether the y-intercept (*b*) is = 0 (FALSE) or not (TRUE).

...

Figure 11.50
The trendline can be plotted on an Excel chart, with or without first generating the values with the *TREND* function.

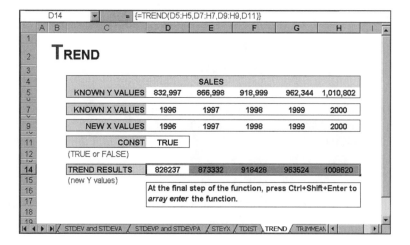

TRIMMEAN

TRIMMEAN returns the mean of the interior of a data set.

=TRIMMEAN(array,percent)

The TRIMMEAN function is used when you want to exclude data points from the top and bottom of the data set, for example when the data set contains unusually high or low values which skew the mean. In Figure 11.51, the percent argument is 15% and the data set contains 50 values; 15% of 50 is 7.5. The TRIMMEAN function rounds down to the nearest multiple of 2. In this example, it will trim three values from the top and three from the bottom.

ARRAY   Is the data set, which can be cell references, arrays, or range names.

PERCENT   Is the fractional number of data points to exclude from the calculation.

Figure 11.51
Because values are trimmed from the data set, the *TRIMMEAN* will vary from the arithmetic mean (*AVERAGE*).

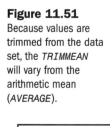

❶ The array is the list of amounts

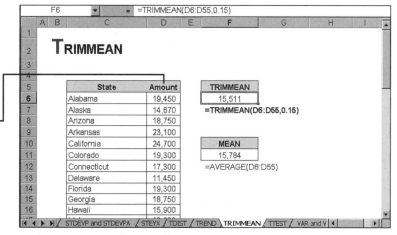

TTEST

TTEST returns the probability associated with t-test.

`=TTEST(array1,array2,tails,type)`

Sometimes called Student's t-test, this function is used to determine whether two samples are likely to have come from the same two underlying populations that have the same mean. In Figure 11.52, the probability that the two samples came from different populations with the same mean is 25%.

ARRAY1	Is the first data set.
ARRAY2	Is the second data set.
TAILS	Is an indication whether to return a one-tailed distribution or two-tailed distribution.
TYPE	Is the type of t-test to perform: 1 indicates paired; 2 indicates two-sample equal variance; 3 indicates two-sample unequal variance.

Figure 11.52
Both the *TAILS* and *TYPE* arguments should be integers.

❶ Choose 1 or 2 tails.

❷ Choose type 1, 2, or 3.

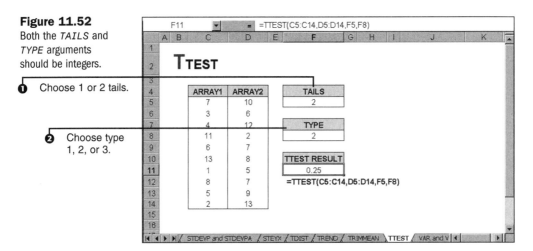

VAR

VAR returns an estimate for the variance of a population, based on a sample data set.

`=VAR(number1,number2,...)`

Figure 11.53 shows a sample data set of 20 people and the time they spend (one way) commuting to work from a specific suburb. The VAR function provides an estimate of the variance for all the commuters from that suburb.

NUMBER N	You can specify up to 30 arguments for the VAR function. The arguments can be cell references, arrays, or range names. Blank cells or cells containing text are ignored. Cells that contain a zero (0) are included in the VAR calculation.

Figure 11.53

The *VAR* and *VARA* functions are used when you have only a sample of the entire population. If the data set is the entire population, use the *VARP* and *VARPA* functions.

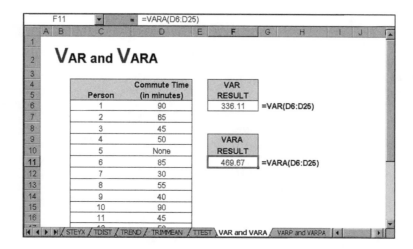

VARA

VARA estimates variance based on a sample, including samples that contain text or logical values.

`=VARA(value1,value2,...)`

The VARA function differs from the VAR function in that it will also evaluate logical values such as TRUE and FALSE. TRUE evaluates to one (1); FALSE evaluates to zero (0). Arguments that contain text also evaluate to zero. Refer to Figure 11.53 for a comparison of VAR and VARA.

> VALUE N   Is the cell reference(s), range name, text representations of numbers, array, or logical values that makes up the data set. Up to 30 arguments can be specified.

VARP

VARP calculates variance based on the entire population.

`=VARP(number1,number2,...)`

The VARP function is used when you have all the data and not just a random sample. Figure 11.54 lists the amount spent by each state on maps at their visitor centers.

> NUMBER N   You can specify up to 30 arguments for the VARP function. The arguments can be cell references, arrays, or range names. Blank cells or cells containing text are ignored. Cells that contain a zero (0) are included in the VARP calculation.

Figure 11.54
The entry for Alaska is None and is ignored by the *VARP* function, but picked up by the *VARPA* function.

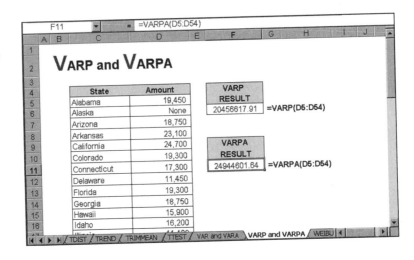

VARPA

VARPA calculates variance based on the entire population. In addition to numbers, text, and logical values such as TRUE and FALSE are included in the calculation.

=VARPA(value1,value2,...)

Refer to Figure 11.54 for a comparison of VARP and VARPA.

VALUE N   Is the cell reference(s), range name, text representations of numbers, array, or logical values that makes up the data set. Up to 30 arguments can be specified.

WEIBULL

WEIBULL returns the Weibull distribution.

=WEIBULL(x,alpha,beta,cumulative)

The WEIBULL function is used in reliability testing, such as calculating an equipment's average time to failure, shown in Figure 11.55.

X   Is the value at which to evaluate the function.

ALPHA   Is a parameter to the distribution.

BETA   Is a parameter to the distribution.

CUMULATIVE   Is a logical value that indicates which form of the exponential function to provide. If TRUE, then WEIBULL returns the cumulative distribution function. If FALSE, then WEIBULL returns the probability density function.

The equation for the cumulative distribution function is

$$F(x;\alpha,\beta) = 1 - e^{-(x/\beta)^{\alpha}}$$

The equation for the probability density function is

$$f(x;\alpha,\beta) = \frac{\alpha}{\beta^{\alpha}} x^{\alpha-1} e^{-(x/\beta)^{\alpha}}$$

Figure 11.55
Use either TRUE or
FALSE for the cumula-
tive argument with the
WEIBULL function.

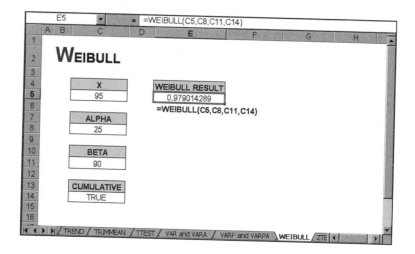

ZTEST

ZTEST returns the two-tailed P-value of a z-test.

`=ZTEST(array,x,sigma)`

The ZTEST function is used to generate a standard score for *x* for the data set, and returns the two-tailed probability for the normal distribution. Use this function to assess whether a partic-ular data value is from a particular population. Figure 11.56 shows an example of ZTEST.

ARRAY   Is the data set against which to test *x*.

X   Is the value to test.

SIGMA   Is the population standard deviation. If omitted the sample standard deviation is used.

The equation for ZTEST is

$$ZTEST(array,x) = 1 - NORMSDIST\left(\frac{\mu - x}{\sigma + \sqrt{n}}\right)$$

Figure 11.56
If you omit *SIGMA*,
the sample standard
deviation is used.

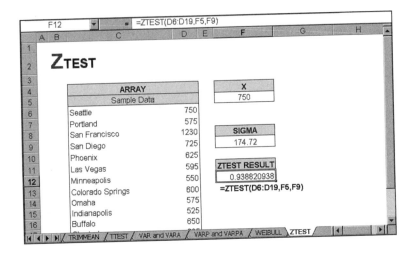

CHAPTER 12

Text Functions

Text Functions Overview

Text functions can be used in several ways. They can return the number of characters in text strings, remove extra spaces and nonprintable characters from cells, return exact data within a string, change the case of text strings, and even combine text from other cells. If you inherit workbooks from other people, you will eventually run into situations where you have to clean or manipulate the data. Text functions allow you to create consistency throughout the workbook. Because certain functions are case-sensitive, it is good practice to create consistency throughout lists and tables.

The following functions are discussed in this chapter.

- ASC
- CHAR
- CLEAN
- CODE
- CONCATENATE
- DOLLAR
- EXACT
- FIND
- FIXED
- JIS
- LEFT
- LEN
- LOWER
- MID
- PHONETIC
- PROPER
- REPLACE
- REPT
- RIGHT
- SEARCH
- SUBSTITUTE
- T
- TEXT
- TRIM
- UPPER
- VALUE
- YEN

ASC

`=ASC(text)`

The ASC function changes full-width double-byte characters to half-width single-byte characters.

When using the different language packs in Excel 2000, you have to use this function to change full-width double-byte characters back to half-width regular English letters or Katakana. See also, JIS function. For example: ASC("EXCEL") = EXCEL. Also notice the example for Japanese characters using the JIS function later in this chapter.

```
ASC("EXCEL"} equals "EXCEL"
ASC("エクセル"} equals "ｴｸｾﾙ"
```

> TEXT   This is text or cell reference that contains the text that you want to change from full-width double-byte characters to regular half-byte English letters or Katakana.

CHAR

CHAR returns the character specified by a number.

`=CHAR(number)`

The CHAR function returns the character set specified by a number. The character set is a set of characters from the ANSI character set for either the Windows or Macintosh character sets. You can use the CHAR function to translate code page numbers from other types of computers into characters. Figure 12.1 shows the CHAR function in use. The characters in the figure are in groups. For example, the alphabet character set falls within the number range of 65 to 90.

> NUMBER   This number is from the character set used by the computer. It's a number between 1 and 255.

Figure 12.1
The *CHAR* function returns the character corresponding to the number from the ANSI character set or Macintosh character set.

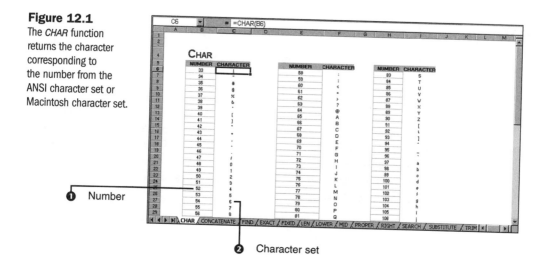

❶ Number

❷ Character set

CLEAN

CLEAN removes all nonprintable characters from text.

`=CLEAN(text)`

The CLEAN function removes all nonprintable characters from the text. For example, `=CLEAN(char(1) &"TEXT"& char(1))` will return the result of "Text." Let's say you had to download yearly corporate data from a mainframe computer and the characters appear as follows:

If cell A1 contains Yearly Corporate Project 1998 Analysis Survey
then `=CLEAN(A1)` will return Yearly Corporate Project 1998 Analysis Survey.

TEXT   The text is any nonprintable character you want to remove from a cell.

CODE

Use the CODE function to return a numeric code from the first character in a text string.

`=CODE(text)`

The CODE function does the opposite of the CHAR function. It uses both the Windows ANSI character set and the Macintosh character set. (For additional details, see the CHAR function earlier in this chapter.)

For example, `=Code("A")` returns the result of 65, because 65 is the computer's numeric code for the "A" character.

TEXT   This is the text that returns the character number.

CONCATENATE

Join several text strings into one text string by using CONCATENATE.

=CONCATENATE(text1,text2,...)

The CONCATENATE function is another one of the useful functions you'll find in Excel. CONCATENATE can be used to join text in several forms. Using this function by itself joins a city and state as shown in the first example in Figure 12.2, however, you also can place characters in between the adjoined text by inserting open and close quotes. The characters or text can include spacing, dashes, commas, numbers, other functions, and so on. Notice some of the different ways the CONCATENATE function can join text in separate cells. You can also use the ampersand "&" as shown in Figure 12.2.

TEXT 1, TEXT 2,...   Text is the text to be joined. You can join from 1 to 30 items per cell.

Figure 12.2
The *CONCATENATE* function allows you to join text from separate cells into the same cell.

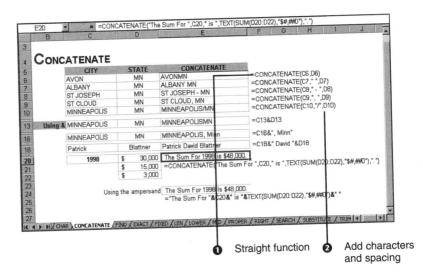

❶ Straight function   ❷ Add characters and spacing

DOLLAR

DOLLAR converts a number to text using Currency format, with the decimals rounded to the specified place.

=DOLLAR(number,decimals)

The DOLLAR function converts numbers to currency.

For example:

=DOLLAR("15000") results in $15,000.00.

=DOLLAR("15000.23") results in $15,000.23.

If you input a negative number, the DOLLAR function will convert the negative number as follows: =DOLLAR("-15000") results in ($15,000.00). You can also use the DOLLAR function with a cell reference. For example, if you have a list of numbers you want to convert to currency format, you could apply the formula =DOLLAR(C5), where C5 equals 25, the result would be $25.00. Keep in mind, however, using this function overrides the use of the format cells command.

NUMBER	This can be a number or cell reference or even a number that evaluates to a number.
DECIMALS	The decimal is the number of digits or decimal places to the right of the decimal. If they are omitted, Excel assumes two places.

EXACT

EXACT compares two text strings and returns TRUE if they're exactly the same, and FALSE otherwise.

=EXACT(text1,text2)

The EXACT function compares two text strings to see if they are the same. The EXACT function can operate from text within the function or via cell referencing.

TEXT 1, TEXT 2,...   The text is the first text string and then the second text string.

For example:

=EXACT("BILL","bill") results in FALSE.

=EXACT("BILL","BILL") results in TRUE.

As you see in Figure 12.3, there are two examples comparing ranges of cells with the EXACT function. The first, displays TRUE when an asset is complete using cell referencing. The second compares a single cell reference to a range in the form of an array. If you had a list of assets, and all assets had unique identities, you might want to see if the asset is in the list. For this, you would use the formula as shown in Figure 12.3:

{=Or(Exact(Cell Reference, Compare Range))}

Figure 12.3
The *EXACT* function tests
two sets of information
and displays a logical
value of TRUE or FALSE
depending on whether
the information is equal.

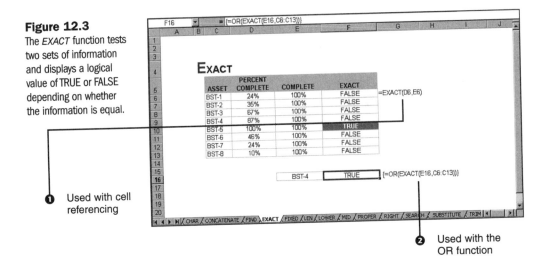

❶ Used with cell
referencing

❷ Used with the
OR function

FIND

FIND locates one text string with another text string, and returns the number of the starting
position of find_text, from the leftmost character of within_text.

=FIND(find_text,within_text,start_num)

The FIND function locates one text string with another and returns the numeric position of
the text string.

FIND_TEXT	The find_text is the text you want to locate or find.
WITHIN_TEXT	The within_text refers to the text string your looking within.
START_NUM	The start_num refers to the number from left to right. For example, Patrick where the "a" character would be 2 as the start_num.

For example:

=FIND("W","Wally Bill") results in 1.

=FIND("a","Wally Bill") results in 2.

What if you had a cell that contained the names of people and the city and state they lived in. You could combine the FIND function with the MID function to extract a text string. Take a look at Figure 12.4. The formula =Mid(C6,1,Find(" ",C6,1)-1) results in the extraction of the first word, which in this case is a name in the cell, regardless of the length of the first name. See entries in this chapter for LEN and MID for additional details.

Figure 12.4

The *FIND* function combined with the *MID* function can extract text strings in cells regardless of the string length.

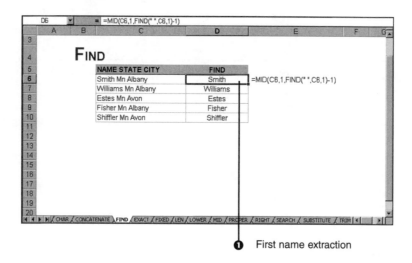

❶ First name extraction

FIXED

The FIXED function rounds a number to a specified number of decimals, formats the number in decimal format using a period and commas, and returns the result as text.

```
=FIXED(number,decimals,no_commas)
```

The FIXED function can round numbers in a cell. You can use the FIXED function with text in the function or with cell referencing. Use the FIXED function to round numbers to decimals, hundreds, and thousands. You should notice that the examples in Figure 12.5 round a number to decimals, tens, hundreds, and thousands using the FIXED function.

NUMBER	The number refers to the number you want to round or convert to text.
DECIMALS	The decimals refer to the number of decimal places to the right.
NO COMMAS	The no commas is a logical result in that if True, it prevents the function from including any commas in the text returned result.

Figure 12.5
Use the *FIXED*
function to round
numbers in a cell.

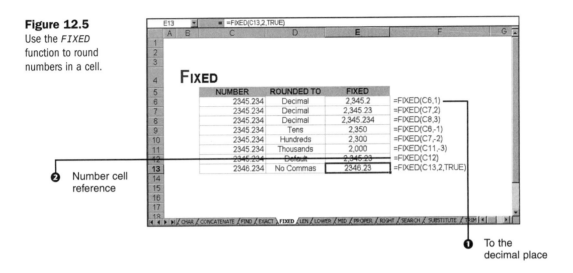

❷ Number cell
reference

❶ To the
decimal place

JIS

The JIS function changes half-width single-byte characters to regular English letters.

`=JIS(text)`

When using the different language packs in Excel 2000, you'll have to use this function to change half-width characters back to regular English letters or Katakana. For example: JIS("EXCEL") = EXCEL. Also notice the example for Japanese characters using the JIS function in the following equation.

JIS("EXCEL") equals "EXCEL"

JIS("ｴｸｾﾙ") equals "エクセル"

TEXT This is text or cell reference that contains the text that you want to change to regular English letters or Katakana.

LEFT

Return the first character or characters in a text string with the LEFT function.

`=LEFT(text,num_char)`

The LEFT function returns the text string up to the number in the number character.

TEXT This is the text string or word that contains the characters you want to extract.

NUM_CHAR This is the number (greater than zero) of characters you want to extract starting from the left.

For example:

=LEFT("John Doe",4) results in John.

=LEFT(A5,4) results in John where cell A4 contains the name John Doe.

You can also use cell referencing within the function. Also see the LEN function.

LEN

LEN returns the number of characters in a text string.

=LEN(text)

The LEN function on its own returns the number of characters in a text string.

TEXT   The text refers to the text string, word, or multiple words that you want to find the number of characters for from left to right. Spaces count as one character.

=LEN("Mn Albany") would result in 9. The number of characters also includes spaces. However, combined with other functions in Excel, the LEN function becomes a powerful tool for extracting text strings. If you work in an environment where you have to clean workbooks that were set up improperly, or you've inherited lists of information and have to extract text strings within cells for your own particular purposes, use the LEN function in conjunction with other Excel functions. Notice the example in Figure 12.6. Let's say I wanted to extract the equipment brand from the equipment type. The function =RIGHT(C17,LEN(C17)-FIND(" ",C17)) results in Caterpillar, because the function extracts the text to the right of the space. See also the RIGHT function later in this chapter.

Figure 12.6
Use *LEN* with other functions in Excel for text extraction.

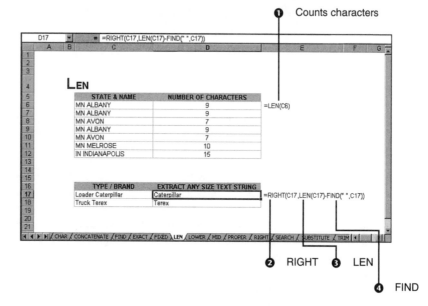

LOWER

LOWER converts all letters in a text string to lowercase.

`=LOWER(text)`

The LOWER function is primarily a cleaning function. If you have inconsistent data in lists and you want all characters to result in lowercase, simply use the LOWER function. Notice the example in Figure 12.7. The LOWER function converts all the uppercase names to lowercase. Use Paste Special and paste as values back into the original location in the list after you've converted all characters to lowercase. This function can be used with text in a cell or with cell referencing as shown.

TEXT   This is the text within the cell you want to convert to lowercase characters.

Figure 12.7
Use the *LOWER* function to clean lists of information that are inconsistent.

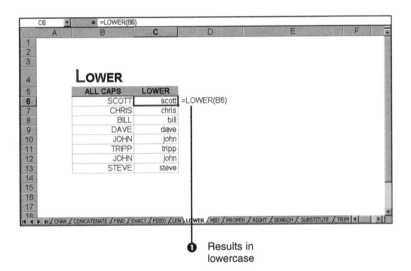

❶ Results in lowercase

MID

Use the MID function to return a specific number of characters from a text string, starting at the position you specify.

`=MID(text,start_num,num_char)`

The MID function returns a specific number of characters from a text string. You can use text within the formula or use cell referencing. If you take a look at the example in Figure 12.8, you'll notice that `=MID("Chris",1,4)` only returns the first four characters in the string. The second example `=MID("Hobbe",2,4)` returns the text string starting with the second character in the string, Hobbe. Combined with the FIND function and used with cell referencing, you can extract first names in text strings. For example, `=MID(C11,1,FIND((" ",C11)-1)` returns the result of the first text string to the left of the first space. The FIND function locates the space based on a space in quotes.

TEXT	The text is the text string or word you want to extract from.
START_NUM	The start_num is the number of the character within the text string or word you want to extract from.
NUM_CHAR	The num_char is the number of characters to extract from the start_num point to the right.

Figure 12.8
Use the *MID* function as a standalone function or in combination with other functions such as *FIND*.

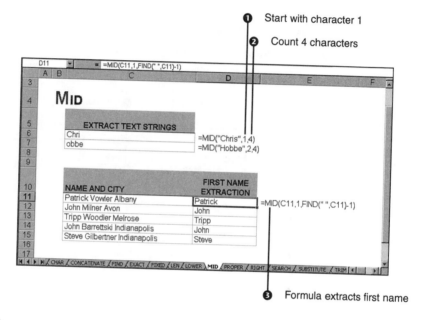

❶ Start with character 1

❷ Count 4 characters

❸ Formula extracts first name

PHONETIC

=PHONETIC(Reference)

The PHONETIC function extracts the phonetic or furigana characters from a text string in Japanese characters.

When using the different language packs in Excel 2000, you'll have to use this function to adjust or change characters from the text string.

| REFERENCE | This is text or cell reference that contains the text that you want to extract the phonetic or furigana characters from. |

PHONETIC(C4) equals "トウキヨキト"

PHONETIC(B7) equals "オオサカフ"

PROPER

`PROPER` capitalizes the first letter of each word in a text string or sentence.

`=PROPER(text)`

The `PROPER` function is another cleaning tool function. It places initial caps on each word within the text string specified in the formula, or text within a cell if you are using cell referencing. The result of `=PROPER("PATRICK")` would be Patrick. Notice that the example in Figure 12.9, used with cell referencing on lists, can quickly clean up the list.

TEXT   The text is the text in the text string, word, or sentence to convert to proper. Meaning, the first character is capitalized in each word.

Figure 12.9
The *PROPER* function creates text with initial caps.

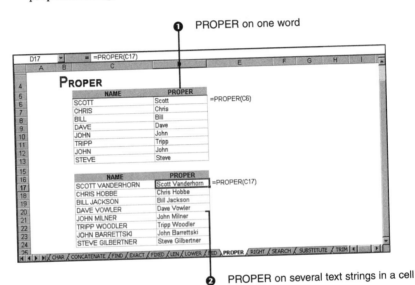

PROPER on one word

PROPER on several text strings in a cell

REPLACE

Use the `REPLACE` function to replace part of a text string with a different text string based on the number of characters you specify.

`=REPLACE(old_text,start_num,num_chars,new_text)`

The `REPLACE` function can be used on a list as a cell reference or with text in the formula.

OLD_TEXT   This is the old text you want to replace with new characters.

START_NUM   This is the number of characters in starting position.

NUM_CHARS   This is the number of characters to replace within the text string.

NEW_TEXT   This is the new text starting with the start number and number of characters that will replace the old text.

For example, =REPLACE("Chris",1,5,"Scott") would result in Scott. Where 1 represents the first character in Chris and 5 is the number of characters in Scott. If you entered the formula =REPLACE("Chris",2,5,"Scott") the result would be Cscott. You could also replace the names with cell references such as: =REPLACE(C5,1,5,D5). In this example, the result would replace the C5's text string starting with 1 to D5's text string up to 5.

REPT

REPT repeats text a given number of times.

=REPT(text,number_times)

The REPT function repeats text in a cell as many times as you specify.

TEXT	This is the text you want to repeat.
NUMBER_TIMES	This number times specifies the number of times you want to repeat the text.

For example:

=REPT("X",5) would result in XXXXX.

=REPT("Stop",2) would result in StopStop.

=REPT(C1,2) would result in the cell reference text repeated twice.

To use the REPT function correctly, the number you provide must be a positive number and cannot exceed 255 characters.

RIGHT

RIGHT returns the last character or characters in a text string.

=RIGHT(text,num_chars)

The RIGHT function returns the rightmost characters in a text string. The text can be in the form of text within the formula or as a cell reference. (Also see LEFT earlier in this chapter.) The NUM_CHARS argument is the number of characters to return.

TEXT	This is the text string or word, or even sentence you want to extract characters from.
NUM_CHARS	This indicates the number of characters you want to extract starting from the right moving left.

For example:

=RIGHT("Patrick",4) would return rick.

Notice the example in Figure 12.10. The RIGHT function used with the LEN and FIND functions can be used to extract text from the cell. Where LEN counts the characters in the text string including spaces, FIND locates the space to the left of the rightmost text string and returns a result of the last word, state, city, and so on.

Figure 12.10
The *RIGHT* function in conjunction with the *LEN* and *FIND* functions can be used to extract the rightmost words.

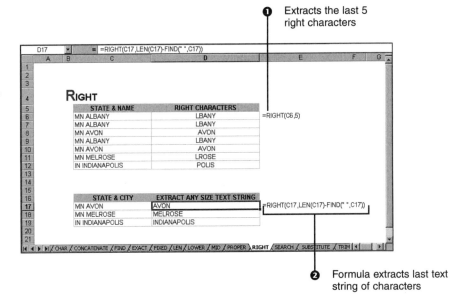

❶ Extracts the last 5 right characters

❷ Formula extracts last text string of characters

SEARCH

The SEARCH function returns the number of the character at which a specific character or text string is first found, reading from left to right.

=SEARCH(find_text,within_text,start_num)

The SEARCH function finds the character within a text string and counts how many places over from left to right based on the start number. For example, the formula =SEARCH("e","Builders",1) would result in 6. Meaning e is the sixth character to the right starting from the first character.

FIND_TEXT	This is the text you're looking for or want to find. The wildcard characters can be used to find a specific character using the (?) and a string of characters using the (*).
WITHIN_TEXT	This is the text you're looking for. It can be included in the formula or referred to using cell referencing.
START_NUM	The number of characters starting from left to right you want to include in the search.

SUBSTITUTE

Use the SUBSTITUTE function to substitute new_text for old_text in a text string.

=SUBSTITUTE(text,old_text,new_text,instance_num)

The SUBSTITUTE function replaces old text within a text string with new text. The text can be in the formula or used as a cell reference. The examples in Figure 12.11 demonstrate that the

SUBSTITUTE function in the first example uses complete cell referencing from one cell to another. The second example gives a mix of cell referencing and text directly in the formula. For the formula =SUBSTITUTE("Melrose",C11,"Farming"), where Cll equals Melrose, the result is Farming.

TEXT	This is the text or text in a cell you want to substitute.
OLD_TEXT	This is the text you want to replace.
NEW_TEXT	This is the new text to replace the old text with.
INSTANCE_NUM	This is the number of instances you want to replace the old text with. For example, if you want to replace every occurrence of old text, use "]["·. If replacing just one occurrence, use 1.

Figure 12.11
The *SUBSTITUTE* function replaces one text string or cell for another.

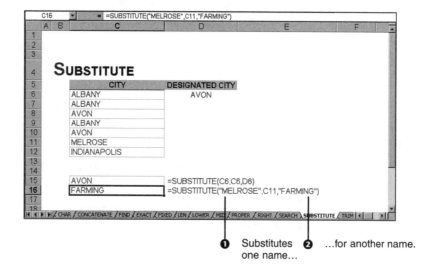

➊ Substitutes one name… ➋ …for another name.

T

T returns the text referred to by VALUE.

`=T(value)`

The T function is provided for compatibility with other spreadsheet programs. Microsoft Excel automatically converts values as necessary. For example, the formula =T("Bob") would result in Bob.

| VALUE | The value is the text or value using a cell reference you want to test. If value is a number, T returns nothing or empty text. |

TEXT

The TEXT function converts a value to text in a specific number format.

`=TEXT(value,format_text)`

The TEXT function converts text from one specific number format to another. You can also access the formatting of text by choosing Format, Cells, and select the Numbers tab. Under Category, choose Custom. From there you add custom formats.

For example, let's say you want to create a custom format that includes the word "Ton" after all the numbers. In a cell where the number is 75, select the General type and include "Ton" in quotes after General. Your result would be 75 Ton. This also allows you to calculate numbers from cells even though Ton shows up in the cell.

VALUE	This is a numeric value, reference to a cell, or a formula that calculates to a numeric value.
FORMAT_TEXT	This is a number format in text. Also see the custom number formats from format cells as mentioned above.

For example:

=TEXT("3/16/64","mmmm dd, yyyy") would result in March 16, 1964.

=TEXT(.3,"$0.00") would result in $0.30.

You can also use cell referencing for the value.

TRIM

Use the TRIM function to remove all spaces from text except for single spaces between words.

=TRIM(text)

The TRIM function is another cleaning function that removes spacing between words. For example, if you inherit a list of information and there happens to be random spacing between the text at different locations, you can trim away the spacing by referencing the cell. For example, you'll notice in Figure 12.12 that the random spacing in the left column shows multiple mixtures in spacing. However, by applying the TRIM function to the right, you can eliminate the spacing. Use the Paste Special command to paste the cleaned text back into the original column as values. This function is specifically useful when data is imported from other applications, particularly mainframe and DOS applications, where spacing often is used as separators in lists and forms.

TEXT	This is the text or cell reference containing text you want to remove all the spaces from.

Figure 12.12

The *TRIM* function can trim random spacing from cells.

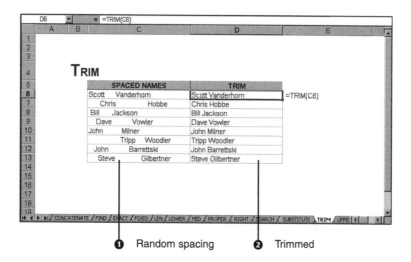

❶ Random spacing   ❷ Trimmed

UPPER

UPPER converts text to uppercase.

=UPPER(text)

Similar to the LOWER function, the UPPER function converts all text within a cell to uppercase. For example, =UPPER("upper") would result in UPPER. Cell referencing can also be used as shown in Figure 12.13.

TEXT   This is the text or cell reference containing text that you want to change to uppercase.

Figure 12.13

The *UPPER* function converts all text to uppercase.

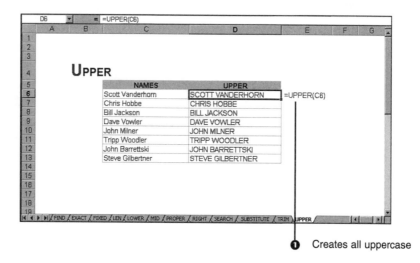

❶ Creates all uppercase

VALUE

Use the VALUE function to convert a text string that represents a number to a number.

=VALUE(text)

The VALUE function is not generally needed because Excel automatically converts text to numbers as necessary and was provided for other spreadsheet compatibility issues.

TEXT   This is the text in quotes or referred to in a cell reference that you want to change to a value. If it's in the form of $11.00 for example, VALUE would convert it to 11.

YEN

The YEN function converts a number to text in Yen. The number is in the format of text.

=YEN(number,decimals)

The difference between using a number format from the format cells dialog box and the YEN function is the YEN function converts a cell to text. This makes the cell inoperable. You cannot add up cells that are converted to text. I would suggest using the Format Cells dialog box as opposed to the YEN function.

NUMBER   This is the number in quotes you want to convert to text in Yen.

DECIMALS   This is the number of decimal places you want to include to the right of the decimal.

Index

Symbols

1904 date system, 67, 74, 78

A

ABS function, 16, 192

absolute deviations of data points, average, 226

absolute value, 95, 192

accounting periods

asset depreciation using double-declining balance method, 124

coupon period settlement date, 118

depreciation, 116

fixed declining balance method, 123

within the formula, 115

interest paid during a defined period of investments, 132

interest payment based on investments with periodic constant payments and constant interest rates, 130

total number of periods for investment, 134

Accounts Payable to Net Sales ratio, 46

ACCRINT function, 11, 114

ACCRINTM function, 11, 115

accrued interests, 114-115

ACOS function, 16, 192

ACOSH function, 16, 193

Add-Ins command (Tools menu), 68, 76-78, 86

ADDRESS function, 15, 174

Allowance for Bad Debt as Percentage of AR ratio, 43

AMORDEGRC function, 11, 115

AMORLINC function, 11, 116

Amortization and Depreciation Expense to Net Sales ratio, 44

Analysis Toolpak

EDATE function, 68

WEEKNUM function, 76

WORKDAY function, 77

YEARFRAC function, 78

AND function, 15, 168-169

annual yields (securities)

discounted, 154

pays interest at maturity, 155

annuities, per period interest, 145

arccosine, 192

arcsine, 193

arctangent, 195

areas, number of, 174

AREAS function, 15, 174

arguments. *See also*
formulas; functions
average, 226
averaging, 27
DATE function, 66
DATEVALUE
  function, 66
DAVERAGE, 54
DAY function, 67
DAYS360 function, 68
DCOUNT, 55
DCOUNTA, 56
defined, 5
DFUNCTIONS, 54
DGET, 56
DMAX, 57
DMIN, 58
DPRODUCT, 58
DSTDEV, 59
DSTDEVP, 59
DSUM, 60
DVAR, 61
DVARP, 62
EDATE function, 68
EOMONTH function, 69
GETPIVOTDATA
  function, 63
HOUR function, 70
largest value, 253
MINUTE function, 70
MONTH function, 71
NETWORKDAYS
  function, 72
NOW function, 73
number of cells contain-
  ing numbers, 233

SECOND function, 73
smallest value, 254
theta, 97
TIME function, 74
TIMEVALUE
  function, 74
TODAY function, 74
types, 6
value average, 227
WEEKDAY function,
  75-76
WEEKNUM function, 76
WORKDAY function, 77
YEAR function, 77-78
arithmetic operators, 6
arrays
element value selected
  by row number and
  column letter indexed,
  179
geometric mean, 244
inverse matrix, 207
matrix determinant, 206
matrix product, 207
most frequently
  occuring/repetitive
  value, 254
relative position of items
  matching specified val-
  ues in speicfied order,
  or position of items,
  184
specified value from
  same position in last
  row or column, 183
specified value search,
  177

ASC function, **280**
ASIN function, **16, 193**
ASINH function, **16,
  194**
**asset depreciation
  (accounting periods),
  151**
double-declining balance
  method, 124
straight-line, 147
sum-of-years digits, 148
**assumed par value
  (Macauley duration),
  127**
ATAN function, **16, 195**
ATAN2 function, **16,
  195**
ATANH function, **16,
  196**
**automating projected
  cash flows, 36**
AVEDEV function, **18,
  226**
AVERAGE function, **18,
  27, 226**
AVERAGEA function,
  18, 227
averaging
absolute deviations of
  data points, 226
arguments, 27, 226-227
positive numbers in
  ranges, 38-39

B

Bad Debt as Percentage of Net Revenues ratio, 43

base 2 logarithm, 102

base-10 logarithm, 206

BESSEL function, 80-82

BESSELI function, 9, 80

BESSELJ function, 10, 80-81

BESSELK function, 10, 81-82

BESSELY function, 10, 82

BETADIST function, 18, 227

BETAINV function, 18, 228

BIN2DEC function, 10

BIN2HEX function, 10

BIN2OCT function, 10

binary numbers

  converting to

    decimal form, 83

    hexadecimal form, 84

    octal form, 84

  decimal numbers, converting to, 89

  hexadecimal numbers, converting to, 93

  octal numbers, converting to, 109

BIND2DEC function, 83

BIND2HEX function, 84

BIND2OCT function, 84

BINOMDIST function, 18, 228-229

binomial distribution probability, 228

breakeven sales formula, 42

building custom functions, 48-49

C

calculations. *See* **functions**

CALL function, 9

capitalizing text, 31, 290

cascading schedules, 33, 35

cash flow schedule, 152

cash flows, 36

CEILING function, 16, 197

CELL function, 14, 158, 160

cells

  addresses, 174

  column/row intersection reference, 180

  empty

    number of, 164

    specified range, 160-161

  error value, 166

  INFO TYPE examples, 158-159

  information, 158-160

  logical test return results, 163-164

  number of, 233-234

  ranges, 199

  reference to range of specific number of rows and columns, 185

  return types, 159

  returning horizontal/ vertical ranges as vertical/horizontal, 188

  value, 164-166

channel velocity, 32

CHAR function, 21, 280

characters

  full-width double-byte, 280

  furigana, 289

  half-width single-byte, 286

  Japanese, 289

  nonprinting, 281

  number of in text strings, 287

  phonetic, 289

  specified by numbers, 280

  text strings, 286, 288, 291-292

chi-squared distribution, 230

CHIDIST function, 18, 230

CHIINV function, 230

CHINV function, 18

CHITEST function, 18, 231

CHOOSE function, 15, 175-176

CLEAN function, 21, 281

CODE function, 21, 281

code resources, 9

coefficients
  complex numbers, 96
  imaginary, 85
  real, 85, 105

COLUMN function, 15, 176

columns
  numbers, 176-177
  row intersection, 25, 180
  value from same position in second column based on range of one column, 184

COLUMNS function, 15, 177

COMBIN function, 16, 197

combinations (numbers), 197

commands
  Data menu, Filter, Advanced Filter, 34
  Edit menu
    Paste Special, 38
    Replace, 37
  Insert menu
    Module, 48
    Name, Defined, 41
    Name, Paste, 42
  Tools menu
    Add-Ins, 68, 76-78, 86
    Options, 67, 74, 78

common logarithm, complex numbers, 101

comparison operators, 6

COMPLEX function, 10, 85

complex numbers
  base 2 logarithm, 102
  coefficient, 96
  common logarithm, 101
  conjugating, 97
  cosine, 98
  difference of two, 107
  exponent, 100
  modulus, 95
  natural logarithm, 101
  product from 2-29 numbers, 104
  quotient, 99
  real coefficient, 105
  sine, 106
  square root, 106
  sum of two, 108

CONCATENATE function, 21, 31, 282

conditional SUM formula, 32

CONFIDENCE function, 18, 231

confidence interval of population means, 231

constant interest rate, 29

contribution margin formula, 42

contribution margin ratio formula, 42

CONVERT function, 10, 86-88

converting
  binary numbers to
    decimal form, 83
    to hexadecimal form, 84
    to octal form, 84
  decimal dollar prices to fraction dollar price, 126
  decimal numbers to
    binary numbers, 89
    hexadecimal numbers, 90
  degrees to radians, 211
  fraction dollar prices to decimal dollar price, 126
  hexadecimal numbers to
    binary numbers, 93
    decimal numbers, 94
    octal numbers, 94
  measurement units, 86-88
  octal numbers to
    binary numbers, 109
    decimal numbers, 110
    hexadecimal numbers, 110
  radians into degrees, 200

CORREL function, 18, 232-233

correlation coefficient, 232

COS function, 16, 198

COSH function, 16, 199

cosine, 198

   complex numbers, 98

   hyperbolic, 199

   inverse hyperbolic, 193

COUGCD function, 204

COUNT function, 18, 233

COUNTA function, 19, 27, 234

COUNTBLANK function, 14, 160-161, 234

COUNTIF function, 16, 27, 199, 205, 235

counting unique list items, 51

COUPDAYBS function, 11, 117

COUPDAYS function, 12, 118

COUPDAYSNC function, 12, 119

COUPNCD function, 12, 119

COUPNUM function, 12, 120

coupon dates

   number of days between settlement dates to next coupon date, 119

   number of previous coupon dates before settlement date, 121

   number representing next coupon date after settlement date, 119

   total number of coupons to be paid, 120

coupon period settlement dates, 117-118

COUPPCD function, 12, 121

COVAR function, 19, 236

covariance, 236

CRITBINOM function, 19, 236

criterion value, 236

CUMIPMT function, 12, 28, 122

CUMPRINC function, 12, 29, 122

cumulative beta probability density function, 227

cumulative binomial distribution, 236

cumulative loan interest, 28, 122

cumulative lognormal distribution, 252

cumulative principal, 29, 122

currency

   converting numbers to, 282

   EUROCONVERT formula, 40-41

   international converters, 39

   rate exchange tables, 40

Current Liabilities to Inventory ratio, 45

Current Liabilities to Net Worth ratio, 45

Current Ratio, 43

custom functions, 7-8, 48-49

D

Data menu commands, Filter, Advanced Filter, 34

data points absolute deviations, 226

database lists, 217

database subtotals, 25

database/list-management functions, 53

   arguments, 54

   DAVERAGE, 8, 54-55

   DCOUNT, 8, 55-56

   DCOUNTA, 8, 56

   DGET, 8, 56-57

   DMAX, 8, 57-58

   DMIN, 8, 58

   DPRODUCT, 8, 58-59

   DSTDEV, 8, 59

   DSTDEVP, 59-60

   DSUM, 8, 60-61

   DVAR, 8, 61-62

   GETPIVOTDATA, 8, 63-64

   syntax, 54

DATE function, 8, 66

date system, 67, 74, 78

date/time functions, 65

   DATE, 8, 66

   DATEVALUE, 8, 66-67

   DAY, 8, 67

   DAYS360, 8, 68

   EDATE, 8, 26, 68-69

   EOMONTH, 8, 69

   HOUR, 9, 70

MINUTE, 9, 70

MONTH, 9, 71

NETWORKDAYS, 9, 27, 72

NOW, 9, 26, 73

SECOND, 9, 73

TIME, 9, 74

TIMEVALUE, 9, 74

TODAY, 9, 26, 74-75

WEEKDAY, 9, 75-76

WEEKNUM, 76

WORKDAY, 77

YEAR, 9, 77-78

YEARFRAC, 9, 78

DATEVALUE function, 8, 66-67

DAVERAGE function, 8, 54-55

DAY function, 8, 67

Days Inventory ratio, 44

Days Purchases ratio, 44

Days Sales in AR ratio, 43

DAYS360 function, 8, 68

DB function, 12, 123

DCOUNT function, 8, 55-56

DCOUNTA function, 8, 56

DDB function, 12, 124

DDE/external functions, 9

DEC2BIN function, 10, 89

DEC2HEX function, 10, 90

DEC2OCT function, 10

decimal dollar prices, 126

decimal form, converting binary numbers to, 83

decimal numbers

hexadecimal numbers, converting to, 94

octal numbers, converting to, 110

converting to

binary numbers, 89

hexadecimal numbers, 90

degrees, 200-211

DEGREES function, 16, 200

deleting

nonprintable characters, 281

text spaces, 294

DELTA function, 10, 90

depreciation

accounting periods, 116

assets, 124

fixed declining balance method, 123

within the formula, 115

assets, 151

DEVSQ function, 19, 237

DFUNCTIONS function, 54

DGET function, 8, 56-57

dialog boxes

Options, 67, 74, 78

Paste Special, 38

direct contribution (P&L), 42-43

DISC function, 12, 125

discounted securities

annual yield, 154

based on price per $100 face value, 142

rates, 125

DLLs (dynamic link libraries), 9

DMAX function, 8, 57-58

DMIN function, 8, 58

DOLLAR function, 21, 282

DOLLARFR function, 12, 126

double factorial, 203

DPRODUCT function, 8, 58-59

DSTDEV function, 8, 59

DSTDEVP function, 59-60

DSUM function, 8, 60-61

DURATION function, 12, 127

DVAR function, 8, 61-62

DVARP function, 8, 62-63

dynamic link libraries (DLLs), 9

E

EDATE function, 8, 26, 68-69

Edit menu commands
Paste Special, 38
Replace, 37

editing dates, 67, 74, 78

EFFECT function, 12, 127-128

effective annual interest rates, 127

empty cells, 234

engineering functions
BESSELI, 9, 80
BESSELJ, 10, 80-81
BESSELK, 10, 81-82
BESSELY, 10, 82
BIN2DEC, 10, 83
BIN2HEX, 10, 84
BIN2OCT, 10, 84
COMPLEX, 10, 85
CONVERT, 10, 86-88
DEC2BIN, 10, 89
DEC2HEX, 10, 90
DEC2OCT, 10
DELTA, 10, 90
ERF, 10, 91
ERFC, 10, 92
GESTEP, 10, 92
HEX2BIN, 10, 93
HEX2DEC, 10, 94
HEX2OCT, 10, 94
IMABS, 10, 95-96
IMAGINARY, 10, 96

IMARGUMENT, 10, 97
IMCONJUGATE, 10, 97
IMCOS, 10, 98
IMDIV, 10, 99
IMEXP, 11, 100
IMLN, 11, 101
IMLOG10, 11, 101
IMLOG2, 11, 102
IMPOWER, 11, 103
IMPRODUCT, 11, 104-105
IMREAL, 11, 105
IMSIN, 11, 106
IMSQRT, 11, 106
IMSUB, 11, 107
IMSUM, 11, 108-109
OCT2BIN, 11, 109
OCT2DEC, 11, 110
OCT2HEX, 11, 110
overview, 79
SQRTPI, 11

English letters, 286

EOMONTH function, 8, 69

ERF function, 10, 91

ERFC function, 10, 92

error types, corresponding number values, 161-162

ERROR.TYPE function, 14, 161-162

EUROCONVERT formula, 40-41

EVEN function, 16, 201

EXACT function, 21, 283

EXP function, 16, 201

EXPONDIST function, 19, 238

exponents, complex numbers, 100

exponential curve (fit data), 250

exponential distribution, 238

exponential growth prediction, 245

external/DDE functions, 9

F

F probability distribution, 239

F-test, 242

FACT function, 16, 202

FACTDOUBLE function, 16, 203

factorial, 202
double, 203
ratio, 208

FALSE function, 15, 169

FDIST function, 19, 239

Filter, Advanced Filter command (Data menu), 34

financial functions
ACCRINT, 11, 114
AMORDEGRC, 11, 115
AMORLINC, 11, 116
COUPDAYBS, 11, 117
COUPDAYS, 12, 118

COUPDAYSNC, 12, 119

COUPNCD, 12, 119

COUPNUM, 12, 120

COUPPCD, 12, 121

CUMIPMT, 12, 122

CUMPRINC, 12, 122

DB, 12, 123

DDB, 12, 124

DISC, 12, 125

DOLLARDE, 12, 126

DOLLARFR, 12, 126

DURATION, 12, 127

EFFECT, 12, 127-128

FV, 12, 128

FVSCHEDULE, 12, 129

INTRATE, 12, 129

IPMT, 12, 130

IRR, 12, 131

ISPMT, 132

MDURATION, 12, 132

MIRR, 13, 133

NOMINAL, 13, 134

NPER, 13, 134

NPV, 13, 135

ODDFPRICE, 13, 136

ODDFYFIELD, 13

ODDFYIELD, 138

ODDLPRICE, 13, 138-139

ODDLYIELD, 13, 139

overview, 113

PMT, 13, 140

PPMT, 13, 140

PRICE, 13, 141

PRICEDISC, 13, 142

PRICEMAT, 13, 143

PV, 13, 144-145

RATE, 13, 145-146

RECEIVED, 146

SLN, 13, 147

SYD, 13, 148

TBILLEQ, 13, 148

TBILLPRICE, 13, 149

TBILLYIELD, 13, 150-151

VDB, 13, 151

XIRR, 13, 152

XNPV, 14, 152-153

YIELD, 14, 153

YIELDDISC, 14, 154

YIELDMAT, 14, 155

financial ratios, 43-46

financial results functions

CUMIPMT, 28

CUMPRINC, 29

FV, 29

IPMT, 29

FIND function, 21, 284

finding text strings, 284

FINV function, 19, 240

FIRST function, 242

FISHER function, 19, 240

Fisher transformation, 240

FISHERINV function, 19, 240

FIXED function, 21, 285

FLOOR function, 16, 203

FORECAST function, 19, 28, 241

formulas. *See also* **arguments; functions**

breakeven sales, 42

conditional SUM, 32

contribution margin, 42

contribution margin ratio, 42

defined, 5

EUROCONVERT, 40-41

IF AND, 36

monthly breakeven sales, 42

named ranges, 41-42

profit during the period, 42

SUMIF, 41

total fixed expenses, 42

velocity, 36

VLOOKUP, 47

four-quadrant arctangent, 195

fraction dollar prices, 126

French accounting system, 115

FREQUENCY function, 19, 241

FTEST function, 19, 242-243, 280

fully invested securities

amount received at maturity, 146

interest rates, 129

functions. *See also*
arguments; formulas
ABS, 16, 192
ACCRINT, 11, 114
ACCRINTM, 11, 115
ACOS, 16, 192
ACOSH, 16, 193
ADDRESS, 15, 174
AMORDEGRC, 11, 115
AMORLINC, 11, 116
AND, 15, 168-169
AREAS, 15, 174
ASC, 280
ASIN, 16, 193
ASINH, 16, 194
ATAN, 16, 195
ATAN2, 16, 195
ATANH, 16, 196
AVEDEV, 18, 226
AVERAGE, 18, 27, 226
AVERAGE A, 18
AVERAGEA, 227
BESSEL, 80-82
BESSELI, 9, 80
BESSELJ, 10, 80-81
BESSELK, 10, 81-82
BESSELY, 10, 82
BETADIST, 18, 227
BETAINV, 18, 228
BIN2DEC, 10
BIN2HEX, 10
BIN2OCT, 10
BIND2DEC, 83
BIND2HEX, 84
BIND2OCT, 84

BINOMDIST, 18,
228-229
CALL, 9
CEILING, 16, 197
CELL, 14, 158, 160
CHAR, 21, 280
CHIDIST, 18, 230
CHIINV, 230
CHINV, 18
CHITEST, 18, 231
CHOOSE, 15, 175-176
CLEAN, 21, 281
CODE, 21, 281
COLUMN, 15, 176
COLUMNS, 15, 177
COMBIN, 16, 197
COMPLEX, 10, 85
CONCATENATE, 21,
31, 282
CONFIDENCE, 18, 231
CONVERT, 10, 86-88
CORREL, 18, 232-233
COS, 16, 198
COSH, 16, 199
COUNT, 18, 233
COUNTA, 19, 27, 234
COUNTBLANK, 14,
160-161, 234
COUNTIF, 16, 27, 199,
205, 235
COUPDAYBS, 11, 117
COUPDAYS, 12, 118
COUPDAYSNC, 12, 119
COUPNCD, 12, 119
COUPNUM, 12, 120
COUPPCD, 12, 121

COVAR, 19, 236
CRITBINOM, 19, 236
CUMIPMT, 12, 122
CUMIPT, 28
CUMPRINC, 12, 29, 122
custom, 7-8
  building, 48-49
DATE, 8
DATEVALUE, 8, 66-67
DAVERAGE, 8, 54-55
DAY, 8, 67
DAYS360, 8, 68
DB, 12, 123
DCOUNT, 8, 55-56
DCOUNTA, 8, 56
DDB, 12, 124
DEC2BIN, 10, 89
DEC2HEX, 10, 90
DEC2OCT, 10
defined, 5
DEGREES, 16, 200
DELTA, 10, 90
DEVSQ, 19, 54, 237
DGET, 8, 56-57
DISC, 12, 125
DMAX, 8, 57-58
DMIN, 8, 58
DOLLAR, 21, 282
DOLLARDE, 12, 126
DOLLARFR, 12, 126
DPRODUCT, 8, 58-59
DSTDEV, 8, 59
DSTDEVP, 59-60
DSUM, 8, 60-61
DURATION, 12, 127

DVAR, 8, 61-62

DVARP, 8, 62-63

EDATE, 8, 26, 68-69

EFFECT, 12, 127-128

engineering, 79

EOMONTH, 8, 69

ERF, 10, 91

ERFC, 10, 92

ERROR.TYPE, 14, 161-162

EVEN, 16, 201

EXACT, 21, 283

EXP, 16, 201

EXPONDIST, 19, 238

FACT, 16, 202

FACTDOUBLE, 16, 203

FALSE, 15, 169

FDIST, 19, 239

financial, 113

FIND, 21, 284

FINV, 19, 240

FIRST, 242

FISHER, 19, 240

FISHERINV, 19, 240

FIXED, 21, 285

FLOOR, 16, 203

FORECAST, 19, 28, 241

FREQUENCY, 19, 241

FTEST, 19

FV, 12, 29, 128

FVSCHEDULE, 12, 129

GAMMADIST, 19, 243

GAMMAINV, 19, 244

GAMMALN, 19, 244

GCD, 16, 204

GEOMEAN, 19, 244

GESTEP, 10, 92

GETPIVOTDATA, 8, 63-64

GROWTH, 19, 245

HARMEAN, 19, 246

HEX2BIN, 10, 93

HEX2DEC, 10, 94

HEX2OCT, 10, 94

HLOOKUP, 15, 177-178

HOUR, 9, 70

HYPERLINK, 15, 178-179

HYPGEOMDIST, 19, 246

IF, 15, 30, 170-171

IMABS, 10, 95-96

IMAGINARY, 10, 96

IMARGUMENT, 10, 97

IMCONJUGATE, 10, 97

IMCOS, 10, 98

IMDIV, 10, 99

IMEXP, 11, 100

IMLN, 11, 101

IMLOG10, 11, 101

IMLOG2, 11, 102

IMPOWER, 11, 103

IMPRODUCT, 11, 104-105

IMREAL, 11, 105

IMSIN, 11, 106

IMSQRT, 11, 106

IMSUB, 11, 107

IMSUM, 11, 108-109

INDEX, 15, 25

INDEX (Array Form), 179-180

INDEX (Reference Form), 180, 182

INDIRECT, 15, 182-183

INFO, 14, 162-163

information, 157-158, 160-166

INT, 16, 204

INTERCEPT, 19, 247

INTRATE, 12, 129

IPMT, 12, 130

IPT, 29

IRR, 12, 131

ISBLANK, 14, 30, 164

ISERR, 14

ISERROR, 14

ISEVEN, 14

ISLOGICAL, 14

ISNA, 14

ISNONTEXT, 14

ISNUMBER, 14, 30, 164-165

ISODD, 14

ISPMT, 132

ISREF, 14

JIS, 286

KURT, 19, 248

LARGE, 19, 248

LCM, 205

LCMN, 17

LEFT, 21, 286

LEN, 22, 287

LINEST, 19, 249-250

LN, 17

LOG, 17, 206

LOG10, 17, 206

LOGEST, 19, 250

logical, 167-172

LOGINV, 19, 251

LOGNORMDIST, 19, 252

LOOKUP, 15

LOOKUP (Array Form), 183

LOOKUP (Vector Form), 184

LOWER, 22, 288

MATCH, 16, 24, 184

math and trigonometry, 191

MAX, 20, 28, 252

MAXA, 20, 253

MDETERM, 17, 206

MDURATION, 12, 132

MEDIAN, 20, 253

MID, 22, 31, 288

MIN, 20, 28, 254

MINA, 20, 254

MINUTE, 9, 70

MINVERSE, 17, 207

MIRR, 13, 133

MMULT, 17, 207

MOD, 17, 208

MODE, 20, 254

MONTH, 9, 71

MROUND, 17, 208

MULTINOMIAL, 17, 208

N, 14, 165

NA, 14, 166

NEGBINOMDIST, 20, 255

NETWORKDAYS, 9, 27, 72

NOMINAL, 13, 134

NORMDIST, 20, 256

NORMINV, 20, 257

NORMSDIST, 20, 258

NORMSINV, 20, 258

NOT, 15, 171

NOW, 9, 26, 73

NPER, 13, 134

NPV, 13, 135

OCT2BIN, 11, 109

OCT2DEC, 11, 110

OCT2HEX, 11, 110

ODD, 17, 209

ODDFPRICE, 13, 136

ODDFYFIELD, 13

ODDFYIELD, 138

ODDLPRICE, 13, 138-139

ODDLYIELD, 13, 139

OFFSET, 16, 24, 185, 187

OR, 15, 172

PEARSON, 20, 258

PERCENTILE, 20, 259

PERCENTRANK, 20, 260

PERMUT, 20, 209, 261

PHONETIC, 289

PI, 17, 210

PMT, 13, 140

POISSON, 20, 261

POWER, 17, 210

PPMT, 13, 140

PRICE, 13, 141

PRICEDISC, 13, 142

PRICEMAT, 13, 143

PROB, 20, 262

PRODUCT, 17, 210

PROPER, 22, 31, 290

PV, 13, 144-145

QUARTILE, 20, 263

QUOTIENT, 17, 211

RADIANS, 17, 211

RAND, 17, 212

RANK, 20, 264

RATE, 13, 145-146

RECEIVED, 146

REGISTER.ID, 9

REPLACE, 22, 290

REPLACEB, 22

REPT, 22, 291

RIGHT, 22, 31, 291

ROMAN, 17, 213

ROUND, 17, 213

ROUNDDOWN, 17, 214

ROUNDUP, 17, 214

ROW, 16, 188

ROWS, 16, 188

RSQ, 20, 264

SEARCH, 22, 292

SEARCHB, 22

SECOND, 9, 73

SERIESSUM, 17, 214

SIGN, 17, 215

SIN, 17, 215

SINH, 17, 216

SKEW, 20, 265

SLN, 13, 147

SLOPE, 20, 266

SMALL, 20, 267

SQL.REQUEST, 9
SQRT, 17, 216
SQRTPI, 11, 17, 216
STANDARDIZE, 20, 267
statistical, 225
STDEV, 268
STDEVA, 20, 28, 269
STDEVE, 20
STDEVP, 21, 269
STDEVPA, 21, 270
STEYX, 21, 270
SUBSTITUTE, 22, 292
SUBTOTAL, 18, 25, 217
SUM, 18, 218
SUMIF, 18, 24-25, 219
SUMPRODUCT, 18, 220
SUMSQ, 18, 221
SUMX2MY2, 18, 222
SUMX2PY2, 18, 222
SUMXMY2, 18, 222
SYD, 13, 148
T, 22, 293
TAN, 18, 223
TANH, 18, 223
TBILLEQ, 13, 148
TBILLPRICE, 13, 149
TBILLYIELD, 13,
  150-151
TDIST, 21, 271
TEXT, 22, 293
text, 279
TIME, 9, 74
TIMEVALUE, 9, 74
TINV, 21, 272

TODAY, 9, 26, 74-75
TRANSPOSE, 16, 188
TREND, 21, 272
TRIM, 22, 294
TRIMMEAN, 21, 273
TRUE, 15, 172
TRUNC, 18, 223
TTEST, 21, 274
TYPE, 14, 166
U, 14
UPPER, 22, 31, 295
VALUE, 22, 296
VAR, 274
VARA, 21, 275
VARP, 21, 275
VARPA, 21, 276
VDB, 13, 151
VLOOKUP, 16, 24, 189
WEEKDAY, 9, 75-76
WEEKNUM, 76
WEIBULL, 21, 276
WORKDAY, 77
XIRR, 13, 152
XNPV, 14, 152-153
YEAR, 9, 77-78
YEARFRAC, 9, 78
YEN, 296
YIELD, 14, 153
YIELDDISC, 14, 154
YIELDMAT, 14, 155
ZTEST, 21, 277
**furigana/phonetic
  characters, 289**

**future value predictions,
  241**
  periodic constant
    payments/constant
    interest rates, 128
  principal amount after
    applying several/seris
    of compound interest
    rates, 129
**FV function, 12, 29,
  128**
**FVSCHEDULE function,
  12, 129**

G

**gamma distribution,
  243**
**GAMMADIST function,
  19, 243**
**GAMMAINV function,
  19, 244**
**GAMMALN function,
  19, 244**
GCD function, 16
**GEOMEAN function,
  19, 244**
**geometric mean of posi-
  tive data arrays/ranges,
  244**
**GESTEP function,
  10, 92**
**GETPIVOTDATA func-
  tion, 8, 63-64**
**greatest common divisor
  (integers), 204**

Gross Margin Percentage ratio, 43

Gross Profit Percentage ratio, 44

GROWTH function, 19, 245

H

half-width single-byte characters
  converting to English letters, 286
  full-width double-byte characters, converting into, 280

HARMEAN function, 19, 246

harmonic mean of data sets, 246

HEX2BIN function, 10, 93

HEX2DEC function, 10, 94

HEX2OCT function, 10, 94

hexadecimal numbers
  converting to
    binary numbers, 84, 93
    decimal numbers, 94
    octal numbers, 94
  decimal numbers, converting to, 90
  octal numbers, converting to, 110

HLOOKUP function, 15, 177-178

HOUR function, 9, 70

hyperbolic cosine, 199

hyperbolic sine, 216

hyperbolic tangent, 223

hypergeometric distribution, 246

HYPERLINK function, 15, 178-179

HYPGEOMDIST function, 19, 246

I

IF AND formula, 36

IF function, 15, 30, 170-171

IMABS function, 10, 95-96

IMAGINARY function, 10, 96

imaginary/real coefficients, 85

IMARGUMENT function, 10, 97

IMCONJUGATE function, 10, 97

IMCOS function, 10, 98

IMDIV function, 10, 99

IMEXP function, 11, 100

IMLN function, 11, 101

IMLOG10 function, 11, 101

IMLOG2 function, 11, 102

IMPOWER function, 11, 103

IMPRODUCT function, 11, 104-105

IMREAL function, 11, 105

IMSIN function, 11, 106

IMSQRT function, 11, 106

IMSUB function, 11, 107

IMSUM function, 11, 108-109

Income Before Tax to Net Worth ratio, 45

Income Before Tax to Total Assests ratio, 45

independence test, 231

INDEX (Array Form) function, 179-180

INDEX (Reference Form) function, 180, 182

INDEX function, 15, 25

index number from list, 175

INDIRECT function, 15, 182-183

individual term binomial distribution probability, 228

INFO function, 14, 162-163

INFO TYPE (cells) examples, 158-159

information functions
  CELL, 14, 158, 160
  COUNTBLANK, 14, 160-161
  ERROR.TYPE, 14, 161-162
  INFO, 14, 162-163
  IS, 163-164

ISBLANK, 14, 164

ISERR, 14

ISERROR, 14

ISEVEN, 14

ISLOGICAL, 14

ISNA, 14

ISNONTEXT, 14

ISNUMBER, 14, 164-165

ISODD, 14

ISREF, 14

N, 14, 165

NA, 14, 166

TYPE, 14, 166

U, 14

informational/logical data functions, 30

Insert menu commands

Module, 48

Name, Defined, 41

Name, Paste, 42

INT function, 16, 204

integrated error function, 91-92

INTERCEPT function, 19, 247

interest (cumulative loan), 28

Interest Expense to Net Sales ratio, 45

interest payments, 29

interest rates, 29

interior data set mean, 273

internal rate of return

cash flow schedule, not periodic, 152

periodic cash flows, 133

series of cash flows represented by numbers in value form, 131

international rate converters, 39

INTRATE function, 12, 129

Inventory Turnover ratio, 43

inverse cumulative beta probability density function, 228

inverse F probability distribution, 240

inverse Fisher transformation, 240

inverse gamma cumulative distribution, 244

inverse hyperbolic cosine, 193

inverse hyperbolic sine, 194

inverse hyperbolic tangent, 196

inverse lognormal cumulative distribution, 251

inverse matrix, 207

inverse normal cumulative distribution, 257

inverse one-tailed probability of chi-squared distribution, 230

inverse standard normal cumulative distribution, 258

inverse t-distribution, 272

investments

interest paid during a defined period, 132

net present value with discount rate, several future payments and income, 135

present value, 144

total number of periods for, 134

IPMT function, 12, 29, 130

IRR function, 12, 131

IS function, 163-164

ISBLANK function, 14, 30, 164

ISERR function, 14

ISERROR function, 14

ISEVEN function, 14

ISLOGICAL function, 14

ISNA function, 14

ISNONTEXT function, 14

ISNUMBER function, 14, 30, 164-165

ISODD function, 14

ISPMT function, 132

ISREF function, 14

J - K

Japanese characters, 289
JIS function, 286

k-th largest value, 248
k-th percentile, 259
k-th smallest value, 267
keystroke operaters, 6-7
Kronecker, 10, 90
KURT function, 19, 248
Kurtosis, 248

L

LARGE function, 19, 248
LCM function, 205
LCMN function, 17
least common multiple (integers), 205
LEFT function, 21, 286
LEN function, 22, 287
letters, converting to lowercase, 288
line intersections, 247
line items
  milestone management charts, 49-50
  production ramping, 50-51
linear regression lines r2 value, 264
linear trendlines, 272

LINEST function, 19, 249-250
list subtotals, 25
list/database-management functions, 53
  arguments, 54
  DAVERAGE, 8, 54-55
  DCOUNT, 8, 55-56
  DCOUNTA, 8, 56
  DGET, 8, 56-57
  DMAX, 8, 57-58
  DMIN, 8, 58
  DPRODUCT, 8, 58-59
  DSTDEV, 8, 59
  DSUM, 8, 60-61
  DVAR, 8, 61-62
  DVARP, 8, 62-63
  GETPIVOTDATA, 8, 63-64
  syntax, 54
lists, unique items, 51
LN function, 17
loans
  cumulative interest, 28, 122
  cumulative principal between start and stop dates, 122
  payment based on constant payments and constant interest rates, 140
LOG function, 17, 206
LOG10 function, 17, 206

logarithms, 206
  base-10, 206
  complex numbers, 101-102
  natural, 205
LOGEST function, 19, 250
logical functions
  AND, 15, 168-169
  FALSE, 15, 169
  IF, 15, 170-171
  NOT, 15, 171
  OR, 15, 172
  overview, 167
  TRUE, 15, 172
logical test return results (cells), 163-164
logical tests
  AND function, 168-169
  FALSE function, 169
  IF function, 170-171
  NOT function, 171
  OR function, 172
  TRUE function, 172
logical/informational data functions, 30
LOGINV function, 19, 251
LOGNORMDIST function, 19, 252
LOOKUP (Array Form) function, 183
LOOKUP (Vector Form) function, 184
LOOKUP function, 15

lookup/reference functions

ADDRESS, 15, 174

AREAS, 15

CHOOSE, 15, 175-176

COLUMN, 15, 176

COLUMNS, 15, 177

HLOOKUP, 15, 177-178

HYPERLINK, 15, 178-179

INDEX, 15

INDEX (Array Form), 179-180

INDEX (Reference Form), 180, 182

INDIRECT, 15, 182-183

LOOKUP, 15

LOOKUP (Array Form), 183

LOOKUP (Vector Form), 184

MATCH, 16, 184

OFFSET, 16, 185, 187

overview, 173

ROW, 16, 188

ROWS, 16, 188

TRANSPOSE, 16, 188

VLOOKUP, 16, 189

LOWER function, 22, 288

M

Macauley duration, 127

MATCH function, 16, 24, 184

math functions, 191

ABS, 16, 192

ACOS, 16, 192

ACOSH, 16, 193

ASIN, 16, 193

ASINH, 16, 194

ATAN, 16, 195

ATAN2, 16, 195

ATANH, 16, 196

CEILING, 16, 197

COMBIN, 16, 197

COS, 16, 198

COSH, 199

COUNTIF, 16, 199, 205

DEGREES, 16, 200

EVEN, 16, 201

FACT, 16, 202

FACTDOUBLE, 16, 203

FLOOR, 16, 203

GCD, 16, 204

INDEX, 25

INDEX with MATCH condition, 25

INT, 16, 204

LCM, 205

LCMN, 17

LN, 17

LOG, 17, 206

LOG10, 17, 206

MATCH, 24

MDETERM, 17, 206

MINVERSE, 17, 207

MMULT, 17, 207

MOD, 17, 208

MROUND, 17, 208

MULTINOMIAL, 17, 208

ODD, 17, 209

OFFSET, 24

PERMUT, 209

PI, 17, 210

POWER, 17, 210

PRODUCT, 17, 210

QUOTIENT, 17, 211

RADIANS, 17, 211

RAND, 17, 212

RANDBETWEEN, 17, 212

ROMAN, 17, 213

ROUND, 17, 213

ROUNDDOWN, 214

ROUNDUP, 17, 214

SERIESSUM, 17, 214

SIGN, 17, 215

SIN, 17, 215

SINH, 17, 216

SQRT, 17, 216

SQRTPI, 17, 216

SUBTOTAL, 18, 25, 217

SUM, 18, 218

SUMIF, 18, 24-25, 219

SUMPRODUCT, 18, 220

SUMSQ, 18, 221
SUMX2MY2, 18, 222
SUMX2PY2, 18, 222
SUMXMY2, 18, 222
TAN, 18, 223
TANH, 18, 223
TRUNC, 18, 223
VLOOKUP, 24
matrix determinant (arrays), 206
matrix product, 207
MAX function, 20, 28, 252
MAXA function, 20, 253
MDETERM function, 17, 206
MDURATION function, 12, 132
mean distributions, 267
measurement units, 86-88
median, 253
MEDIAN function, 20, 253
MID function, 22, 31, 288
milestone management charts, 49-50
MIN function, 20, 28, 254
MINA function, 20, 254
MINUTE function, 9, 70
MINVERSE function, 17, 207
MIRR function, 13, 133
MMULT function, 17, 207

MOD function, 17, 208
MODE function, 20, 254
modified durations (securities), 132
modified internal rate of return, periodic cash flows, 133
Module command (Insert menu), 48
modulus (absolute value), 95
MONTH function, 9, 71
monthly breakeven sales formula, 42
mortgages, 122
MROUND function, 17, 208
MULTINOMIAL function, 17, 208

N

N function, 14, 165
NA function, 14, 166
Name, Defined command (Insert menu), 41
Name, Paste command (Insert menu), 42
named ranges, 41-42
natural logarithms, 205
  complex numbers, 101
  gamma function, 244
negative binomial distribution, 255
NEGBINOMDIST function, 20, 255

net present value, investments, 135
Net Sales ratio, 44
Net Sales to AR ratio, 44
Net Sales to Net Fixed Assest ratio, 44
Net Sales to Net Worth ratio, 44
Net Sales to Total Assests ratio, 44
Net Sales to Working Capital ratio, 44
Net Worth to Total Liabilities ratio, 46
NETWORKDAYS function, 9, 27, 72
nominal annual interest rates, 134
NOMINAL function, 13, 134
non-empty cells, 234
nonprinting characters, 281
normal cumulative distribution, 256
normal distribution, two-tailed probability, 277
normalized value from mean/standard dev distributions, 267
NORMDIST function, 20, 256
NORMINV function, 20, 257
NORMSDIST function, 20, 258
NORMSINV function, 20, 258

NOT function, 15, 171

NOW function, 9, 26, 73

NPER function, 13, 134

NPV function, 13, 135

number of areas, 174

number of columns, 161-162, 177

numbers

averaging positive in ranges, 38-39

converting to currency, 282

converting to Yen, 296

rounding, 285

numeric codes for text string characters, 281

O

OCT2BIN function, 11, 109

OCT2DEC function, 11, 110

OCT2HEX function, 11, 110

octal numbers

hexadecimal numbers, converting to, 94

converting to

binary numbers, 84, 109

decimal numbers, 110

hexadecimal numbers, 110

ODD function, 17, 209

ODDFPRICE function, 13, 136

ODDFYIELD function, 13

ODDFYIELD function, 138

ODDLPRICE function, 13, 138-139

ODDLYIELD function, 13, 139

OFFSET function, 16, 24, 185, 187

one-tailed probability of chi-squared distribution, 230

operating environment information, 162-163

Operating Expense as a Percent of Net Sales ratio, 45

operators, 6-7

Options command (Tools menu), 67, 74, 78

Options dialog box, 67, 74, 78

OR function, 15, 172

order (operators), 7

P

P&L (direct contribution), 42-43

Paste Special command (Edit menu), 38

Paste Special dialog box, 38

PEARSON function, 20, 258

Pearson product moment correlation coefficient, 258

per $100 face value (securities), 138

per period interest, annuities, 145

PERCENTILE function, 20, 259

PERCENTRANK function, 20, 260

periodic cash flows, 133

periodic constant payments, 128

periodic payments, 29

PERMUT function, 20, 209, 261

permutations, 209, 261

PHONETIC function, 289

phonetic/furigana characters, 289

pi, 210

PI function, 17, 210

PMT function, 13, 140

Point of Sale (POS), 36

POISSON function, 20, 261

Poisson probability distribution, 261

population means, confidence interval, 231

population variance, 274-276

POS (Point of Sale), 36

positive numbers in ranges, 38-39

**positive square roots,
216**

**POWER function, 17,
210**

PPMT function, 13, 140

present value

cash flow schedule, not
periodic, 152

investments, 144

**PRICE function, 13,
141**

**PRICEDISC function,
13, 142**

**PRICEMAT function,
13, 143**

principal

amount after applying
several/series of com-
pound interest rates,
129

cumulative, 29

investment period based
on periodic constant
payments and constant
interest rate, 140

PROB function, 20, 262

probability, 262

**PRODUCT function, 17,
210**

**production, ramping,
50-51**

**profit during the period
formula, 42**

projected cash flows, 36

**PROPER function, 22,
31, 290**

Q

quartile, 263

**QUARTILE function,
20, 263**

**queries, SQL.REQUEST
function, 9**

**quotient, complex num-
bers, 99**

**QUOTIENT function,
17, 211**

R

**r² of linear regression
lines, 264**

radians

converting into degrees,
200

degrees, converting to,
211

**RADIANS function, 17,
211**

**ramping production,
50-51**

RAND function, 17, 212

**RANDBETWEEN
function, 17, 212**

ranges

cells, 199

geometric mean, 244

named, 41-42

number of cells meeting
given criteria, 235

positive numbers, 38-39

values, 241

RANK function, 20, 264

ranking

data set values, 260

numbers in lists, 264

**RATE function, 13,
145-146**

rates (currency)

EUROCONVERT formu-
la, 40-41

exchange tables, 40

international
converters, 39

ratios (financial), 43-46

**real coefficients, 85,
105**

**RECEIVED function,
146**

reference operators, 7

**reference/lookup
functions**

ADDRESS, 15, 174

AREAS, 15, 174

CHOOSE, 15, 175-176

COLUMN, 15, 176

COLUMNS, 15, 177

HLOOKUP, 15, 177-178

HYPERLINK, 15,
178-179

INDEX, 15, 25

INDEX (Array Form),
179-180

INDEX (Reference
Form), 180, 182

INDIRECT, 15, 182-183

LOOKUP, 15

LOOKUP (Array Form),
183

LOOKUP (Vector Form), 184

MATCH, 16, 24, 184

OFFSET, 16, 24, 185, 187

overview, 173

ROW, 16, 188

ROWS, 16, 188

SUBTOTAL, 25

SUMIF, 24-25

TRANSPOSE, 16, 188

VLOOKUP, 16, 24, 189

references

cells (column/row intersection), 180

range of specific number of rows and columns from cell/range of cells, 185

row number, 188

text strings, 182

REGISTER.ID function, 9

regression lines, 266

remainders, 208

repeating text a given number of times, 291

Replace command (Edit menu), 37

REPLACE function, 22, 290

REPLACEB function, 22

REPT function, 22, 291

resource pools, 46-48

Retained Earning to Net Income ratio, 45

Return on Net Sales ratio, 45

Return on Net Worth ratio, 45

Return to Total Assets ratio, 45

return types (cells), 159

RIGHT function, 22, 31, 291

ROMAN function, 17, 213

ROUND function, 17, 213

ROUNDDOWN function, 17, 214

rounding numbers, 285

ROUNDUP function, 17, 214

ROW function, 16, 188

rows

column intersection, 25, 180

number, 188

value from same position in second row based on range of one row, 184

ROWS function, 16, 188

RSQ function, 20, 264

S

sample variance estimate, 275

schedules, 33, 35

SEARCH function, 22, 292

SEARCHB function, 22

SECOND function, 9, 73

securities

accrued interests, 114-115

amount received at maturity (fully invested), 146

discounted

annual yield, 154

based on price per $100 face value, 142

rate, 125

fully invested, 129

interest rate of fully invested, 129

modified duration with par value assumed of $100, 132

pays interest at maturity, 155

per $100 face value having odd last coupon period, 138

values

based on price per $100 face value and periodic interest payments, 141

based on price per $100 face value and odd first period, 136

pays interest at maturity and price per $100 face value, 143

yield, 153, 138-139

sell through, 32

sell in, 32

sentences, capitalizing, 290

SERIESSUM function, 17, 214

shortcuts, documents stored on network servers, 178

SIGN function, 17, 215

SIN function, 17, 215

sine, 215

   complex numbers, 106

   hyperbolic, 216

   inverse hyperbolic, 194

SINH function, 17, 216

SKEW function, 20, 265

skewness of distributions, 265

SLN function, 13, 147

Slope, regression lines, 266

SLOPE function, 20, 266

SMALL function, 20, 267

SQL.REQUEST function, 9

SQRT function, 17, 216

SQRTPI function, 11, 17, 216

square roots

   complex numbers, 106

   positive, 216

squares of deviations of data sets, 237

standard dev distributions, 267

standard deviation (based on), 28

   entire populations, 269-270

   samples, 268-269

standard error, predicted y values for x in regression, 270

standard normal cumulative distribution, 258

standard score for x in data sets, 277

STANDARDIZE function, 20, 267

statistical functions

   AVEDEV, 18, 226

   AVERAGE, 18, 27, 226

   AVERAGE A, 18

   BETADIST, 18, 227

   BETAINV, 18, 228

   BINOMDIST, 18, 228-229

   CHIDIST, 18, 230

   CHIINV, 230

   CHINV, 18

   CHITEST, 18, 231

   CONFIDENCE, 18, 231

   CORREL, 18, 232-233

   COUNT, 18, 233

   COUNTA, 19, 27, 234

   COUNTBLANK, 234

   COUNTIF, 27, 235

   COVAR, 19, 236

   CRITBINOM, 19, 236

   DEVSQ, 19, 237

   EXPONDIST, 19, 238

   FDIST, 19, 239

   FINV, 19, 240

   FIRST, 242

   FISHER, 19, 240

   FISHERINV, 19, 240

   FORECAST, 19, 28, 241

   FREQUENCY, 19, 241

   FTEST, 19

   GAMMADIST, 19, 243

   GAMMAINV, 19, 244

   GAMMALN, 19, 244

   GEOMEAN, 19, 244

   GROWTH, 19, 245

   HARMEAN, 19, 246

   HYPGEOMDIST, 19, 246

   INTERCEPT, 19, 247

   KURT, 19, 248

   LARGE, 19, 248

   LINEST, 19, 249-250

   LOGEST, 19, 250

   LOGINV, 19, 251

   LOGNORMDIST, 19, 252

   MAX, 20, 28, 252

   MAXA, 20, 253

   MEDIAN, 20, 253

   MIN, 20, 28, 254

   MINA, 20, 254

   MODE, 20, 254

   NEGBINOMDIST, 20, 255

   NORMDIST, 20, 256

   NORMINV, 20, 257

   NORMSDIST, 20, 258

   NORMSINV, 20, 258

overview, 225

PEARSON, 20, 258

PERCENTILE, 20, 259

PERCENTRANK, 20, 260

PERMUT, 20, 261

POISSON, 20, 261

PROB, 20, 262

QUARTILE, 20, 263

RANK, 20, 264

RSQ, 20, 264

SKEW, 20, 265

SLOPE, 20, 266

SMALL, 20, 267

STANDARDIZE, 20, 267

STDEV, 268

STDEVA, 20, 28, 269

STDEVE, 20

STDEVP, 21, 269

STDEVPA, 21, 270

STEYX, 21, 270

TDIST, 21, 271

TINV, 21, 272

TREND, 21, 272

TRIMMEAN, 21, 273

TTEST, 21, 274

VAR, 274

VARA, 21, 275

VARP, 21, 275

VARPA, 21, 276

WEIBULL, 21, 276

ZTEST, 21, 277

STDEV function, 268

STDEVA function, 20, 28, 269

STDEVE function, 20

STDEVP function, 21, 269

STDEVPA function, 21, 270

STEYX function, 21, 270

straight lines (fit data), 249

straight-line depreciation (assets), 147

SUBSTITUTE function, 22, 292

substituting new text for old text, 292

SUBTOTAL function, 18, 25, 217

SUM function, 18, 218

sum-of-years digits depreciation (assets), 148

SUMIF formula, 41

SUMIF function, 18, 24-25, 219

SUMPRODUCT function, 18, 220

SUMSMY2 function, 222

SUMSQ function, 18, 221

SUMX2MY2 function, 18, 222

SUMX2PY2 function, 18, 222

SUMXMY2 function, 18

SYD function, 13, 148

T

T function, 22, 293

t-distribution, 271

t-test probability, 274

tables. *See also* **rows; columns**

   element value selected by row number and column letter indexes, 179

   rate exchange, 40

   top row specified value search, 177

   transposing, 37-38

   value from specified column number based on leftmost column value, 189

TAN function, 18, 223

tangents, 196, 223

TANH function, 18, 223

TBILLEQ function, 13, 148

TBILLPRICE function, 13, 149

TBILLYIELD function, 13, 150-151

TDIST function, 21, 271

testing independence, 231

text
  capitalizing, 31
  cell address created as, 174
  converting
    between number formats, 293
    numbers to Yen, 296
    to uppercase, 295
  deleting all spaces, 294
  operators, 7
  referred to by value, 293
  repeating a given number of times, 291
  strings
    characters, 286-288, 291
    combining, 282
    comparing, 283
    converting all letters to lowercase, 288
    finding, 284
    first character's numeric code, 281
    first letter of each word, 290
    joining, 31
    number where first found, 292
    phonetic/furigana characters, 289
    reference, 182

  replacing parts of, 290
  representing numbers, 296
  substituting new text for old text, 292
  types, 162
  uppercase, 31
text functions, 22, 293
  ASC, 280
  CHAR, 21, 280
  CLEAN, 21, 281
  CODE, 21, 281
  CONCATENATE, 21, 31, 282
  DOLLAR, 21, 282
  EXACT, 21, 283
  FIND, 21, 284
  FIXED, 21, 285
  JIS, 286
  LEFT, 21, 286
  LEN, 22, 287
  LOWER, 22, 288
  MID, 22, 31, 288
  overview, 279
  PHONETIC, 289
  PROPER, 22, 31, 290
  REPLACE, 22, 290
  REPLACEB, 22
  REPT, 22, 291
  RIGHT, 22, 31, 291
  SEARCH, 22, 292
  SEARCHB, 22
  SUBSTITUE, 22, 292

  T, 22, 293
  TEXT, 22, 293
  TRIM, 22, 294
  UPPER, 22, 31, 295
  VALUE, 22, 296
  YEN, 296
theta argument, 97
time and date functions, 26-27
TIME function, 9, 74
time/date functions, 65
  DATE, 8, 66
  DATEVALUE, 8, 66-67
  DAY, 8, 67
  DAYS360, 8, 68
  EDATE, 8, 68-69
  EOMONTH, 8, 69
  HOUR, 9, 70
  MINUTE, 9, 70
  MONTH, 9, 71
  NETWORKDAYS, 9, 72
  NOW, 9, 73
  SECOND, 9, 73
  TIME, 9, 74
  TIMEVALUE, 9, 74
  TODAY, 9, 74-75
  WEEKDAY, 9, 75-76
  WEEKNUM, 76
  WORKDAY, 77
  YEAR, 9, 77-78
  YEARFRAC, 9, 78
Times Interest Earned ratio, 45
TIMEVALUE function, 9, 74

TINV function, 21, 272

TODAY function, 9, 26, 74-75

Toolpak, Analysis
EDATE function, 68
WEEKNUM function, 76
WORKDAY function, 77
YEARFRAC function, 78

Tools menu commands
Add-Ins, 68, 76-78, 86

Total Assests to Net Sales ratio, 44

total fixed expenses formula, 42

Total Liabilities to Net Worth ratio, 46

total velocity, 36

TRANSPOSE function, 16, 188

transposing tables, 37-38

treasury bills
bond equivalent yield, 148
price per $100 face value, 149
yield, 150

TREND function, 21, 272

trigonometry functions, 191
ABS, 16, 192
ACOS, 16, 192
ACOSH, 16, 193
ASIN, 16, 193
ASINH, 16, 194

ATAN, 16, 195
ATAN2, 16, 195
ATANH, 196
CEILING, 16, 197
COMBIN, 16, 197
COS, 16, 198
COSH, 16, 199
COUNTIF, 199, 205
DEGREES, 16, 200
EVEN, 16, 201
EXP, 16, 201
FACT, 16, 202
FACTDOUBLE, 16, 203
FLOOR, 16, 203
GCD, 16, 204
INDEX, 25
INT, 16, 204
LCM, 205
LCMN, 17
LN, 17
LOG, 17, 206
LOG10, 17, 206
MATCH, 24
MDETERM, 17, 206
MINVERSE, 17, 207
MMULT, 17, 207
MOD, 17, 208
MROUND, 17, 208
MULTINOMIAL, 17, 208
ODD, 17, 209
OFFSET, 24
PERMUT, 209
PI, 17, 210

POWER, 17, 210
PRODUCT, 17, 210
QUOTIENT, 17, 211
RADIANS, 17, 211
RAND, 17, 212
RANDBETWEEN, 17, 212
ROMAN, 17, 213
ROUND, 17, 213
ROUNDDOWN, 17, 214
ROUNDUP, 17, 214
SERIESSUM, 17, 214
SIGN, 17, 215
SIN, 17, 215
SINH, 17, 216
SQRT, 17, 216
SQRTPI, 17, 216
SUBTOTAL, 18, 25, 217
SUM, 18, 218
SUMIF, 18, 24-25, 219
SUMPRODUCT, 18, 220
SUMSQ, 18, 221
SUMX2MY2, 18, 222
SUMX2PY2, 18, 222
SUMXMY2, 18, 222
TAN, 18, 223
TANH, 18, 223
TRUNC, 18, 223
VLOOKUP, 24

TRIM function, 22, 294

TRIMMEAN function, 21, 273

TRUE function, 15, 172

TRUNC function, 18, 223

TTEST function, 21, 274

two-tailed probability for normal distribution, 277

TYPE function, 14, 166

U

U function, 14

unique list items, counting, 51

units of measure, converting, 86-88

UPPER function, 22, 31, 295

uppercase, 31

V

VALUE function, 22, 296

values

securities

based on price per $100 face value, 142

based on price per $100 face value and odd first period, 136

based on price per $100 face value and periodic interest payments, 141

pays interest at maturity and price per $100 face value, 143

set, 252-254

VAR function, 274

VARA function, 21, 275

VARP function, 21, 275

VARPA function, 21, 276

VDB function, 13, 151

velocity, 36

VLOOKUP formula, 47

VLOOKUP function, 16, 24, 189

W

WEEKDAY function, 9, 75-76

WEEKNUM function, 76

Weibull distribution, 276

WEIBULL function, 21, 276

WORKDAY function, 77

X - Z

XIRR function, 13, 152

XNPV function, 14, 152-153

y-values along linear trendlines, 272

YEAR function, 9, 77-78

YEARFRAC function, 9, 78

Yen, 296

YEN function, 296

YIELD function, 14, 153

YIELDDISC function, 14, 154

YIELDMAT function, 14, 155

yields

discounted annual, 154

odd first period, 138

odd last period, 139

pays interest at maturity, 155

treasury bills, 150

ZTEST function, 21, 277

CD-ROM Installation

Windows 95 Installation Instructions

1. Insert the CD-ROM disc into your CD-ROM drive.

2. From the Windows 95 desktop, double-click on the My Computer icon.

3. Double-click the icon representing your CD-ROM drive.

4. Double-click the icon titled START.EXE to run the CD-ROM interface.

N O T E If Windows 95 is installed on your computer and you have the AutoPlay feature enabled, the START.EXE program starts automatically whenever you insert the disc into your CD-ROM drive. ▓

Windows NT Installation Instructions

1. Insert the CD-ROM disc into your CD-ROM drive.

2. From File Manager or Program Manager, choose Run from the File menu.

3. Type <drive>\START.EXE and press Enter, where <drive> corresponds to the drive letter of your CD-ROM. For example, if your CD-ROM is drive D: type D:\START.EXE and press Enter. This will run the CD-ROM interface.

By opening this package, you are agreeing to be bound by the following agreement:

You may not copy or redistribute the entire CD-ROM as a whole. Copying and redistribution of individual software programs on the CD-ROM is governed by terms set by individual copyright holders.

The installer and code from the author(s) are copyrighted by the publisher and the author(s).

This software is sold as-is, without warranty of any kind, either expressed or implied, including but not limited to the implied warranties of merchantability and fitness for a particular purpose. Neither the publisher nor its dealers or distributors assumes any liability for any alleged or actual damages arising from the use of this program. (Some states do not allow for the exclusion of implied warranties, so the exclusion may not apply to you.)

NOTE: This CD-ROM uses long and mixed-case filenames requiring the use of a protected-mode CD-ROM driver.